Rural Development through People's Participation

Rural Development through People's Participation

Dr. Neha Arora

RANDOM PUBLICATIONS
NEW DELHI (INDIA)

Rural Development through People's Participation

ISBN 978-93-5111-483-3

Published in 2015 in India by

RANDOM PUBLICATIONS

4376-A/4B, Gali Murari Lal, Ansari Road
New Delhi-110 002
Phone : +9111-43580356, 011-23289044, 011-43142548
e-mail: sales@randompublications.com,
info@randompublications.com, randomexports@gmail.com

Reprinted 2025

Type Setting by : Friends Media, Delhi-110089
Digitally Printed at : Replika Press Pvt. Ltd.

Preface

Over the past two decades, many governments, development agencies and non-governmental organizations have recognized that the "top-down" approach characteristic of traditional development strategies has largely failed to reach and benefit the rural poor. Pressed by a lack of resources, deteriorating terms of trade and mounting external debt repayments many governments are looking for alternative approaches to development. In this search, people's participation as a mechanism for promoting rural development is of paramount importance.

People's participation implies the active involvement in development of the rural people, particularly disadvantaged groups that form the mass of the rural population and have previously been excluded from the development process. The World Conference on Agrarian Reform and Rural Development (WCARRD) in 1979 affirmed that "participation by the people in the institutions and systems which govern their lives is a basic human right and also essential for realignment of political power in favour of disadvantaged groups and for social and economic development". Through participatory programmes and activities it is possible to mobilize local knowledge and resources for self-reliant development and, in the process, reduce the cost to governments of providing development assistance. People's participation is also recognized as an essential element in strategies for sustainable agriculture, since the rural environment can only be protected with the active collaboration of the local population.

This book provides a detailed description of people's participation in rural development, the role of NGOs in mobilizing people's participation and innovative strategies to strengthen people's participation. It is bound to benefit social scientists, planners, rural technologists, academicians, teachers and all those interested in learning about rural development.

Author

Contents

1

People's Participation in Rural Development

The term 'rural development' in general is used to denote the actions and initiatives taken to improve the standard of living in non-urban neighborhoods, countryside, and remote villages. These communities can be exemplified with a low ratio of inhabitants to open space. Agricultural activities may be prominent in this case whereas economic activities would relate to the primary sector, production of foodstuffs and raw materials.

The meaning of rural development has been the subject of much debate and little agreement. The definition of rural development varies from one point of view to the other. The definition or rural development may be centered around income criterion in which the concept is made to address the problem of rural poverty. Or it may be defined in sociological concept in which the rural poor represents a reservoir of untapped talent a target group that should be given the opportunity to enjoy the benefits of development through improved education, health and nutrition. This is one of the most important definitions of rural development as the provision of social infrastructures could provide the catalyst that would transform the rural areas.

Rural development may also be seen as an ideology and a practice. It may mean planned change by public agencies based outside the rural areas such as the national Government and International organization; It may also be the bringing of the countryside into an active state, as well as the transformation of the inferior nature of the country side into something more superior in terms of activities.

Rural development as the improvement in the living standard of the rural dwellers by engaging them in productive activities such as the establishment of rural industries that will increase their income. It is seen by these scholars as a means of raising the sustainable living of the rural poor by giving them the opportunity to develop their full potentials.

Rural development can be distinguished from agricultural development which it entails and transcends. In essence Rural Development may imply a broad based re-organization and mobilization of rural masses in order to enhance their capacity to cope effectively with the daily task of their lives and with changes consequent upon this. According to the World Bank Rural Development must be clearly designed to increase production. It recognizes that improved food supplies and nutrition, together with basic services, such as health and education, not only directly improve the physical well-being and quality of life of the rural poor, but can also indirectly enhance their productivity and their ability to contribute to the national economy.

Rural development ensures the modernization of the rural society and the transition from its traditional isolation to integration with the national economy. It is concerned with increased agricultural production for urban and international markets. This is essential so as to generate foreign exchange, and to attract revenue to finance public and private consumption and investment. In order to encourage increased production rural development may offer a package of inputs and welfare services for the rural masses. Such inputs and welfare services include physical inputs (such as the provision of feeder roads, water and electrification), social inputs—(namely health and educational facilities) and institutional inputs such as credit facilities, agricultural research facilities, rural expansion services among others.

However the reports from variuos countries shows that many rural development efforts have failed to deliver on their promises. One evaluation found that half of rural development projects funded by the World Bank in Africa were outright failures. A review of assistance to agricultural cooperatives reported similar results. A study by the International Labour Organisation of "poverty-oriented" projects worldwide showed that the poorest were excluded from activities and benefits What has gone wrong? Recent years have seen growing criticism of rural development strategies followed, with only minor adjustments, since the 1960s. These conventional strategies have seen development primarily as a series of technical transfers aimed at boosting production and generating wealth. In practice, conventional projects usually target medium to large scale "progressive" producers, supporting them with technology, credit and extension advice in the hope that improvements will gradually extend to more "backward" strata of rural society. In many cases, however, the channeling of development assistance to the better-off has led to concentration of land and capital, marginalization of small farmers and alarming growth in the number of landless labourers.

The basic fault in the conventional approach is that the rural poor are rarely consulted in development planning and usually have no active role in development activities. This is because the vast majority of the poor have no organizational structure to represent their interests. Isolated, undereducated and often dependent on rural elites, they lack the means to win greater access to resources and markets, and to prevent the imposition of unworkable programmes or technologies. The lesson is clear: unless the rural poor are given the means to participate fully in development, they will continue to be excluded from its benefits. This realization is provoking new interest in an alternative rural development strategy, that of people's participation through organizations controlled and financed by the poor.

The WCARRD Concept of Rural Development

People's participation in rural development is by no means a new concept. It was formulated in the mid-1970s, amid growing awareness that development efforts were having little impact on poverty. At the World Conference on Agrarian Reform and Rural Development (WCARRD), held in Rome in 1979, the international community identified the reason for this failure —the lack of active participation of the poor in programmes designed, supposedly, to assist them.

> WCARRD declared that participation by rural people in the institutions that govern their lives is a basic human right. If rural development was to realize its potential, the Conference said, disadvantaged rural people had to be organized and actively involved in designing policies and programmes and in controlling social and economic institutions. WCARRD saw a close link between participation and voluntary, autonomous and democratic organizations representing the poor. It called on development agencies to work in close cooperation with organizations of intended beneficiaries, and proposed that assistance be channeled through small farmer and peasant groups.

Since WCARRD, developing countries have suffered economic set-backs unforeseen in 1979. With their economic survival at stake, many countries have been forced to cut back on rural development, giving priority to growth ahead of WCARRD's concern for participation and equity. During this same period, however, great progress has been made in the elaboration of participatory principles and methodologies. Spurred by WCARRD, the Food and Agricultural Organization launched the People's Participation Programme, or PPP, in 1980. Since then, PPP has implemented pilot projects throughout the developing world in an attempt to test and develop an operational method of people's participation for incorporation in larger rural development schemes.

The experience of PPP has demonstrated that true participation is possible only when the rural poor are able to pool their efforts and resources in pursuit of objectives they set for themselves. The most efficient means for achieving this objective, FAO has found, are small, democratic and informal groups composed of eight to 15 like-minded farmers. For governments and development agencies, people's participation through small groups offers distinct advantages:

- *Economies of scale.* The high cost of providing development services to scattered, small scale producers is a major constraint on poverty-oriented programmes. Participatory groups constitute a grassroots "receiving system" that allows development agencies to reduce the unit delivery or transaction costs of their services, thus broadening their impact.
- *Higher productivity.* Given access to resources and a guarantee that they will share fully in the benefits of their efforts, the poor become more receptive to new technologies and services, and achieve higher levels of production and income. This helps to build net cash surpluses that strengthen the groups' economic base and contribute to rural capital formation.
- *Reduced costs and increased efficiency.* The poor's contribution to project planning and implementation represent savings that reduce project costs. The poor also contribute their knowledge of local conditions, facilitating the diagnosis of environmental, social and institutional constraints, as well as the search for solutions.
- *Building of democratic organizations.* The limited size and informality of small groups is suited to the poor's scarce organizational experience

and low literacy levels. Moreover, the small group environment is ideal for the diffusion of collective decision-making and leadership skills, which can be used in the subsequent development of inter-group federations.

- *Sustainablility.* Participatory development leads to increased self-reliance among the poor and the establishment of a network of self-sustaining rural organizations. This carries important benefits: the greater efficiency of development services stimulates economic growth in rural areas and broadens domestic markets, thus favouring balanced national development; politically, participatory approaches provide opportunities for the poor to contribute constructively to development.

The pivotal role of people's participation in development is now re-emerging in economic and social development thinking. One striking example of this trend comes from the World Bank. In its proposed strategy for sustainable development in Africa, the Bank calls for a "people-centred" approach that will improve the poor's access to productive assets, allow them to participate in designing and implementing development programmes, and foster their involvement in institutions from village to national level. UNICEF has proposed similar measures in its strategy for structural adjustment "with a human face", stressing people's participation in the formulation of development policy, and efforts to make full use of local potential. FAO believes that the participatory approach described in the following pages will be an essential part of any strategy to meet the challenges ahead.

Changes Perceptions of People's Participation and Development

Internationally, resources for social welfare services are shrinking. Population pressures, changing priorities, economic competition, and demands for greater effectiveness are all affecting the course of social welfare. The utilization of nonprofessionals through citizen involvement mechanisms to address social problems has become more commonplace. In their modern form, the concepts of community development and people's participation took shape in the 1950s. From the situation in the 1950s, when community development was perceived to be synonymous with people's participation, the situation has now changed to one in which there appears to be no clear understanding of the relationship between the two. Clearly, this impacts or changes perception of what constitutes people's participation and development.

Participation is a rich concept that varies with its application and definition. The way participation is defined also depends on the context in which it occurs. For some, it is a matter of principle; for others, practice; for still others, an end in itself. Indeed, there is merit in all these interpretations as Rahnema notes:

> Participation is a stereotype word like children use Lego pieces. Like Lego pieces the words fit arbitrarily together and support the most fanciful constructions. They have no content, but do serve a function. As these words are separate from any context, they are ideal for manipulative purposes. 'Participation' belongs to this category of word.

Often the term participation is modified with adjectives, resulting in terms such as *people's participation, citizen participation, people's participation, public participation,* and *popular participation*. The Oxford English Dictionary defines participation as "to have a share in" or "to take part in," thereby emphasizing the rights of individuals and the choices that they make in order to participate. Arnstein states that the idea of citizen participation is a little like eating spinach: no one is against it in principle because it is good for you. But there has been little analysis of the content of citizen participation, its definition, and its relationship to social imperatives such as social structure, social interaction, and the social context where it takes place.

Brager, Specht, and Torczyner defined participation as a means to educate citizens and to increase their competence. It is a vehicle for influencing decisions that affect the lives of citizens and an avenue for transferring political power. However, it can also be a method to co-opt dissent, a mechanism for ensuring the receptivity, sensitivity, and even accountability of social services to the consumers. Armitage defined citizen participation as a process by which citizens act in response to public concerns, voice their opinions about decisions that affect them, and take responsibility for changes to their community. Pran Manga and Wendy Muckle suggest that citizen participation may also be a response to the traditional sense of powerlessness felt by the general public when it comes to influencing government decisions: "people often feel that health and social services are beyond their control because the decisions are made outside their community by unknown bureaucrats and technocrats".

Westergaard defined participation as "collective efforts to increase and exercise control over resources and institutions on the part of groups and movements of those hitherto excluded from control". This definition points toward a mechanism for ensuring people's participation. The World Bank's Learning Group on Participatory Development defines participation as "a process through which stakeholders influence and share control over development initiatives, and the decisions and resources which affect them"

A descriptive definition of participation programs would imply the involvement of a significant number of persons in situations or actions that enhance their well-being, for example, their income, security, or self-esteem. Chowdhury states that the ideal conditions contributing towards meaningful participation can be discussed from three aspects:

1. What kind of participation is under consideration?
2. Who participates in it?
3. How does participation occur?

Evens also points out the importance of the following issues in order to assess the extent of people's participation:

1. Who participates?
2. What do people participate in?
3. Why do people participate? There are:
    a) Cultural explanations (values, norms, and roles, etc.)
    b) Cognitive explanations (verbal skills and knowledge about the organizations)
    c) Structural explanations (alternatives, resources available, and the nature of benefit sought)
4. Implications (how the benefit contributes to the ends or principles they value).

Oakley and Marsden defined people's participation as the process by which individuals, families, or communities assume responsibility for their own welfare and develop a capacity to contribute to their own and the community's development. In the context of development, people's participation refers to an active process whereby beneficiaries influence the direction and execution of development projects rather than merely receive a share of project benefits. Paul's five objectives to which people's participation might contribute are:

1. *Sharing project costs*: participants are asked to contribute money or labor (and occasionally goods) during the project's implementation or operational stages.
2. *Increasing project efficiency:* beneficiary consultation during project planning or beneficiary involvement in the management of project implementation or operation.
3. *Increasing project effectiveness*: greater beneficiary involvement to help ensure that the project achieves its objectives and that benefits go to the intended groups.
4. *Building beneficiary capacity*: either through ensuring that participants are actively involved in project planning and implementation or through formal or informal training and consciousness-raising activities.
5. *Increasing empowerment:* defined as seeking to increase the control of the underprivileged sectors of society over the resources and decisions affecting their lives and their participation in the benefits produced by the society in which they live.

Bamberger says the objectives and organization of project-level activities are different from those of programs at the national or regional levels. The level or scope of the activity must be taken into consideration when defining objectives. According to Bamberger, three distinct kinds of local participation included the following:

1. Beneficiary involvement in the planning and implementation of externally initiated projects or people's participation.
2. External help to strengthen or create local organizations, but without reference to a particular project, or local organizational development.
3. Spontaneous activities of local organizations that have not resulted from outside assistance or indigenous local participation.

The first two are externally promoted participatory approaches used by governments, donors, or NGOs, while the third is the kind of social organization that has evolved independently of (or despite) outside interventions. At a community level, there is a separation of people's participation into two distinct approaches:

(1) the community development movement and

(2) community involvement through conscientization.

The basis of conscientization, according to De Kadt, started from "the existence of socioeconomic inequalities, the generation of these by the economic system, and their underpinning by the state".

Concept of Development

The word 'development' is fraught with ideological, political, and historical connotations that can greatly change its meaning depending on the perspective being discussed. The following three definitions of development are most helpful and suitable in relation to this research project. The first definition is provided by Korten:

> Development is a process by which the members of a society increase their personal and institutional capacities to mobilise and manage resources to produce sustainable and justly distributed improvements in their quality of life consistent with their own aspirations.

Korten's definition emphasizes the process of development and its primary focus on personal and institutional capacity. It also touches on justice, equity, quality of life, and participation.

The second definition is from Robinson, Hoare, and Levy's work. He adds the dimension of empowerment to Korten's idea of development.

> [Empowerment is] a social action process that promotes participation of people, organisations, and communities towards the goals of increased individual and community control, political efficacy, improved quality of life, and social justice.

Finally, Zachariah and Sooryamoorthy emphasize that development must promote economic growth, but not at any cost:

> The encouragement of economic growth must take account of and be restrained by three other equally important objectives:
>
> 1. Protection of the environment and consideration of the ecological impact of industrialisation and commercialisation.
> 2. Fair and equitable distribution as well as redistribution of goods and services to enable poorer people to get a fairer share of society's wealth and to participate fully in the economy.
> 3. Creation of opportunities for everyone to increasingly participate in the political, artistic and other activities of society. (1994: 22–23)

Zachariah and Sooryamoorthy's criteria for development recognize the environmental and ecological facets of communities going through the process of development. The environment is considered an integral part of development, since any impacts on a person's environment also influence the state of well-being or welfare. Environment and development are thus linked so intricately that separate approaches to either environmental or developmental problems are piecemeal at best.

Some Important People's Participation Approaches

The community development approach emphasizes self-help, the democratic process, and local leadership in community revitalization. Most community development work involves the participation of the communities or beneficiaries involved. Thus, people's participation is an important component of community development and reflects a grassroots or bottom-up approach to problem solving. In social work, people's participation refers to "... the active voluntary engagement of individuals and groups to change problematic conditions and to influence policies and programs that affect the quality of their lives or the lives of others".

One of the major aims of community development is to encourage participation of the community as a whole. Indeed, community development has been defined as a social process resulting from citizen participation. Through citizen participation, a broad cross-section of the community is encouraged to identify and articulate their own goals, design their own methods of change, and pool their resources in the problem-solving process.

It is widely recognized that participation in government schemes often means no more than using the service offered or providing inputs to support the project. This is contrasted with stronger forms of participation, involving control over decisions, priorities, plans, and implementation; or the spontaneous, induced, or assisted formation of groups to achieve collective goals.

The most important and complicated issue bearing on local level planning and development is people's participation. Effective people's participation may lead to social and personal empowerment, economic development, and sociopolitical transformation. Yet there are obstacles: the power of central bureaucracies, the lack of local skills and organizational experience, social divisions, and the impact of national and transnational structures. There is no clear-cut agreement in the literature of community development on the nature of people's participation or on a prescription to ensure it. The need for people's participation in development and management is nonetheless accepted and recognized in the professional literature.

Although there is no consensus, some of the most important approaches to participation are presented below.

United Nations Research Institute on Social Development (UNRISD) Approach

The most important and original aspect of UNRISD is the focus on people power and organization of disadvantaged groups, hitherto bypassed in development. The significant factor in this approach was not that it concentrated on the poorest of the poor but that it emphasized questions of power and organization and also viewed the allies and adversaries of the hitherto excluded as included in the scope of investigation.

Norman Uphoff's Team: Framework on Participation

In 1976, USAID asked the interdisciplinary Rural Development Committee at Cornell University to come up with some practical concepts and measures of people's participation in development. The committee focused on participation and its framework. In fact, they gave a new thrust to old Community Development (CD) approaches. The four kinds of participation they identified are: decision-making, implementation, benefits, and evaluation. Even if these kinds of participation are distinguishable, there are usually connections and feedback among them; for example, participation in decision making is likely to contribute to participation in benefits. The more there is of any one kind, the more participation there is in total.

Self-reliance and Self-help Approach

During the development decade of the 1960s, self-reliance and self-help projects became the order of the day. Chowdhury also notes that this trend is further developed by the social worker S. Tilakratna of Sri Lanka in his participatory rural development strategy, which aims to combine the best of community development and UNRISD ideas. According to Tilakratna, the idea of people's participation in development means improving the potential of the previously neglected rural poor, enabling them to make decisions for their own welfare. Chowdhury also notes:

> Essentially, the main components of this developmental process are participation in taking initiatives to identify unmet needs, and self-reliance—

breaking away from dependencies that suppress the creativity of the poor. This approach is nearest to the type of people's participation practice in Bangladesh. It is more a psychological than an economic or physical process.

It is evident from these discussions that participation as it relates to development is a process that includes a set of activities and takes place through different stages. The definitions, approaches, and the various literatures on participation suggests participation in development projects needs to be understood based on the following elements.

Identification of Appropriate Stakeholders

The public involvement of stakeholders in development projects is widely recognized as a fundamental element of the process. Timely, well-planned, and well-implemented public involvement programs have contributed to the successful design, implementation, operation, and management of proposals. For instance, the range of stakeholders involved in an Environmental Impact Assessment (EIA) project typically includes:

1. The people, individuals, or groups in the local community
2. The proponent and other project beneficiaries
3. Government agencies
4. Nongovernmental Organizations (NGOs)
5. Others, such as donors, the private sectors, academics, and so forth

Needs Identification and Goal Determination

Participation of the masses in development activities implies enhanced capacity to perceive their own needs. Through participation, local people identify their needs as well as the relevant goals of a program. By participating in decision making and implementation activities, local people help project officials identify (1) needs, (2) strategies to meet those needs, and (3) the necessary resources required to implement the various strategies. For example, people's participation will be discouraged if environmental issues are given priority in agendas without addressing issues such as poverty, homelessness, health, and other basic necessities perceived to be more important by the coastal communities.

Information Dissemination

This is a one-way flow of information from the proponent of the development project to the public. The proponent should provide sufficient relevant information about the project such as the benefits of the project to the beneficiaries, the costs of implementation, the potential for financing and implementation, and possible risk factors. The proponent must allow sufficient time for individuals to read and discuss the information provided, and listen to the views held by individuals as well as to issues and problems. Lack of transparency often fosters mistrust and misunderstanding between project authorities and local communities.

Consultation

Consultation involves inviting people's views on the proposed actions and engaging them in a dialogue. It is a two-way flow of information between the proponent and the public. Consultation provides opportunities for the public to express their views on the project proposal initiated by the project proponent. Rigorous planning and implementation of projects should be undertaken only after considerable discussion and consultation. Consultation includes education, information sharing, and negotiation, with the goal being a better decision making process through organizations consulting the general public. This process allows neglected people to hear and have a voice in future undertakings. Depending on the project, various methods are used during consultation such as public hearings, public meetings, general public information meetings, informal small group meetings, public displays, field trips, site visits, letter requests for comments, material for mass media, and response to public inquiries. The knowledge of local people should be recognized and they should be enrolled as experts in designing development projects. Participants should be encouraged to articulate their ideas and the design of the project should be based on such ideas.

Genuine Interests

Participation depends on people's legitimate interests in the project or development activities. Therefore, participation needs to be considered as an active process, meaning that the person or group in question takes initiatives and asserts an independent role.

Public Involvement in Decision Making

The project should encourage a maximum number of people in the participation of development projects. Such involvement should give the participants full inclusion in designing, organizing, and implementing activities and workshops in order to create consensus, ownership, and action in support of environmental change in specific areas. It should include people and groups rather than exclude any individuals. Public involvement is a process for involving the public in the decision making of an organization. Participation actually brings the public into the decision-making process.

White stressed community involvement in management of marine protected areas. According to the author, public involvement can take place at several stages in the establishment and management of marine protected areas. These stages are:

(1) the recognition of a need;

(2) discussions with interested parties and integration with the community;

(3) baseline studies and monitoring;

(4) education;

(5) core group building and formalization of reserves; and

(6) enforcement.

Accountability

The requirement of accountability applies to all parties involved in the project, such as project management, external organizers, and traditional leaders, as well as any emergent leadership from the ranks of the poor and the disadvantaged. The authors also note that the agencies involved in project management and implementation are procedurally and periodically answerable to the people in the project area, as well as the citizens of the country in general. All people should be aware of their roles in the project and the planning of activities of the project. Accountability of concerned community members must be ensured, particularly after the decision is taken.

Repeated Interaction

Often there is interaction at the beginning of the project but no dialogue or any other form of interaction occurs during the project. This ultimately creates a big gap between the proponents of the development projects and the communities. Consequently, the local people abandon a project based on such an idea. Therefore, it is suggested that there should be ongoing communication throughout the project period.

Ownership and Control

Participation plays a major role in people's management of their own affairs. Ownership and control of resources have a profound impact on participation in development projects. Ferrer emphasized four areas to be worked toward in a participatory coastal resource management program: greater economic and social equality, better access to services for all, greater participation in decision making, and deeper involvement in the organizing process resulting from the empowerment of people.

Sharing Benefits

It is evident that without sharing the benefits of the project, participation is a frustrating process for the poorer people. Zachariah and Sooryamoorthy note that there should be a fair and equitable distribution of benefits, as well as redistribution of goods and services, to enable poorer people to get a fairer share of society's wealth and to participate fully in the development process.

The Centre on Integrated Rural Development for Asia and the Pacific, a regional rural development organization in South Asia, mentions that participation entails three distinct processes: first, the involvement of the people in decision making; second, eliciting of their contribution to development programs; and third, their participation in *sharing the benefits* from the development process.

Partnerships

Partnership in development processes allows stakeholders to work, talk, and solve problems with individuals who are often perceived as the masters. Instead of demonstrating the relationship as a worker-client tie, the parties involved should agree on working in partnerships. An expression used by the Latin American activists to describe their relationship with the people with whom they are working is *accompanamiento*, or "accompanying the process". Wilson and Whitmore identified a set of principles for collaboration in a variety of settings and situations. These include non-intrusive collaboration, mutual trust and respect, a common analysis of what the problem is, a commitment to solidarity, equality in the relationship, an explicit focus on process, and the importance of language.

Environmental Legislation

The environment is considered as an integral part of development, since any impacts on an individual's environment also impacts on well-being or welfare. It has been shown that the lack of environmental legislation in developing countries limits environmental protection. This ultimately creates considerable environmental problems in the name of development in third world countries. Therefore, lack of legislation to protect human rights as well as the environment may impede public participation in development projects.

USE AND ABUSE OF PEOPLE'S PARTICIPATION

It is noteworthy that until recently participation as it relates to the poor was not acknowledged in the literature, even though notes that the disadvantaged were always expected to become actively involved in procuring their own services. For example, the poor in the United States are involved inter alia in state schools, welfare departments, hospitals, and public housing. Participation for them is time-consuming, but not voluntary, and they exercise a relatively low degree of influence or control over organizations in which they participate, given that the services are usually controlled by people who are not poor or recipients of the services.

How can poor people's participation be of greatest use? Rankopo utilizing Midgley identifies four typical state responses toward participation in majority world nations: the antiparticipatory mode, the manipulative mode, the incremental mode, and (the most desirable) the participatory mode. In the latter case, the state sponsors participatory activities through training and deployment of social development workers, and the provision of material, financial, and other forms of assistance.

Arnstein contends that citizen participation is citizen power, but that there is a critical difference between going through the empty ritual of participation and having the real power needed to affect the outcome of the process. This difference was briefly exhibited in a poster painted by French students to explain the student-worker rebellion (in English): "I participate; you participate; he participates; participate; you participate... They profit". The poster highlights the fundamental point that participation without redistribution of power is an empty and frustrating process for the powerless. Abbott also supports the foundation for a new, more appropriate approach to people's participation, based upon the concept of community power and control.

In order to assess the types of participation and nonparticipation, Arnstein suggested a typology of eight levels of participation using a ladder technique:

> The bottom rungs of the ladder are (1) Manipulation and (2) Therapy. These two rungs describe levels of "non-participation" that have been contrived

> by some to substitute for genuine participation. Rungs (3) Informing and (4) Consultation, progress to levels of 'tokenism' that allow the have-nots to hear and to have a voice. Rung (5) Placa-tion is simply a higher level tokenism because the ground rules allow have-nots to advice, but retains for the power holders the continued right to decide. Citizens can enter into a (6) Partnership that enables them to negotiate and engage in trade-offs with traditional power-holders. At the topmost rungs, (7) delegated power and (8) Citizen Control; have-not citizens obtain the majority of decision-making seats, or full managerial power.

The use of people's participation yielded significant results in one of the community-based forestry regions in Gujrat, India. During the 1980s, an average of 18,000 offenses were recorded annually: 10,000 cases of timber theft, 2,000 of illegal grazing, 700 fires, and 5,300 other offense.

> Twenty forestry officials were killed in confrontations with communities and offenders; assaults on forestry officials were frequent. In response, an experiment in joint management with communities was begun by the conservator. This included community meetings, widely publicized creation of forest protection committees, and profit sharing of 25 percent of timber returns with local groups. As a result, con-flicts between officials and community groups diminished, community groups assumed responsibility for patrolling forests, and productivity of the land and returns to villages increased sharply. In one year, one village of eighty-eight households harvested and sold 12 tons of fi rewood, 50 tons of fodder, and other forest products, while also planting and protecting teak and bamboo trees.

Abuse of the concept of participation is illustrated by using two examples of community forestry programs in South Asia. Community forestry programs have been designed and implemented to address the problem of declining forest resources. Yadama compared the use and abuse of the concept of participation from an institutional context:

> A growing number of non-governmental organizations (NGOs) are planning, organizing, and implementing community forestry programs in South Asia, the rise due in part to the perceived failure of government development programs. There is much documentation on how governmental community forestry programs have not paid attention to who participates and who benefits. The general criticism is that governmental programs ignore the social welfare effects of the community forestry programs. Many of the governmental programs were successful in generating new wood-based resources but were not effective in involving the poor and as a result had minimal impact on their economic well being.

While evaluations of community forestry programs managed by the government have found rural participation lacking, there is a growing belief that nongovernmental organizations involved in community forestry have more effectively included rural people in the planning and decision making processes. It was found that one of the advantages NGOs claim over the government sector is their ability to implement participatory programs that help the poorer people gain control of any new resources that are generated. Moreover, many of the NGOs are locally based and are familiar with the cultures and values of the communities in which they operate.

The second example of the abuse of people's participation is the Bangladesh government's response to the management of coastal reforestation projects. Deforestation has become a critical problem in Bangladesh because only nine percent of its area is forested (less than in most countries), and forest resources are an important national resource base. The southern part, which are the coastal regions of Bangladesh, has been favored by nature with this important resource endowment. The forest in this area is not only of economic significance, but also works as a barrier to devastating cyclones, tidal-bores, salinity, and erosion. It also provides shelter for many species of wild and aquatic animals and provides a living for many people who fish and collect honey, thatching materials, and timber for fuel and housing. The loss of mangrove trees and other forest resources has become extreme in the last fifty years. There is continuous deforestation by natural disasters such cyclones, tidal surges, and storms. Self-interested groups, who cut many trees for preparation of their shrimp projects, further aggravate the problem.

Consequently, the government has taken up reforestation projects in the area. One of the main issues in the reforestation project is the promotion of monoculture. As a matter of fact, reforestation was proceeding with only a very few, fast-growing nonindigenous species such as eucalyptus. In the process, indigenous species were displaced. Short-term gain from fast-growing species was sought, to the neglect of long-term benefit.

The planting of fast-growing species created several impacts. First was the depletion of water resources in the region, as fast-growing species require more water and are adapted to compete for the water resource. With the loss of indigenous species and monoculture there was loss of biodiversity. There was also loss of livelihoods as people who from a diverse ecosystem made their living by collecting honey, fuel woods and timbers, thatching materials, and fishing were no longer able to do so. This of course has a negative impact on communities and families living in the area.

In response, there were acts of violence against those seen as perpetrating these changes. Government offices were ransacked and destroyed, and government officials in some cases were beaten up. Many NGOs in the region had been obliged to oppose the government because it promoted monoculture plantation.

In fact, the government approach to reforestation projects was overcentralized, with little participation existing in the protection of coastal environmental projects. Indeed, there was no two-way communication between government staff and the local people. This phenomenon, or the paternalistic fallacy, assumes that planners, technicians, and experts possess all the knowledge, wisdom, and virtue needed to achieve development, the poor being deemed responsive and grateful beneficiaries. The traditional popular knowledge system and culture, which value the sustainable use of natural resources, are degraded and devalued in the name of science and technology by government officials. It has been found that in many cases, the proper utilization and implementation of coastal development projects such as mangrove vegetation, inshore fisheries, and coral reefs depends upon the community's understanding of the delicate nature of these resources and the beneficial role the proposed project will have in their daily lives and future welfare.

In the process, coastal people ultimately felt cheated by the government because the project caused damage to the communities instead of creating opportunities in the area. The knowledge of these two situations provides with an empirical scenario of the abuse of the concept of participation in development practice.

Evidences of Effective People's Participation

There is evidence that people's participation enhances the effectiveness of development projects. The following two examples from South Asia in this regard will explain about it in detail. Over the last two decades, Bangladesh hosted a unique model of community development named Grameen Bank.

The Orangi Pilot Project (OPP) was a successful project involving a maximum number of squatters from the Orangi slums effectively in managing and solving their own problems.

Orangi Pilot Project (OPP)

The Orangi Pilot Project of Karachi in Pakistan started in 1980. This venture now involves most of the residents in a huge squatter settlement outside of Karachi with almost a million people. The founder of the project is Akhter Hamid Khan, a veteran civil servant who helped to establish a cooperative movement in Bangladesh when it was East Pakistan. The Bangladesh Academy for Rural Development (BARD) was also established based on his two tier cooperative model of development.

Orangi is Karachi's largest slum, long considered a no hope area. The children were playing in filth; the streets were filled with excreta and wastewater, making movement difficult and creating health hazards. Typhoid, malaria, diarrhea, dysentery, and scabies were rampant in the area. The residents of Orangi were aware of these problems, but they could not solve them because:

1. They believed that the provision of infrastructure was the responsibility of the government (the psychological barrier).
2. They did not have the technical expertise to construct a sewage system (the technological barrier).
3. They were not organized to undertake collective action (the sociological barrier).
4. They could not afford the costs of a conventional sewage system (the economic barrier).

Appeals for government-funded schemes were in vain. The project was established to fill the gap left by the city's incompetent government, which failed to provide the slum with sanitation. The most urgently felt need of the community was for waste disposal, so low-cost, participatory sanitation became the first priority. The Orangi Pilot Project organized local people into street committees, each committee consisting of twenty to forty families living in the same lane, and lent them money to buy the raw materials to build their own sewage facility. Residents of individual lanes banded together to elect a project manager and contributed cash and voluntary labor to get their own sewer installed.

Besides, local management capabilities developed through lane committees have provided the foundation for housing, health, family planning, community-financed education, women's work centers, micro-enterprises, reforestation, and other activities. Sanitation, combined with the

OPP's health project, has brought the district's infant mortality down from 130 per 1,000 live births in 1980 to 37 in 1991. Nationally, the figure is 95 per 1,000 live births.

Impressed by the project's success, the government, along with international aid agencies, is trying to replicate its model for urban development in other parts of the country. To reiterate the importance of people's participation in development, Akhter Hamid Khan states:

> The collapse of government here is very deep and probably irreversible. The old socialist model that everything will be done for the people has failed. The old institutions are dinosaurs that will decay and die. The new institutions, the vital bodies that can get things done, are arising out of squatter settlements. The state authorities promise to provide most services, but they fail. In future, most communities will provide most services for themselves.... We have broken out of the dependency culture.

Qualities of Participation

Following are the qualities of effective relationship between people's participation and the effectiveness of OPP.

1. Akhter Hamid Khan personally recruited social organizers from within the slum community. Local organizers' intimate knowledge of the locality helps in defining and designing effective programs of the project. In none of these programs did OPP its role as the provider of a service; rather, the community provided the service to itself with appropriate assistance from OPP.
2. The idea of organizing people of the same lane into groups generated mutual trust.
3. The OPP has been able to mobilize major amounts of local resources—seventeen rupees' worth of funds, labor, and materials for every one rupee of external funding received.
4. The OPP was able to identify people's felt needs appropriately. This ultimately creates people's genuine interests in the project.
5. Each program of the project was introduced only after a thorough analysis of community need and identification of the most important factors. The programs have periodically been evaluated and modified to respond to changes within the community.
6. The project carried economic and social benefits to the local people.

7. The OPP has opened opportunities for people in local communities to make improvements in their lives through collective action.

The Grameen Bank (GB)

The community-based Grameen Bank Bangladesh is an institution that pioneered lending to the landless poor in Asia's poorest country. Since the Grameen Bank started in 1976, it has turned peasants' lives around with loans for cows, chickens, irrigation pumps, and plots of land. In total, Grameen customers, whose only collateral is the sari / shirt on their backs, have now borrowed US$1,662 million, and despite their meager incomes, repaid an astonishing 98 percent of it. Because of the Grameen Bank's significant performance, it has been copied in fifty-two countries of the world, including the United States, the United Kingdom, China, Australia, India, and other developed and developing countries.

In 35,568 out of 68,000 villages across Bangladesh, the GB's almost unparalleled success is rooted in a basic belief that its borrowers, no matter how poor they may be, understand their needs and their potential better than anyone else. "We think they are as capable and as enterprising as anybody else in the world," said Dr. Mohammed Yunus, the founder of the Grameen Bank. If the poor are provided credit on reasonable terms, they themselves best know how to increase their incomes.

Grameen provides microcredit facilities to the rural poor, aimed at generating income to help them meet their basic needs and become independent of the moneylenders. The people participate in the loan program by forming groups and attending purposeful meetings. Villagers communicate among themselves and many of them have been taught the precepts of awareness. Chowdhury also mentioned that:

> ... after receiving awareness precepts, people become eager to learn about functional education and family planning along with skilled training to help them better conduct their small-scale business to earn profit. Motivated bank workers, a strict cadre of dedicated youths, work at the grass-roots to help build up groups of five members and explain to them the process of requiring weekly savings before applying for loans on projects of their own.

Qualities of Participation

1. Grameen gives the authority to five-member groups of the local people called *Kendro* (center) to plan at the local level. This *Kendro* discusses concerns related to group and emergency funding with *Gram Sarkers,*

administrative units. The assumption is that if individual borrowers are given access to credit, they will be able to identify and engage in viable income-generating activities.

2. The borrowers plan their loans by themselves and then discuss them with others. The viability of their scheme, how the marketing will be conducted, is also sorted out by the borrowers.
3. Grameen officials believe participation is a process of growth.
4. The GB follows a unique procedure for ensuring accountability of the group members. For example, the mode of repayment of loans: once the borrowers receive the money, they must repay 2 percent of the principal every week for one year. Then they have two weeks to pay the accumulated interest. Grameen experience shows that most of the borrowers pay within one week because they are waiting for another loan.
5. Borrowers' sincere and firm commitments to the sixteen decisions of GB are based on four basic principles: discipline, unity, courage, and hard work.
6. Grameen officials believe Dr. Mohammed Yunus' statement that "credit is a human right that should be treated as a human right. If credit can be accepted as a human right, then all other human rights will be easier to establish".
7. The Grameen Bank has directly attacked poverty (the basic problem of rural communities in Bangladesh) by targeting credit and organizational assistance directly to the poorest people at reasonable terms, and the poor find it acceptable.

In spite of GB's successes, certain criticisms have been leveled against the bank in the recent years. For instance, Chowdhury notes that "credit alone is useless, even at times counterproductive. One must proceed in an integrated manner where credit will be one of many variables such as education, training, family planning, marketing, technology, infrastructure development and so on".

Rahman based his study on anthropological methods and claims that he is the first to use this approach to examine the GB's records reports:

> Previous studies have been quantitative focusing on the numbers of women involved in the program, investment of loans, the loan recovery rate, and profit margins. In the study, it was found that 78 percent of the total micro-

> loans in a village were used for different purposes than those approved by the GB. About 30 percent were used to meet household needs such as paying dowry, buying medicine, or paying fees to broker agencies that arrange overseas employment for household members.

Overall, it was found in the study that the male members of the borrower's family used more than 60 percent of the loans. This situation created a debt burden for women, forcing them to borrow money from other lenders, appeal to men to pay off the loan installments, or sell the household produce that their families would otherwise consume.As a result, there were acts of violence in the borrowers' families. Rahman mentions that in one case, a man threatened to send his wife back to her birthplace and remarry unless she took out another loan from GB. According to GB's policy she is not eligible to take a second loan unless she paid off her first loan. This situation led her to become the victim of violence in the family as well as in the society. Rahman describes: "In the household women are powerless in relation to their husband and in the loan centres they are powerless before influential members and bankers who are mostly men".

References

Agrawal, A. and K. Gupta (2005) 'Decentralization and Participation: The Governance of Common Pool Resources in Nepal's Terai'. *World Development,* Vol. 33, No. 7, pp. 1101–1114.

Bastian, S. and N. Bastian (eds) (1996) *Assessing Participation: A Debate from South Asia.* Delhi: Konark.

Chambers, R. (1994) 'Participatory Rural Appraisal (PRA) Analysis of Experience'. *World Development,* Vol. 22, No. 9, pp. 1253-1268.

Ellis, F. (2000) *Rural Livelihoods and Diversity in Developing Countries.* Oxford: Oxford University Press.

Hickey, S. and G. Mohan, eds. (2004) *Participation: From Tyranny to Transformation.* London: Zed Books.

2

Participatory Assessment of Governance

The definition of governance according to the United Nations Development Programmes (UNDP) is: ". .. the exercise of economic, political and administrative authority to manage a country's affairs at all levels. It comprises mechanisms, and institutions, through which citizens and groups articulate their interests, exercise their legal rights, meet their legal obligations and mediate their differences". Participation is taken as the pillar of good governance. Public participation is regarded as a vital part of the democratic process. Public participation seeks the involvement of those who are targeted as beneficiaries. Those are affected by decision needs to participate in the decision making process. This implies that public contribution will influence the decision. The participatory processes viewed as the facilitator and inclusiveness, the desire to participation of the whole community or society. Public participation is a part of people-centred or human-centric principles which have emerged over the last thirty years. In this respect, public participation challenges logic of centralized hierarchy and paradigm shift. It advances the alternative idea, that collective decision making is better than one, further argues that public participation can sustain productive and durable change. Article 25 of the international covenant on civil and political rights envisaged that, "every citizen shall have the rights and the opportunity ..... to take part in the conduct of public affairs, directly or through freely chosen representatives. .."

In some countries, public participation is the central principle of making public policy. Public participation is viewed as a tool that is intended to the informed planning, organizing, and funding of activities. Public participation may use measure attainable objectives, evaluate impact, and identify lessons for future practices. Public participation in administrative rulemalung refers to the process by which proposed rules are subject to public comment for a specified period of time.

Features of Participatory Governance

Some features of participatory governance are

Participatory Budgeting

Participatory budgeting is a process of democratic deliberation and decision making, in which ordinary residents of a village or city decide how to allocate part of a panchayat or municipal or public budget. Participatory budgeting is usually characterized by several basic design features, such as: identification of spending priorities by community members, election of budget delegates to represent different communities, facilitation and technical assistance by public employees, local and higher level assemblies to deliberate and vote on spending priorities, and the implementation of local direct-impact community projects. Participatory budgeting may be used by the local self governments around the world, and has been widely publicized. In India, the panchayat in some states utilizes its common property resources and generates funds which are added to the total budget of the panchayats. Besides this, people also collect money to manage their common resources such as water works, and street lights.

Public Trust

In recent years, loss of public trust in authorities and politicians has become a widespread concern in many democratic societies. Public participation is regarded as one of the potential solutions to the crisis in public trust and governance. The idea is that the public should be involved in the policy process, and to have state officials seek public views and participation, rather than treating the public as simply passive recipients of policy decisions. The underlying assumption by political theorists, social commentators, and even politicians is that public participation increases public trust in authorities, improving citizen political efficacy, enhancing democratic ideals, and even improving the quality of policy decisions. However, the assumed benefits of public participation are yet to be confirmed.

Transparency and Accountability

Transparency and accountability are critical for the efficient functioning of a modem economy, and to achieving faster growth and development. These are two important pillar of democratic governance. Transparency ensures that information is made available that can be used to measure the authority's performance and to guard against the misuse of power. Transparency enables democracies to achieve accountability.

Participatory Development

In economic development theory, the school of participatory development draws the attention of all today. The desire to increase public participation in humanitarian aid and development has led to the establishment of a numerous context-specific, formal methodologies, matrices, pedagogics, and ad hoe approaches. These include conscientization and praxis- project programmc appraisal (PPA), rapid rural appraisal (RRA) and participatory rural appraisal (PRA); 'open space' approaches; goal-oriented project planning also called 'Zielorientierte Projektplanung' (ZOPP). The World Development Report (1994) on infrastructure reported that in a study of 121 completed rural water supply projects, financed by various agencies, projects with a high degree of local participation in project selection and design were more likely to enjoy good maintenance, subsequently, than those with more centralized decision-making.

Environment and Sustainable Development: In recent years, public participation has come to be seen as a vital part of addressing environmental problems and bringing about environment and sustainable development, In this context, relying solely on a method where technocrats, or, bureaucrats monopolize decision making is no longer seen as effective, and it is argued that public participation allows governments to adopt policies and enact laws that are relevant to communitics and takc into account thcir rcal nccds.

Globalization and Participatory Governance

With globalization, the scenario of governance has changed completely. There are many players in the system of administration which is termed governance. The government and market are now players on equal plane. New actors have entered the system. Two of these actors are: the multinational companies (MNCs) and the non government organizations (NGOs). The state is no longer a coercive power while negotiating with

MNCs. The state is now, one among others, although a significant one. The government and MNCs both remain engaged with each other and prepare a ground on which they have to work together. This will also help the host country to keep a check on an MNC. That gives a bigger role to be played by the government of a host country. Globalization has changed the scenario. Both actors have to work together on equal plane according to a prepared code of conduct and rules of the game, which regulate the behaviour of both actors. MNCs play an important role in working with various actors, such as NGOs and the market.

MNCs, in their role as investor, innovator, experts, manufacturers, lobbyists, and employers, are critical players in developing the architecture of global governance. They are amazingly prominent in negotiating formal inter-governmental regimes, such as the Kyoto Protocol, and the scientific advisory panels of these regimes. MNCs, working as the actors in the decision making process that determine the quality of products, decide about the standards and codes of conduct that govern not just products, but environmental practices and labour conditions too.

MNCs negotiate with a government about the entry into their country to establish their units, but, at the same time, they negotiate with NGOs about the quality of environment which is going to be affected by their industrial enterprise. They want to know the market conditions of a country whether there is any restriction imposed on the market from the government or even through NGOs. MNCs need to know what environmental problems their unit is going to create. If it emits higher than acceptable level of carbon dioxide which is the source of global warming then they have to talk to the government and NGOs about the sustainable technology which can reduce the emission of carbon.

The government, MNCs, and NGOs all have to agree to regulations that are to be followed by all so that acceptable labour standards and environmental standards are in place. For instance, if an MNC uses child labour in their factory, an unacceptable practice, then NGOs and government watchdog bodies have the right to bring the matter to the attention to courts and other bodies. The government, MNCs and NGOs all of them need to agree to have a regulatory authority where they can be subject to code of conduct approved by them to regulate their activities in relation to labour employment. MNCs and NGOs often make common ground for discussions and settle disputed matters amongst themselves, according to the ground rules that have been adhered to, previously. Peter Newell remarked "There has been a notable shift in the relationship between business and NGO around regulatory issues. From a position of clearly defined antagonism, there is increasing emphasis on partnerships and institutionalized forms of collaboration".

Governance is a mechanism for these non state actors to participate in the decision making process. Though, NGOs are not as powerful as MNCs in terms of finance, yet as a network, NGOs, are a significant force to reckon with. NGOs are able to pressurize MNCs and business, in general, for coming to agreement over issues related to environment and climate. Today, a large number of NGOs around the world have received recognition by international funding agencies. For example, participation by NGOs has brought the issue of carbon emission to an international forum which resulted in the Kyoto agreement in which business has to be selective about technology which creates less carbon emission. They have to follow international standards to ensure the quality of their products. This quality is measured in terms of the impact on the environment Thus NGOs are getting importance in global governance. Moreover, because of the active role of civil society and business, the political regime is a critical factor in governance, as the state is no longer the only important actor. To regulate diverse interest groups, the state cannot use administration. In the place of state and bureaucracy, which, earlier, took decisions on behalf of the state, a regulatory authority has been established. The regulatory authority has to mediate with both non state actors and state actors. David Levy and Peter Newell remarked that business is not just a subject of a regulatory system imposed by the state rather business is an intrinsic part of the fabric of governance. Governance is multilayered and all the stakeholders do participate in the decision making process, i.e., the states, the market, and NGOs.

Participatory Assessment of Governance (PAG)

The generic practice developed over recent years is termed as Community Voice Tool (CVT) for assessment of institutional service delivery which is mainly a qualitative assessment made by local communities of local service delivery by different agencies. It is based on the principle that listening to community voices is important since they constitute the primary stakeholders as far as institutional service delivery is concerned. In its broader scope, such local service delivery include all the services provided by the government, semi-government agencies, NGOs, the private sector or even by local CBOs. For instance, any local service provide/rs providing health, education, drinking water, extension, nursing, nutrition, land development, veterinary services, relief services and others as relevant. There could be minor addition and alteration made in the same practice to adapt it suitably to local needs and objectives and hence could have different names/ terminologies. When the local communities apply 'scoring' (use qualitative scores as weights) to assess service delivery of local institutions then the practice is termed as 'Community Score card' (CSC).

The local communities may choose to assess different governance institutions related to them as per different criteria (criteria can range for instance, from those reflecting provision of service delivery to rating in terms of their importance of services to rating in terms of their transparency and corruption) including provision of services and in that case it is termed as 'Participatory Assessment of Governance'(PAG).

Location

The practice is described here as it was applied in three countries of the Asia-Pacific region. The information was collected from both household surveys and Focus Group Discussions (FGDs). The samples included a total of 406 households and 24 FGDs with a gender balance. In addition to scoring for selected services qualitative information was mainly based on the FGDs.

PAG was a tool applied as a part of a Participatory Poverty Assessment (PPA) study covering more than 100 locations in 12 districts of the state of West Bengal, where 95% of the sample constituted rural areas and 5% covered urban and peri-urban localities. The districts represented 12 different agro-ecological zones in the State of West Bengal and selection of districts also took into account the social diversities and the incidence of income and human poverty. For each year, eighteen villages/townships in the 3 provinces were covered – with 6 villages/townships per province. The villages selected were based on different criteria such as remote location of a village; those villages having project-related activities; those with high proportion of ethnic minorities etc.

Socioeconomic Profile

The following provides a description of the socio-economic profile, extent of poverty, and access to basic services at the country level for the three countries where CVT and PAG were applied (India, Nepal and China). The three countries are quite at variance in terms of size of population where China and India's size of population is more than 1 billion, each, while Nepal has a population of 28 million. Amongst the three countries under reference, China and India have medium level of human development while Nepal has a low level of development. China has a 61st rank amongst 177 countries and an HDI index of 0.777 as compared to India, with a rank of 128th and an index of 0.619. Nepal has a rank of 142nd out of 177 countries with an HDI index of 0.534.

China, amongst the three study countries, has demonstrated the highest GDP growth rate of 11.2% over 2006-07 with the highest GDP per capita, (US$ 5046 in 2005 purchasing power parity). India's GDP growth rate was 7.1% with a GDP per capita of US$ 2599 in ppp. Nepal, a low income country had a much lower GDP growth of 0.5% and GDP per capita of US$ 976 in 2005 ppp. Nepal's economy is gradually returning to normal after prolonged conflict.

On the poverty front and achievement of MDG's, India and Nepal's performance have lagged behind. In China 15.9% of the population was found to be living in poverty. Child malnutrition under 5 years of age was 45.9 % and 38.6 % respectively for India in 2005 and Nepal in 2006 as compared to 6.9% in China in 2005. Though under 5– mortality rates per thousand have improved over time for India and Nepal, China's rates are far better.

In terms of access to basic infrastructure, the percent of the rural population with access of rural population to seasonal roads is much better in China (97%) over 1993-2004 as compared to India (61%) and Nepal (17%) while access to electricity by rural households is high for China (latest data not available) but low for India (48.1%) and much lower for Nepal (17.4%) (UN ESCAP, 2008). China topped the chart in 2004 in terms of access of the population to sanitation (65%) followed by India (28%) and Nepal (27%).

The following describes the socio-economic conditions for each of the localities where the tool was used. In West Bengal, India where the tool under reference was applied to 100 locations in 12 districts is located in the Eastern part of India. It has a population of 82 million and covers an area of 88,752 Sq km.

Accounting for 7.8 % of the country's total population, the State of West Bengal has 72% of its people living in rural areas where the proportions of scheduled caste and scheduled tribe population are 28.6 % and 5.8 % respectively, while the same proportions are 19.9 % and 1.5 % respectively in the urban areas. The state has a literacy rate of nearly 70 %. With 12 agro-ecological zones, West Bengal major agricultural state and has recording the highest rate of growth in agricultural productivity. The State has been a forerunner in the implementation of agrarian reforms, since the early eighties.

It has installed a system of decentralized planning and governance, with a three tier *Panchayati Raj* System, since 1977. There was accelerated agricultural productivity in the State after 1983 and this coincides with the period during which the incidence of rural poverty, both percentage and number of rural poor, registered the sharpest decline. Urban poverty alleviation has been less effective due to a fall in the industrial growth in the State after the mid-1980s. The rising income of the State has also been accompanied by declining poverty as given by the estimates of the Planning Commission.

An estimated 27 % population in West Bengal lived below the poverty line in 1999-2000 as compared India's average of 26 %. However, the poverty rates for the Scheduled Caste, Scheduled Tribe and female-headed households. Higher poverty among the female-headed households also became apparent when demographically-adjusted measures were used.

Recent statistics show that poverty and hunger has increased in rural West Bengal. Bandyopadhay based on recent statistics from the 61st Round of NSSO data for 2004-05 highlights the point that the percentage of households not getting enough food every day in some months of the year was the highest in West Bengal (10.6 %) followed by Orissa (4.8 %). Based on the same data, he also shows that West Bengal has the highest food inadequacy in India with 12 % of the rural households facing occasional or continuous hunger and starvation followed by acute morbidity and mortality.

Many rural development programmes are being implemented in West Bengal by the State. The major ones are the National Rural Employment Guarantee Scheme (NREGS), Swarnajayanti Gram Swarojgar Yojana (SGSY), below-the-poverty line 'red' coloured *Antyodaya* ration cards, the *Annapurna Antyodaya* grain transfer scheme for elderly women, cash transfers under the old age pension scheme and subsidized housing.

There are many NGOs and CBOs working in West Bengal in all sectors such as rural and urban development, health, education and micro finance though the local panchayats (governments) lead the development pathway at the local and district level. The coastal districts of West Bengal are situated in a cyclonic belt and are badly affected every year from heavy rains, winds and floods. Many international and bilateral donor agencies such as UNICEF, Asian Development Bank, The World Bank, DFID and others are engaged in providing support for development activities, environmental protection and construction of infrastructure such as urban facilities, bridges and highways.

Yunnan, Sichuan and Guangxi provinces in western China have large proportions of ethnic minorities and rural poor though the 3 provinces exhibit varying levels of development as well as ethnic populations which vary in size. The incidence of poverty in the year 2001 is 3.35, 3.31 and 7.89 iin Guangxi, Sichuan and Yunnan respectively, which does show a considerable reduction in poverty as compared to the earlier years 1985 and 1993.

have failed in 2002 include Guangxi (by 30 %) and Yunnan. Standards of health also tend to be much lower in western China. They all have maternal mortality rate and level of malnutrition below China's national average. Average life expectancy was 68.4 in the West and 71.9 in the East of China. The rural elderly receiving government assistance was the lowest in the Western region – only 5.8 % as compared to 10.99 % and 6.03 % in Eastern and Central region of China. Though the human development indices improved for all the three provinces under reference over the period 2003 to 2006, life expectancy indices deteriorated for all the three provinces while overall education index improved for Guangxi and Yunnan but fell for Sichuan during the same period. Per capita funding for working population and medical care assistance were the lowest for Yunnan as compared to the other two provinces under reference.

In its 11th Five Year Plan (2006-2010) China has committed to devoting more attention to the issue of social equity and social development among ethnic minorities in particular. China's policy goal is to build a well-off and harmonious society and to attain MDGs.

There are some NGOs in the three provinces working in the areas including poverty reduction, reproductive health, child development and disaster management. Bilateral and international donor agencies such as DFID, The World Bank, the Asian Development Bank, UNICEF, UNDP,

IFAD and others are also engaged in the provinces under reference. DFID and the World Bank are supporting the PRCD project covering the three provinces where participatory impact assessment was undertaken by ITAD, a private consultancy firm from UK where the community voice tool was applied for a part of the assessment.

The two districts where the tool under reference was applied in Nepal are Saptari district and Gorkha district. Poverty reduction and social protection programmes in Nepal include social insurance, social assistance, micro credit, labour market programmes and child protection, which constitute just over 2 % of Nepal's GDP (Bhatta, 2006). Saptari and Gorkha districts are the two districts of the 75 districts of Nepal where the tool under reference was applied by an NGO.

Saptari district is a part of Sagarmatha zone with Rajbiraj as its district headquarters is known for its high agricultural output and its fish farms in Hanumannagar and Fattepur. It has an area of 1363 square km and a population of 570,282 as in 2001. Gorkha district is a part of Gandaki zone with Gorkha as its district headquarters.. It has an area of 3610 square km and a population of 288,134 as of 2001. Though Saptari district is from the Eastern development region of Nepal while Gorkha district is from the Western development region of Nepal, their human development index (HDI) lies in the range of 0.450 to 0.499, which is comparable to that of the National level for Nepal, which is 0.463. Both districts have a similar position with regard to gender-development status and have performed better as regards many other districts. Saptari district is in a slightly better position than Gorkha district is terms of human empowerment status with overall empowerment as 0.486, economic empowerment: 0.369 and social empowerment: 0.398. A large number of NGOs and international and bilateral agencies work in both the districts across a range of topics, where forestry constitutes an important area of intervention.

Needs Addressed/Situation Analysis

PAG primarily evolved as a qualitative tool for participatory assessment of services delivered by public (or private) bodies with wide applicability. It had special significance for enabling participation of socially exclude groups. In countries such as India, Nepal and China it enabled excluded and weaker segments of the population to participate and express their views and have better grasp of the issues through open discussions in small group meetings.

The tool helped to provide marginalized segments of society with the space to participate and flexibility to assess criteria related to provision of services by different service delivery organizations.

Specific situational assessments related to the three countries under reference are as follows. In West Bengal, India the tool of PAG was applied as a part of a participatory poverty assessment (PPA) in order to elicit people's perspectives on the poverty situation before negotiations with the government for an external loan. Despite the declining trends in rural poverty since 1977 there were perceived gaps in the performance of social sectors such as health, education and nutrition and it was important to find out about people's perspectives on poverty and programmes and service delivery, especially of social development services like health, education, nutrition and others.

The tool was applied as a part of participatory impact assessment exercise for a poverty reduction project covering the 3 provinces. One major challenge faced by China on the poverty front is that of relative marginalization of ethnic minorities where census data shows that there are 55 ethnic minorities scattered mostly along the Chinese borders in the south, southwest, north and northwest. The 3 provinces – Yunnan, Sichuan and Guangxi have large proportions of ethnic minorities (25 in Yunnan, 12 in Guangxi and multiple groups in Sichuan) while rural poor constitute 14.22 million in Yunnan; 4.6 million in Sichuan and 17.94 million in Guangxi. Different types of investments undertaken since 2000 by the provinces under reference have improved food security, infrastructure and public facilities though much remains to be done for better inclusion of those residing in the remote areas and mountainous regions of the provinces.

Focus of the Practice

PAG for assessing service delivery is a tool by means of which the communities/ citizens/groups provide their views, opinions, scores on performance of service delivery organizations such as government, private sector or NGO's related to 'quality', 'coverage of services', 'efficiency', 'cost', and 'responsiveness' in the area/s of providing different types of services to the community. The tool can be based on semi-structured interview with a set of open questions, or it can be based on small group discussions. The tool can be applied as a combination of both closed and open questions. The main focus of the PAG tool was to gain an overview of people's assessment of service delivery though the larger objectives were different in the three countries under reference.

In China the PAG tool was further refined in 2007 and has been applied as a part of participatory impact assessment in a poverty reduction project. In India the PAG tool was first applied in 2004-05/a part of Participatory Poverty Assessment (PPA) study at a sub-national level to gain insights into people's assessment of delivery of social development services. Lastly in Nepal the PAG tool was applied as a tool for participatory monitoring system for PRSP and MDG-related indicators in the years 2006 and 2007.

Scale of the Practice

There are major data gaps in the scale of practice in terms of total cost and annual expenditure. The following description provides an idea of the above to the extent possible.

The tool has been applied in China for 3 years as a part of participatory impact assessment to a total of 54 villages/townships in 3 provinces. On an annual basis 6 villages/ townships have been covered in each province. The villages were selected based on their remoteness, engagement in project-related activities and the proportion of ethnic minorities, etc. The annual expenditure on the application of the tool expected to be minimal since it was being applied by 3 persons in each province for a few days annually for each of the 3 years. The number of persons covered was through sample groups interviewed and those engaged in group discussion. In the 6 villages per province an estimated average number of 12 persons per group (men + women) = 72 would imply a total of 216 persons in 3 provinces for each year and an estimated 600 persons would have taken part over the three year period.

In West Bengal, India the PPA study was undertaken in more than 100 locations across 12 districts of West Bengal 95 % of which were rural areas and 5% of which were urban/peri-urban localities. The selection of districts was made on the basic of the agro-ecological and social diversities as well as the incidence of income and human poverty. The number of people covered for the tool under reference was covered through participatory sessions with more than 4000 village participants, of which, 55%, on average, were women.

In Nepal the information was collected from a total of 406 households through a household survey and 24 FGDs with a gender balance. In addition to scoring for the services qualitative information are sought mainly from the FGDs. Total costs of the initiative are not available

Duration of the Practice

In India CVT was applied in 2004-2005. In Nepal, CVT/PAG was applied from late 2005 to 2007. Since 2007, the PAG tool has been applied in South-West China.

Institutional Structure

The institutional structures in the three countries under reference are described below.

In India three tier elected bodies are parts of the overall Panchayati Raj System (PRI). In descending hierarchical order they are: district governance (Zilla Parishad), block governance (Panchayat Samiti) and village governance (Gram Panchayat). Panchayats are engaged in implementing and overseeing government's rural development programme in the State at different levels. The current policies involves further decentralization through village assembly (Gram Sabha) at the village governance (Gram Panchayat) level village parliament (Gram Sangshad) and village development committee (Gram Unnayan Samiti). There are also administrative offices and line ministries at district, sub-division and block levels.

The different bodies described above at district, block and village level helped to identify poor areas and villages and also provide background information, they were otherwise not directly engaged in application of the PAG tool. The findings from the application of the tool were meant for the state/provincial level of governance.

In China, for implementing the PRCD project management tiers exist at four levels—(a) the Provincial Project Management Office (PMO); (b) the County PMO; (c) the Township PMO; and (d) the Village/Sub-Village Project Management Group. The main roles and responsibilities of the PMO at the Provincial level include conducting, guiding and reviewing micro-meso-regional planning and policy making for project planning, implementation and monitoring and approving and funding and training. PMO at the County Level is mainly a temporary structure with staff mainly from different government agencies, whose main roles and responsibilities are to organize and coordinate the planning process of different townships, coordinate co-financing, training, review plans of project villages and coordinate technical inspection. PMO at the Township Level is normally led by the township mayor/s, each consists of 5–7 officials.

None of the bodies described here were actually engaged in the PAG tool. Rather all of them facilitated the process undertaken for an independent research and piggybacked on to participatory impact assessment.

Nepal – With the Parliament as the apex body and the National Planning Commission responsible for development policies and programmes in Nepal, the district development committees (DDC's) and the village development committees (VDCs) are responsible for district and village-level development respectively. Much of their functioning is being slowly regained after prolonged years of conflict.

Key Partners

A brief profile is presented below of each country under reference in terms of the activities of the key stakeholders with regard to the usage of the tool under consideration.

In China the provincial government and township governments supported the entire study (PAG was a part of annual study of participatory impact assessment) as a part of PRCD project and were also fed back the field findings by local researchers who undertook the study. This helped to validate the findings. The provincial government also contributed towards local travel and holding of required workshops along with DFID, China. The Project was managed by the Government of China and Provincial Governments. Finally the government was supported by DFID, UK, ITAD and UK in monitoring efforts.

In Nepal the Planning Commission delegated the study to a national NGO, which thereby established linkages with local service providers and district officials for the purpose. The Planning Commission of Nepal and national level NGOs managed the project. The government, NGO and UNDP, Nepal monitored the project.

PAG: Practice Development and Operations

Initiation, Planning and Design

PAG was first applied in 2004-05 in West Bengal, India as a tool for institutional assessment as part of a ADB Funded. Participatory Poverty

Assessment (PPA) sub-national level study carried out for the government of West Bengal. The practice was initiated to assess people's perspectives on poverty and also the role of main stakeholders. There was a formal selection process by the Asian Development Bank to recruit Indian field/ action research organization to carry out the assigned PPA study in the state of West Bengal.

Realizing the potential of the tool and the community response it was refined within an institutional framework for good governance, which helped to evolve a set of criteria for assessing delivery of services. In late 2005, it was further developed as a tool for participatory monitoring system for PRSP and MDG-related indicators and used by the Planning Commission of Nepal, NGOs and UNDP from 2006-2007. Since 2007, the tool was further refined and applied by the Chinese government, ITAD and UK as a part of periodic impact assessment in a poverty reduction project in South-West China covering 3 provinces. PAG has come a long way since 2004 gradually evolving based on cross-country experiences.

Focus on the Poor

In China the participants were the rural ethnic communities which typically exhibit higher poverty incidence in sampled villages/townships in 3 provinces – Guangxi, Sichuan and Yunnan.

In West Bengal, India the Participatory poverty Assessment (PPA) study was done in situ, through participatory sessions with more than 4000 village participants, of which, 55 per cent, on average, were women. The sampling frame was also representative of socially, culturally and ecologically vulnerable groups. Selection of districts took into account the agro-ecological and social diversities and the incidence of income and human poverty as well. The community voice tool was applied to the poor communities and those socially excluded in one terai and one hill district in Nepal.

Participation

Participants who have direct experience of delivery of different services as provided are gathered and asked to discuss delivery of relevant services by different service providers. Small group discussions are encouraged and facilitated under PAG as done by experienced facilitators and scores on different criteria for delivery of services emerge in the process. Small groups of participants are encouraged to discuss amongst them selves and arrive at 'group' assessment as reflected through qualitative scores. Each group assessment and score is examined by the groups before finalizing it. There can also be participants who do not agree with group score and note of their dissent is made.

Once the scoring process is over and scores are finalized, the participants are asked to provide their suggestions for bringing about improvements in the standard and quality of relevant services provided.

The group scores are then validated by means of semi-structured interviews of local persons/key informants.

Once the above process is completed the local service providers are asked to sit for a meeting where the findings of the group scores and discussions are presented in summarized forms in the presence of the local people react and help to validate the findings as well as suggest further action.

Practice in Operation

Application of PAG may be regarded chronology of steps and activities as regarded below:

(1) Team of 12 experienced facilitators (who have good skills in interacting with poor groups) is selected. For conducting facilitation, they forty pairs which imply a total of 6 pairs. 2 field coordinators are chosen from the 12 facilitators to; they collate information and maintain the quality of field interaction.

(2) List of Government/public/private services to be assess made. (Each interactive session could be of 2 to 3 hours. Experience shows that in any one interactive session not more than 4 services are possible to be assessed efficiently. In case there are more than 4 services separate sessions could be held.)

(3) Selected criteria for assessment by user-group/s of services can be divided as follows:

- Awareness, access and inclusion to services
- Attitude and behaviour of service providers
- Quality, responsiveness and efficiency of service providers
- Quality and adequacy of infrastructure for services

- Cost of services
- Sustainability of services

Criterion above a needs to be first defined in the local context and then a list of 4 or 5 open questions with few closed questions can be prepared to explore the criterion in different aspects depending on the service to be assessed. List of open questions (semi-structured questionnaire) will emerge for each service delivered based on the above set of criteria.

(4) While assessing criteria as above by local communities/groups, both social groups and gender could be mainstreamed so also age and ethnic factors can be considered through multi-stage sampling of groups under consideration. For example assessment of services, such as 'education' and 'health' may involve 6 small groups chosen based on socio (poor economic class as well middle class and better off) as well as gender.

(5) Parallel to small group interactions it is also important to field open and semi-structured questionnaire to selected individuals on the six criteria for assessment. This has objectives in terms of validating and cross-checking group responses, scores and those who dissent. This also helps to understand better the basis of scoring by groups and individuals. The set of semi-structured and open questionnaire is to be fielded separately to those individuals, who may be key informants or who are dominating personalities and hence could influence group opinions, or who are generally quiet and shy to participate in group discussions.

(6) Of the 11-15 participants from each group, 10 of them could sit for group discussion and group scoring, while 5 (including women, men, dominant persons and opinion makers) could be fielded questionnaire separately preferably in separate locations so as to reduce the bias.

(7) When the group discussion and group scoring are over the field coordinators overseeing the groups and their facilitators are expected to meet with the facilitators and collate key information from group scoring and individual questionnaire. A meeting at the local level and local community views are shared with them. The facilitators and other citizens may be present at this meeting clarify issues as and when required.

(8) The data are collated in SPSS/Excel package and PAG will be presented in the format as above for each village/town or at other levels such as the meso level.

(9) This exercise may be conducted on an annual basis with the first exercise forming base line data.

Challenges and Responses

A key constraint faced in the application of PAG is the lack of institutional space in most countries for people's assessment of service delivery. One-off exercises are often conducted, but they are of limited use.

Some common challenges faced in the 3 countries are listed below. Ways in which such challenges were overcome or met are also described to the extent possible.

One common challenge faced with regard to participatory tools in general is that academicians and technical experts often under appreciate qualitative data emerging through the voices of the poor. It was often difficult to make use of and interpret such data. Lack of flexibility of project leaders and staff with regard to participatory tools and listening to the voices of the poor was overcome to a considerable extent through training workshops and experiential field learning sessions.

There was dearth of good facilitators in many agencies and sometimes inexperienced facilitators were unable to handle tricky situations such as conflicts which arose during participatory sessions and they took more time than others in conducting sessions. Field coordinators tried to minimize this problem by observing the field sessions and helping resolve problems faced by an experienced facilitator. Inexperienced field facilitators were also often paired with an experienced one for conducting small group discussions.

Another challenge faced is that few government bodies and service delivery agencies were prepared to hear the problems listed by common people and to listen to suggested changes. During application of the PAG tool it was realized that the best way to present findings of user-group discussions was to start with the strengths of a service delivery agency as described by the people before enumerating the weaknesses.

There were rising community expectations from their service providers and the high expectations of the consumers also influenced their assessment of service delivery. The service providers often had many constraints and lacked technical expertise, funds and managerial skills to provide quality services. This was overcome by asking the participants about whether they were also aware of the constraints faced by the service providers and by inquiring about the participants' possible contributions towards bettering delivery of services.

Because the service providers at the local level are not decision makers, senior officials and decision makers were also invited to the sessions. This helped sensitize the senior officials/decision makers to public views and assessment as well as made them respond to such public assessment either instantaneously or over a period of time.

There were challenges in setting criteria for people's assessment of service providers. This list of criteria was therefore kept flexible enough so that new criteria could be added by the participants and/or the facilitators as required.

Outcomes of PAG

Effectiveness

The main objective of PAG is to obtain qualitative assessment of service delivery agencies by users of those services. Some objective indicators of the changes brought about by the practice include frequency of application of the tool, dissemination of user-assessment to service delivery agency, major gaps identified in service delivery and response of service delivery agency and changes in the service delivery agency's decisions with regard to public feedback based on PAG. It is difficult to attribute any change in service delivery as a result of application of such tool.

Though PAG is a powerful tool for assessment and self-learning it could also be perceived to be a threat by any service delivery agency because scores and rates on its provision of services. On many occasions the service delivery agencies experience different problems in providing services and even when their services are assessed and gaps identified by local service users, the agencies may lack much scope to make corrections and respond to such gaps due to lack of funds, skilled personnel, machinery, technology and other factors. In terms of achieving its objectives, the tool merely establishes a record of the performance of service delivery agencies as assessed by the community. However whether the public feedback is followed or acted upon is altogether another dimension. Much depends on the scope of such agencies to follow up on their gaps and shortcomings as identified by local users. It is in this regard that the tool may not bring immediate results, but may help many service delivery agencies to improve service provision in the medium to long term.

The tool in practice has helped different service delivery agencies to learn about public views on their delivery of services. Though the service delivery agency may or may not be enthusiastic to learn of users opinions it may not be in a position to act upon the assessment. Much depends on the organizational culture of the service delivery agency. If the organizational culture is democratic, open and flexible then it has better scope to learn from its users. Most service delivery agencies have a bureaucratic structure and decisions are made at a top level: the local personnel providing the service are not empowered in any manner to respond to user-views. Since women and men assess delivery of local services in separate groups the *space for gendered views* is incorporated in the usage of the tool.

Efficiency

In both India and China the efficiency of the tool was ensured by piggy backing it onto other tools based on the resources available: no additional funds, time or personnel were requested. Such use was achieved by using a similar sample and user groups for the PAG as for the larger study and also by extending the project checklist for field inquiry to allow PAG inquiry.

Participation also helped increase the efficiency of the tool, for example, the better rapport between facilitator and user-groups the better is the usage of the tool and its process of application. Once external facilitators are accepted by user-groups' participatory inquiry becomes much easier.

Innovation

It is important to remember the following features of the tool as applied to poor and those illiterate and semi-literate.

The community voice tool (CVT) is an easy way to identify the strengths and weaknesses of the services delivered and what the agencies could do better to deliver them. With detailed guidelines; facilitators and users of services can apply it with ease. Service-Users as participants in usage of the tool are able to understand its objective/s and applications. The tool is flexible in application and any type of service delivery can be assessed by means of this tool. It is adaptable in different areas/regions/countries irrespective of their level of development.

Regular use of the tool helps to establish regular communication between the community and the service provider. It becomes a tool for participatory monitoring of public services when poor people as users of services are involved in assessing public services on a regular basis.

Unexpected Outcomes

PAG, when piggybacked on PPA/ PIA findings and only shared with higher tiers of delivery agencies rather than the public and lower tiers of delivery agencies resulted in some unexpected action at a lower level. It tended to set a signal for better performance and efficiency for the staff/ officials of delivery agencies once they learned of a potential or actual user assessment.

There was a diversity of user views and many user views were not reflected by a PAG study. Furthermore, in PAG exercises users were empowered to team up with other users and learn from different user views and experiences. To that extent they gained from such exercises even when the status of delivery of services remained the same.

At times users criticized the service delivery of user-agencies but ended up forming coalition and action groups to improve service delivery on their own and in their own way and by their own means. The users often formed a user group that regularly monitors delivery of services and negotiates directly with service agencies.

Key Operational Lessons Learned

Project planning and the limited duration of a project can affect the usage of the tool. While it is easier to apply the tool in a project than without a project, its usage cannot be guaranteed when the project life ends. One-off usage of the tool does not help to create comparative data profiles and changes in public assessment of services and therefore limits comparisons of findings over time.

With regard to the nature and structure of partnership, there are underlying tensions between governmental institutions and NGOs. If an NGO applies the tool for user–assessment of government services then it may or may not be appreciated by the government agencies for various reasons. Hence the type of organization responsible for facilitating user-assessment practices and its credibility/reputation among government agenciesare also important considerations for its acceptance by both the user-groups and also the service delivery organizations.

Roles played by other stakeholders such as civil society, NGO's and CBO's vary from location to location. Lack of capacity building can constrain an organization from efficient application of the tool.

Often, user-views appear threatening to local service delivery organizations which generally have a 'top-down' approach and are seldom used to considering user-groups' perspectives. They generally adopt a defensive approach and have little scope to change or adapt at least in the short-run.

Sustainability of PAG

Degree of Sustainability

One main issue in sustainability of PAG is that it is often perceived as a threat or criticism by local service delivery agencies. The agencies are not receptive because such views of the publication are perceived as undermining their authority because most agencies lack funds and technology to respond. They also lack decision-making powers, in a complex system of governance, where decisions are made mostly from the 'top' on a political basis. In certain socio-political set-ups criticisms of the government in any form and its systems of delivery are discouraged. The practice may be made more sustainable by observing the following:

Organization(s) that are acceptable to both the users and the service delivery agencies should be entrusted with the responsibility of using the tool. Such organization(s) could vary across places, countries and regions.

It is important to have country experience and case studies on the PAG tool ready for sharing and circulation for the decision-making and the implementing agencies and also for the researchers and field facilitators. Such country experience and case studies help them to appreciate the whole gamut of the tool and also enable them to visualize the processes involved and the output/s which could be derived from the application of the tool.

It is desirable to have data processors ready at PAG application workshops and after field visits, preferably based on the SPSS package. This helps to organize, collate and quickly process and analyse the data and also to cross-check data and to identify gaps, if any.

It is prudent for the field team to discussion how to manage people's expectations. Application of the tool makes many users think that their local service delivery would improve immediately once they have made an assessment. However, that this is an exercise in user assessment of service delivery, which would eventually be transmitted to respective service delivery agencies. It may or may not result in improvement of delivery of services as desired by user-groups.

Perhaps the most important part of the whole process to select and prepare a team of good facilitators through a training-workshop. A trained and skillful set of facilitators are expected to make the most of the opportunity in interacting with the users of services and their delivery agencies, apply the tool in a positive mode and manage users' expectations while also being able to diffuse delicate and explosive situations.

The team of facilitators should be ready to share immediate outcome/s and verify and cross-check field data. For any field application the team of facilitators should be ready to summarize and present their field to service delivery agencies and other officials and leaders as required.

Achieving Greater Sustainability

The lack of *institutional space* for CVT/CVT/PAG is often a constraint to its usage. An institutional space at one local user-community level and/or inter-community level would help to strengthen the usage of the tool and also to provide regular feedback for betterment of quality of services.

The size of the practice can be extended from a few user-groups to many user-groups based on random and purposive sampling in order to ensure social and geographical inclusion. It is important to have data processing facilities available for the tool so that such the practice may e easily collated and processed when extended to more user-groups. Data processing software such as SPSS package or any other appropriate statistical packages help to process the data and identify inter-group differences for better analysis.

Challenges Ahead

One major challenge is the lack of motivation for service delivery agents to perform. They are used to a bureaucratic work culture wherein they perform routine activities, with low pay, and few opportunities for promotion or other incentives to perform.

Application of the PAG tool implies conducting interactive sessions with different user-groups and communities. When conflicts arise it is often not easy to the tool. This would depend on the location/s in question and mood of local user-groups and whether they would be able to participate freely in user-assessment. This is especially true for those socially excluded communities and remote areas. A possible remedy is to identify a neutral agency, which is locally respected and can undertake such a task.

For purposes of making the tool meaningful and operational over time, it is important to develop an organizational data base of user-groups. Developing a strategic plan for approaching remote areas and excluded communities for assessment of service delivery will help to make such a larger picture more meaningful. Such a strategic plan must also consider ways of creating an environment of trust and faith amongst the participants engaged in developing the larger picture.

Applications of PAG raises user-groups' expectations. The more people talk about their quality of local services the more they expect good things to happen. So it is important to find ways to manage expectations. One way is to mainstream the findings their problems into the national planning process and to allocate resources for implementation. This would also imply sharing findings of the tool with the user-groups and disseminating relevant actions undertaken government and other agencies. For any PAG, the people would like to many of their suggestions turned into action. One way would be that the relevant authority consider as many suggestions as possible, implement them and share news of their implementation with the public. This would emphasize the accountability part of PAG and motivate people to do further assessment of service delivery organizations. Any lethargy or delay in taking action based on people's suggestions and recommendations would mean that people would be less enthusiastic to participate in repeat PAG exercises.

In case of disseminating follow up actions on the findings of PAG and favorable decision-making by service delivery agencies, wide dissemination and communication with the public would help whether through public announcements, informal group meetings, public meetings, door-to-door meetings, distributing leaflets, announcements through media, advertisements, announcements through notice boards, schools, dispensaries, hospitals, and ration shops. Such steps would help to sustain the process of participation and motivate people to actively engage in assessing their own services and come up with ideas for improvement and also to contribute as users. Such monitoring tools are not that effective if people are generally in a negative mood for different reasons or have little or no hope in their local institutions and the government at large.

Replication and Scaling Up

Replication

Similar initiatives take time to start. In this context, usage of the tool has come a long way as far as the referred countries are concerned. However, additional funding for the tool for regular usage still remains an issue especially after the pilot-stage and completion of project. Recently Cambodia has begun looking for application of a similar tools to monitor MDGs at local and sub-national level from user-perspective though things are yet to firm up in terms of methodology to be used. UNDP Cambodia is in the process of exploring a suitable methodology for user-assessment of MDGs at the local/provincial level and decisions are yet to be taken about the application of a suitable tool.

Potential for Replication

This tool has great potential for replication and adaptation in different countries for participatory monitoring of MDG-related services. It is helpful to start with a pilot exercise in order to assess the applicability of the tool. Based on this a larger application can be planned. The way in which the tool is replicated should be determined by the objective(s). For example, if the objective is to obtain the assessment of service delivery by excluded user-groups then the field would need to be sampled for areas where such excluded communities reside and then sampled further in terms of villages/ towns and then purposively sampled further in terms of gender, age, social strata and others. It will also be necessary to determine how many of such user-communities can form a reasonable sample size and to factor in the extent of heterogeneity accordingly. For covering a larger sample size there is a critical need to have adequate preparation time as well as more than one team of facilitators and data processors.

Scaling up

The usage of the tool under reference can be scaled up on a much expanded basis though it is important to have a team of well trained facilitators for applying the tool in a participatory manner and also have enumerators for computerized data processing and software application. It can be a widely adopted model for user-assessment of services whether covering a few or multiple services, whether from government agencies and/or all service delivery agencies and whether across a district, province or a region or whether selected user-groups or all users. A neutral development agency acceptable to both users and the service delivery agencies will be another prerequisite. It is also desirable that such an agency has strong advocacy and dissemination skills for following up on the findings of PAG, to favouably influence decision-making and support wide dissemination of the results.

Necessary Changes in Policies and Knstitutions

Policies emphasizing the rights of citizens, consumers and users as well as good governance can bolster the use of the tool under reference. Setting up accountability mechanisms for service delivery agencies can also help. Though there are no perceived risks in usage of this tool there could be a showdown between a service agency, whose service are rated low and those user-groups, which actually do the rating. Again there is also a perceived risk that user-groups may be reluctant or not motivated enough to use the tool if their earlier assessments fail to produce any desirable result in terms of follow-up actions. Engaging a busy community for user-assessment of different services is often time-consuming and could take a whole or half day. Lack of good facilitators for application of the tool can end up in half-baked results which may then become cumbersome to handle and may distort findings when combined with user-assessments which have emerged out of a tested procedure based on good facilitation skills.

The need for a institutional mechanism for organizing PAG can not be emphasized enough. If people's voice and feedback are to be regularly considered then PAG needs to be institutionalized in a manner so that it happens on a regular basis for providing continuous feedback as required. It needs to engage different stakeholders in a long term partnership. The institution facilitating PAGs could have some desirable characteristics; it should be able to accomplish the following.

- reflect honesty of purpose and credibility
- organize local communities into group activities
- generate inclusive data
- handle data efficiently and in a timely manner

- provide high quality and dependable data
- provide regular and timely feedback on poverty
- communticate data to different stakeholders and channels in a user friendly way

The operational levels of such an institution would start from the bottom at the grassroots and also be able to reach the decision-makers at the top. An independent field research organization which is dependable, participatory and credible can undertake capacity building for PAG as well as provide mechanisms for follow-up on PAG.

References

Bandyopadhay, D., (2007). "On poverty, food adequacy and hunger in West Bengal"', Delhi, *Mainstream*, 19 June, Tuesday.

Bhatta, S. D. and Sharma, S. K., (2006). The Determinants and Consequences of Chronic and Transient Poverty in Nepal, CPRC Working Paper No. 66, Manchester, Chronic Poverty Research Centre.

Buhl, S., Wei, Q. and Xuixeong, W. (2004). *Report Card – Satisfaction Survey, An initial observation from China*, Technical Report 2, Beijing, GTZ, July.

Chambers, R., (1993). *Challenging the Professions Frontiers for Rural Development*, London, Intermediate Technology Publications, 1993

Mukherjee, A, (ed.). (2004). *Participatory Monitoring*, Delhi, Concept Publishing Company, 2004.

UNDP (2004), *West Bengal Human Development Report*, Delhi, United Nations Development Programme.

3

Gemi Diriya Project for Rural Development in Sri Lanka

May 2009 marked the end of Sri Lanka's nearly three decades long armed conflict, leading to a surge in optimism for stronger economic growth and poverty reduction. Yet even with the conflict, Sri Lanka has posted strong growth rates, putting the country on track to achieve most MDGs by 2015.

During the last five years, poverty has declined rapidly. For example, the poorest Southern Province has cut poverty in half, from 28% in 2002 to 14% in 2006/7. However, significant challenges loom large, not least addressing reconstruction in the North and East of the country.

Further south though, the vast disparity between the wealthier Western Province and the so-called "lagging regions" has long been cited as one of the country's most severe obstacles to growth. After all, two-thirds of the population resides in these "lagging regions" of the country, where poverty rates are more than double that in the Western Province.

To help bridge this gap, an innovative rural development program has empowered local communities in three southern provinces to find their own solutions to their development challenges. The program, known as Gemi Diriya or "the strength of the villages", is helping villagers identify, prioritize, plan, fund, and implement their own development needs.

The program is being implemented over 12 years in three phases. The World Bank supported the first phase of the program with a $51 million IDA grant in 2004, and approved on September 10, 2009 an additional $75 million IDA credit for the second phase. Since its inception in 2004, Gemi Diriya has touched the lives of close to 900,000 poor Sri Lankans in over 1,000 villages in Uva, Southern, and Sabaragamuwa Provinces.

The program has financed 2,140 community infrastructure subprojects, generated about 18,500 jobs, and provided support for livelihood activities to 140,000 households. Before the project, about 70 percent of households in the project villages had no access to credit and marketing facilities. Now, almost 20,000 self-organized savings and production groups are actively mobilizing savings. Savings groups have used their cumulative savings of $5.25 million to leverage credit equal to about ten times that amount, and have invested $17.6 million in more than 125 types of income generating activities.

The participatory nature of the decision making process has led to better targcting of the poor and improved governance, transparency and accountability at the village level. An independent evaluation showed that 90% of community members reported feeling empowered and having a sense of ownership over the project. About 98% repay loans with their savings and make new investments. And about 50% of households indicated an improvement in their economic and living conditions, all exceeding targets.

Unemployment rates in Sri Lanka also reflect regional disparities. They are much higher in rural areas and among youth and women. Gemi Diriya therefore gives priority to youth, women, and the most vulnerable groups in its decision-making. Youth and women now comprise 66% of decision-making positions at the village level. In addition, the community-owned and savings-led microfinance system allows them to generate and accumulate resources that are used to leverage additional funds from other government agencies, banks, and the private sector.

The vast majority of rural households in Sri Lanka depend on agriculture for their incomes. However, weak linkages to markets and poor infrastructure such as irrigation and electricity supply remain severe constraints. Most farmers are disconnected from the market, unaware of market opportunities, and are largely ignored by agribusinesses as sources of raw material. Farmers' incomes are hampered by poor linkage roads, by limited storage facilities and absence of wholesale markets," she said. "This leaves the farmers with no option but selling separately to middlemen whose margins amount to a high share of the farm gate price.

In its second phase, Gemi Diriya is putting more emphasis on how to improve productivity, competitiveness and ultimately the incomes of poor producers. This will be achieved through linking community institutions to local governments and addressing accessibility and connectivity constraints. It also aims to strengthen the value chains of key economic sectors by aggregating producers into federations to facilitate better market and financial sector linkages. Gemi Diriya is also expanding its reach to two more provinces (North Central and Central). By 2016, the program is expected to benefit 7 million people in 5,000 villages.

Brief Description of the Programme

Gemi Diriya is a participatory programme for rural poverty reduction implemented and funded by the Government of Sri Lanka, the World Bank, NGOs and local communities. Its mission is "Empower…; it does this by providing grants to regional government offices which then are used to support communities in forming VOs. Through the VOs communities implement livelihood support funds (using 45% of the budget, 80% of which is savings and credit) and they undertake infrastructure projects of their choosing (35% of the budget goes towards infrastructure). Participation is ensured in various ways most notably by requiring 80% of community to take part in Gemi Diriya, and by having villagers design and implement the projects, serve on committees, run the VOs and approve loans. Replication/ upscaling has been possible since the programme began as pilot projects implemented in 3 villages in 1 district in 1999, reached 27 villages by 2004 and 1036 villages in 7 districts by December 2008. Plans have been made to further up scale the work. Despite its success, challenges have arisen most notably that of political capture of the process. This has been limited through various means including ensuring broad participation of the community.

Location

Gemi Diriya is divided into 3 Phases of 4 years each. The pilot testing of its model preceded Gemi Diriya proper and took place in 3 villages in the Polonnaruwa district from 1999 to 2004 as the Village Self-Help Learning Initiative (VSHLI).

Samurdhi Authority will also implement the programme in 50 rural communities in accordance with Gemi Diriya principles and procedures. These will be in Hambantota, Ratnapura, Polonnaruwa, Moneragala and

Badulla districts. Phase II will also have 38 demonstration villages in two districts: 30 in Kurunegala district (in the North Western province) and 8 in Kalutara district (in the Western province).

Socioeconomic Profile

As Gemi Diriya is a national programme, what is relevant here is the socio-economic profile of the country.

The population of Sri Lanka had increased at 1.2% per annum from 14.8 to 18.8 million between 1981 and 2001. While the rate of increase was less in Matara (0.8%), Galle (1.0%), Badulla (1.0%) and Hambantota (1.1%), it was higher in Polonnaruwa (1.6%) and Moneragala (1.8%). Only Ratnapura conformed to the national rate. The density of population in the country was 344 per km for the 18 districts for which data was available in 2001 but it varied from 72 per km in Monaragala district to 613 per km in Galle district. This was much less than in Colombo district where it was 3,330 per km. The sex ratio in the country was slightly in favour of women (99.2 men for every 100 women). Men made up a smaller proportion in Matara district (94.2) but much larger proportion in Polonnaruwa district (109.7).

The percentage of children aged 6-14 years in the country attending school was 93.2% but it was much less (52.6%) for children 15-19 years. The variation was very little among the 7 districts; it was lowest in Ratnapura district (91.9%) and highest in Hambantota district (95.5%). Unemployment was 8.2% for the 18 districts. Among the Gemidirya districts, it was highest in Hambantota district (11.3%) and lowest in Polonnaruwa district (6.4%).

The per capita GDP and GNP at market prices was USD.2,014 and 1,969 in 2008. The median household income was USD 160.98 per month in 2006/07. The Gini coefficient was 0.49 which indicated a high disparity between the rich and the poor. The population one dollar a day was 5.6% (1990-2005) but it was as high as 41.6% for population below two dollars a day. Employment in agriculture was only 32.7% at the national level but in some of the poor rural communities where Gemi Diriya is implemented, it exceeded 75%.

Sri Lanka has invested substantially in education and health from even before independence in 1948 and provides universal education and health care for free. These facilities have been extended to the rural level throughout the country although they vary considerably from place to place.

The national level of literacy is 90.8% (male – 92.7%, female – 89.1%). Schools are found throughout the country. Among 44 Gemi Diriya villages in one DS division (Uvaparanagama), the distance to the primary school was 1½ km or less in 73% of the villages and in only 3 villages was it 4–6 km. Although rural people can readily access schools, Sri Lanka schools lack proper facilities and teachers.

Medical facilities have improved greatly in the past five decades, also for rural people. This has resulted in lengthening life expectancy of women to 75.8 years and men to 68.2 years. Apart from 8 provincial hospitals and 45 base hospitals in the country, there are 155 district hospitals, 101 peripheral units, 196 rural hospitals and 67 central dispensaries. Only in two of the 44 Gemi Diriya villages mentioned above was a rural hospital less than one km away. The distance to a rural hospital for the other villages ranged from 3 to 25 km; 37% of them were within 10 km from such a medical facility. There are also nurse-midwives in rural areas. However, medical facilities are less developed in rural areas and access to them is made more difficult by bad roads and poor transport services.

With a total road length of 91,907 km, the overall road density in Sri Lanka is 1.4 km/km of land. This is made up of 27,248 km of main roads (11,716 km national roads + 15,532 km provincial roads) and 64,659 km of classified rural roads. In the provinces where Gemi Diriya is implemented, road densities are lowest in North Central province (0.17 km/km for provincial roads and 0.51 km/km for local roads). They are highest in the Southern province (0.30 km/km for provincial roads and 1.48 km/km for local roads). Although roads are available, sometimes they are very poorly maintained making it difficult to use them. The fact that roads formed the largest category of village infrastructure undertaken by the communities under Gemi Diriya highlights the lack of satisfactory roads in rural areas with a high level of poverty. Access to bus transport was beyond ½ km for 63% of the 44 Gemi Diriya villages mentioned above. Poor accessibility also contributes to their poverty.

The telephone density (including cellular phones) was 71.9 per 100 persons in 2008. Until recently telephone communication was hardly found in rural areas but with the advent of cellular phone networks, this disadvantage has been overcome. Electricity was available to 83% of the households in the country but this was available more in urban areas. The government has been pursuing a rural electrification programme to bring electricity to rural communities. The World Bank funded Renewable Energy for Rural Economic Development (RERED) Project has taken electricity to remote rural communities through solar photovoltaic home systems and community based village micro-hydro projects. Among the Gemi Diriya provinces, Uva and Sabaragamuwa provinces have benefited most from rural electrification.

Situation Analysis

Poverty is the need addressed by Gemi Diriya as well as by other programmes (Samurdhi and Gama Neguma) and various policies followed by the government for several decades. Poverty is defined in economic terms but it has important social, psychological and spatial dimensions. The Gemi Diriya project addresses five widely accepted reasons for poverty in the country.

- The dependence mentality and the resultant absence of self-help and self determination which is a legacy of the colonial rule.
- The non inclusion of Women and Youth, which constitute more than 50% of the population, in the mainstream poverty reduction movement.
- Expectation of village development by plans formulated outside the villages at urban centres with less knowledge on the village realities and imposed upon village communities from the top.
- Absence of adequate reinvestment of the savings within the village economy while production decreases with increasing costs with no adequate insurance for village ventures.
- Absence of effective social mobilization.

Sri Lanka has achieved a Human Development Index (HDI) of 0.771 in 1998 which is higher than most developing countries. At the same one study estimated that the level of poverty in the country was 40%. However, other studies indicate different results.

One study shows that the period from 1985 to 1986 to 22.4% from 1990 to 1991. Poverty in the country has declined from 26.1% in the period of 1990 to 1991 to 15.2% in the years 2006 to 2007.

This poverty is more serious among the rural population not only because 79% of the poor are in rural areas but also because 24.4% of the rural population is poor compared to 18.3% in the urban sector and 12.6% in the estate sector.

As income data is unreliable and not always irrelevant to measure rural poverty Gemi Diriya followed a participatory process whereby communities assessed poverty in their own villages. The assessment is made by the community using income, materials used for the roof of the house, employment, level of education and lighting mode. The magnitude of the composie indicators is determined by the community and varies according to the conditions in the area. The selection is displayed within the community and members of the community can request for corrections. On the basis of data collected for 44 villages in the Uvaparanagama DS division, nearly 70% of the families were poor in a typical Gemi Diriya village.

Limited ownership of land is characteristic of these villages. Most of the families (76%) have some land but it is less than 1.0 hectare and 4% of the families are landless. Gemi Diriya addresses this issue by finding ways to increase productivity. Lack of infrastructure is an important need the programme addresses. Because of the lack of roads or their poor condition these communities find it difficult to get fair prices for their products and children find it difficult to go to school. People, especially women, have to spend a lot of time on getting water for domestic use. Since the community decides on how they use the funds made available by the Gemi Diriya Foundation for infrastructure development, roads and water supply are often their priority projects.

Focus of the Practice

The focus of the Gemi Diriya programme, as its name signifies, is strengthening the village by empowering the village community to initiate and take responsibility for its development.

As with other programmes such as Janasaviya, Samurdhi and Gama Neguma, poverty alleviation is a major objective of Gemi Diriya also but it gives rural communities authority to decide on their development. Gemi Diriya Foundation gives funds direct to the communities. It has laid down participatory procedures and guidelines to use resources effectively. Gemi Diriya emphasised the participation of a majority of the community and especially the poor, women and youth, in decision making. This differentiates Gemi Diriya from other poverty alleviation programmes implemented in Sri Lanka. The adoption of ethical principles laid down in the ten golden rules of Gemi Diriya is a critical requirement for communities to join the programme. Procedures have been designed to ensure their practice.

The programme focuses on capacity building of the key players to enable them to play their roles. A substantial proportion of programme resources is invested for this purpose. Capacity building programmes have been carried out for:

- Boards of Directors of Village Organisations (VOs)
- Financial Committee Members
- Procurement Committee Members
- Social Audit Committee Members
- Sub-Project Members
- VSCO Committee Members
- Community Professionals (CPs)

Scale of the Practice

With the experience gained from the pilot project, the Gemi Diriya programme was started in 2004; it was made available to 7,956 poor families in 27 villages. By December 2008 Phase I had concluded and had been extended to 1,036 villages in 7 provinces.

Of the 203,760 households are members of the VOs set up under Gemi Diriya. This satisfies the Gemi Diriya requirement that more than 80% of the community should be members and it means that the programme was reaching nearly 769,000 people in those villages. In Phase II it would reach a further 1 million people living in 850 villages including estate communities. It is eventually envisaged to reach between 4,000 to 5,000 village communities.

Duration

Gemi Diriya was started in 2004 with the understanding that the World Bank would provide support for it for 12-years. This period was to be divided into 3 Phases of 4 years each. The initial 4-year Phase I was started in December 2004. The second 4-year Phase II is now being implemented under a changed name: "Gama Neguma Community Development and Livelihood Improvement Project". It is envisaged that there would be some sort of merging between this programme and two other poverty alleviation programmes, Samurdhi and Gama Neguma, to achieve a more unified approach to poverty alleviation.

Institutional Structure

An elected executive president is the head of state of the Republic of Sri Lanka.An elected Parliament exercises the legislative power of the people. The Cabinet of Ministers and the Prime Minister are appointed by the President from among Members of the Parliament. The President is also the Head of the Cabinet and Government. The President can also appoint non-Cabinet Ministers.

The Central Government is made up of Ministries headed by the Ministers who are responsible for Departments, Boards, Authorities and other statutory bodies assigned to the Ministry.

The country is divided into 9 provinces and 25 districts. A District Secretary appointed by the central government administers the district. The 25 districts are divided into 256 Divisions which are administered by Divisional Secretaries (DS). The smallest administrative unit is the Grama Niladhari (GN = Village Officer) division. Central government departments are decentralised to the District and DS division levels and some of them to the GN level.

Some of the Central Government functions have been devolved to Provincial Councils which are representative bodies responsible for many functions in the Provinces. Local government functions are exercised by Pradeshiya Sabha (Regional Councils) at the DS Division level, Municipal Councils and Urban Councils.

Key Partners

The main stakeholders are the rural communities who are the beneficiaries and the Gemi Diriya Foundation that implements the programme but many others play a role as stakeholders at different levels.

At the VO level, the following are the stakeholders:

- Shareholders: These are the beneficiaries. They appoint the Board of Directors of the People's Company and decide on village development plans and activities. Encourage and supervise Small Groups, Clusters and the Village saving and Credit Organization.
- Hub and District teams: Advise, support, supervise and monitor performance of village institutions. Coordinate with village, divisional and district levels government officers, political autorities (Pradeshiya Sabha and other political leaders) and the Gemi Diriya Foundation.

- Village level government officers (Grama Niladari, Samurdhi Development Officer, Agriculture Research and Production Assistant, Family Health Officer, etc.). Provide government services to the village communities. Using facilities and information of village organisations in order to provide their services to communities (e.g., providing office space for Grama Nilidari; using baseline data for planning and making decisions)
- Community Professionals: Provide services related to social mobilisation, capacity building and institutional development to Gemi Diriya communities. Contribute to the strengthening of Community Professional Learning and Training Centers (CPLTCS).

At the Hub level, the following are the stakeholders:

- Regional Saving and Credit Organisation and Sub-Federations: Co-ordinate with VSCOs, VOs and Federations. Provide services to VSCOs and VOs. Supervise functions of VSCOs and VOs identify capacity building gaps and organising relevant training with CPLTCs; review progress of and provide services to VSCOs (appraising loans, linking banks, safety nets, micro insurance) and to VOs (develop weak areas, support to develop and link with producer groups, assist to link with private and other organisations, grading VOs, etc.)
- Divisional Secretary and Head of Government Departments at Divisional level: Approve village activities when necessary. Ensure services are provided by officers in their Departments.
- Divisional level government officers (Divisional Secretary, Samurdhi Managers, Agrarian Services Officers, Police, etc.) Provide government services to the village communities. Assist VOs to implement infrastructure sub projects (releasing lands).
- Pradeshiya Sabha (PS): Support VOs to construct and maintain infrastructure sub projects. Design and Implement interconnectivity infrastructure projects with the VOs. Attend to infrastructure needs. Approve village activities when necessary.

At the District / Provincial level, the following are the stakeholders:

- District Community Professional Learning & Training Centres and District Federations: Support VOs and other village institutions in social mobilisation and institutional development and activities of Sub-

Federations. Coordinate with private, government and non-government sector organisations.

- District Secretary and Head of Government Departments at District level: Approve village activities that need approval at that level. Ensure that officers in their Departments provide the relevant services. Coordinate with Gemi Diriya Federation, District Office. Educate political and other government organisations on project progress and lessons learned from the project.
- Chief Secretaries and Head of Department of Provincial Councils (PC): Provide technical services for PS interconnectivity development programme. Approve village activities as needed. Ensure officers in PC Departments provide the relevant services. Coordinate with Gemi Diriya Federation, District Office.
- District level line departments (Regional Forest Officers, Assistant Commissioner of Samurdhi, Assistant Commissioner of Agrarian Services, Commissioner of Local Government, National Water Supply & Drainage Board, National Youth Council, Mahaweli..etc). Provide services by staff in their Departments that are not provided by respective Departments at the Division level. Coordinate with Gemi Diriya Federation, District Office.
- Projects (e.g., Community Water Supply and Sanitation Project—CWSSP): Coordinate with VOs to upgrade water projects assisted by CWSSP.
- Plantation Managements and Plantation Trust. Approve project implementation in their estates. Educate estate officers on the project to assist estate communities.
- Banks (Bank of Ceylon, People's Bank, Regional Development Banks). Provide USD.460 and above loans to VSCO members. Offer lower interest rate and rewards for promoting savings (computers, name boards, wall clocks, etc.).
- NGOs (e.g. Plan Sri Lanka): Provide financial assistance to complex water supply projects.

At the National level, the following are the stakeholders:

- Ministry of Nation Building and Estate Infrastructure Development. Gemi Diriya Projects through the Foundation. Mobilize resources from

GOSL, The World Bank and other donor. Coordinates with the general treasury, The World Bank and other line Ministries.

- The World Bank: Provide financial and technical resources. Supervise, monitor and evaluate programme implementation. Coordinate with the Ministry of Finance, The General Treasury, Ministry of Nation Building and Estate Infrastructure Development and the Gemi Diriya Foundation.
- National Community Professional Training and Learning Centre. Develop capacity and grade Community Professionals. Audit District CPLTCs. Assist in development implementation and monitoring of the business plans of District CPLTCs. Provide services for organising workshops and seminars of Gemi Diriya Foundation. Strengthen VOs through mobilization and training (VSCO, SAC, etc.).
- Relevant Line Ministries: Provides services through Departments, Authorities and Boards in their Ministries.
- Relevant Departments, Authorities and Boards (Samurdhi Development Authority, Central Environment Authority, Export Development Board, Industrial Development Board, Sri Lanka Institute of Development Administration, National Apprentice and Industrial Training Authority, National Water Supply & Drainage Board, Registrar of Companies, Department of Auditor General). Provide services through their staff at National (where relevant), District, DS Division and GN Division levels.
- Related Projects (Gama Neguma Project, Information and Communication Technology Agency.
- Banks: Negotiate with Gemi Diriya Foundation to make savings and credit facilities available to VOs and VSCOs through their bank branches.
- Private sector (Cargills Ceylon Limited, Prima, Agribusiness Council). Provides inputs (e.g. seeds, fertilizer) to Federations and VOs on favourable terms. Purchases outputs at agreed prices on agreed terms (e.g. potato marketing programmes).
- Universities (University of Colombo, Kelaniya, Ruhuna). Provide research support. Undertake research and consultancy for Gemi Diriya Foundation. Provide higher level training.
- Non-Governmental Organisations (TSHED, Centre for Women's Research). Provide IT services to Gemi Diriya to maintain ITSHED

commercial web portal in VOs. Assist District Federations to create business linkages. Train Community Professionals on maintaining ITSHED web portal.

Practice Development and Operations

Initiation, Planning and Design

Being a national programme, Gemi Diriya was not started as the brain child of some individual or NGO. It evolved out of the history of efforts to alleviate rural poverty in Sri Lanka and other countries. "The Gemi Diriya project design offers a very carefully thought out model backed by a wealth of experience in project implementation in many parts of the world. During its design, many leaders of major poverty alleviation programs locally and abroad were involved in identifying impediments and risk factors in implementation." Its immediate precursor VSHLI. It was the outcome of discussions between Sri Lankan, World Bank and Japan Social Development Fund (JSDF) experts to find a community driven development (CDD) approach to alleviating rural poverty. was started in 1999 as a pilot project under the Mahaweli Restructuring and Rehabilitation Programme and was supported by the Japan Social Development Fund and the IDA.

When the VSHLI project demonstrated that the CDD approach of empowering communities to take charge of their development was successful the GOSL negotiated with the World Bank for 12 year Adaptable Program Lending (APL) to fund the scaling up of this successful CDD approach to cover 4,000 to 5,000 villages.

Gemi Diriya Community Development and Livelihood Improvement

Project came into being Gemi Diriya was based on lessons learned not only from VSHLI but also the Gama Neguma and Samurdhi poverty reduction programmes of the government of Sri Lanka.

Gemi Diriya Foundation was set up as an independent body to implement Gemi Diriya and became the World Bank's partner on behalf of the GOSL.

Initially Gemi Diriya contracted NGOs as partners to empower the communities. They were selected on the basis of their competence in social mobilization and organizational development. Gemi Diriya Foundation prepared training manuals to orient these NGOs in the Gemi Diriya model, values, procedures, etc. They were replaced as partners by Commujnity

Professionals (CPs) in 2007; the CPs were provided with detailed community operations manuals o use in educating the communities. The CPs were mainly young members of the communities where the programme has been implemented successfully. They have formed CPLTCs at district level.

Focus on the Poor

To achieve its focus Gemi Diriya worked out a carefully thought out methodology that comprised:

- selection of communities that are poor
- community willingness to adopt Gemi Diriya approach
- educating the communities in this approach laid out in the Community Operations Manuals
- organizing the community and putting in place the institutional structure
- training the functionaries in these institutes to manage them

To select districts and DS divisions that are poor, it used data collected on poverty by the Department of Census and Statistics. Poverty pockets or clusters within them were identified by applying poverty criteria accepted by the GOSL to the data available in Divisional Secretariats. Villages in these clusters were invited on the basis of their expressed willingness to accept the TGRs which were the "non-negotiable" principles of Gemi Diriya. "Overall the selection process appears to be working appropriately and the outcomes indicate that the clusters selected are from the poorest." At the village level the community is involved in gathering baseline data which includes the identification of the poorest, poor, medium and rich families using living standard profile and wealth ranking.

Participation

The Gemi Diriya model has provided many opportunities for members of the community to participate in decision-making. At least 80% of the families in a community should become shareholders of the People's Company which is the VO and serve in various capacities in the Board of Directors and its sub-committees. Members of the community form Small Groups that meet weekly to transact business at that level and discuss issues that affect the community or themselves. This ensures maximum participation. Furthermore, the office-bearers from 3 to 6 Small Groups form Clusters that also meet weekly; members of different groups are thus able to interact with each other.

Community members also have the opportunity to participate in the sub-committees of the VO. Permanent sub-committees exist for finance, procurement and social auditing.

In addition to these permanent sub-committees, community members can participate in the Livelihood Support Fund Sub-project Committee, Capacity Building and Communication Committee, Environment Committee, Youth Circle and other sub-project committees that the VO appoints to plan and implement specific community projects. Some community members have the opportunity to be selected as Community Facilitators. In that capacity they facilitate the work of the VO in the community.

The level of female participation in VO activities was consistently high. By restricting the number of shares any one family can own in the People's Company to 10%, Gemi Diriya ensured that poor members of the community also became shareholders.

Gemi Diriya Foundation provided funds to be given as one off grants to the poorest to start livelihood projects and for youth to get loans for skill development. This enabled even the poorest and the youth in the village to participate in and benefit from this programme. Despite all of the efforts to ensure participation of he poorest there has been criticism in some communities that the poorest had not been identified properly.

However, collective responsibility and consensus building are important principles that received much emphasis when strengthening the capacity of rural communities to implement the programme. To qualify for funds allocated for infrastructure development the community must determine the priorities through a participatory process. This also facilitated the participation of the community in meeting the requirement of contributing 10% of the cost in cash and 20% in labour and materials.

The VSCO manages the savings and credit activities in the village. Apart from members' own savings, it also handles the funds provided by the Gemi Diriya Foundation through its Livelihood Support Fund. Members of the community can borrow from the VSCO for livelihood improvement projects. To get a loan for such a purpose, the person must be a member of a Small Group and it must guarantee the loan. The member must also have a business plan and be able to repay the loan to the satisfaction of her/his Small Group. The Small Group, Cluster and other "officials" of the Company are involved in supervising the proper utilisation of the loan and its repayment.

Practice in Operation

Communities were mobilized to form village organisations. This averted the delays, difficulties and malpractices that take place when funds are channelled through government organisations. Gemi Diriya foundation credits funds directly to the VO accounts for implementation of development activities the communities decide on.

The interdependent steps to build community strength are:

- Developing vision and objectives
- Establishing organizational framework and understanding partners
- Participatory village development planning and preparation of sub-projects
- Building capacities
- Participatory implementation of development proposals
- Community procurement
- Managing finances and keeping accounts
- Managing operation and maintenance
- Community monitoring and learning
- Resolving conflicts

The ideology of the programme is stated in the Ten Golden Rules a set of core values which distinguish Gemi Diriya from other government programmes. Gemi Diriya strives to be demand driven by requiring 80 per cent or more of the members in a community to request to join the Gemi Diriya programme. They have to pledge that they will abide by the following 10 Golden Rules (TGRs) of Gemi Diriya.

1. *We must contribute to our development*—Every one in the village must work as a team and contribute time, money and labour to plan and implement Gemi Diriya activities to improve the living conditions in our village.
2. *We must have Confidence in Ourselves and Practice Self help* We must learn to manage affairs by ourselves in a sustainable manner and be self-reliant to reduce dependence on others.

3. *We tre Accountable to The Village for all Actions*—We have full freedom in decision-making process and management of financial resources, and hence must be responsible and accountable for all our actions.
4. *Good Governance is Key to Success*—Gemi Diriya Program is built on the principle of trust among all the villagers and between the village community and other partners. Any breach of trust can result in cancellation of funds and support.
5. *Let us Develop our Village Step-by-step*—Development is a gradual step-by-step process and we must plan what we can afford and successfully manage.
6. *Cost Effectiveness Pays*—Treat the funds provided under Gemi Diriya as our own funds. Realise that, if we can avoid wastage of funds, we will be able to take up more programs for the village.
7. *Be Open and Transparent in Our Dealings*—Everybody should have access to all the information related to village development activities. Any misuse of Gemi Diriya funds by anybody in the village shall be immediately reported and punished
8. *Uphold The Principles of Equity and Inclusion*—It is our responsibility to ensure that, all members of the village, especially those who need support the most, like the landless, the women, the unemployed youth etc. are involved in the development process and equally share the benefits of development
9. *Act Timely and Ensure Quality*—We must strive to complete implementation of development activities as per planned time schedules, maintaining national standards and specific quality, so that we become eligible to receive subsequent installments of project funds.
10. *Seek Help when Required*—Seek timely support from Gemi Diriya partners like, Divisional Facilitation Team, Divisional Coordinators, Divisional Community Facilitators, Line Department Officials NGOs etc., before problems and issues grow to unmanageable proportions

During the first two years of implementation Gemi Diriya contracted NGOs as SOs to empower the communities through social mobilisation. SOs were required to achieve this within one year. They operated at the village level through Village Facilitators (VFs) who were trained in the Gemi Diriya model, principles, practices and processes before they were assigned to work with the rural communities.

During the first 6 months, they educated and motivated the community members to participate in the establishment of the village institutional structure and to formulate a Village Development Plan. Through this process the communities learned not only the Gemi Diriya model and approach, its values and procedures but also to identify and prioritise community needs by educating them about preparing development plans for the community. The communities are expected to contribute 20 per cent in labour and 10 per cent in cash towards the cost of developing the village infrastructure identified in the plan; this ensures that the plan is based on the communities priorities by the middle of Phase I. About 80 per cent of the VOs had fully met community cash and labour contributions."

The effectiveness of the Gemi Diriya model in practice depended very much on how well the communities were mobilised by the VFs. They helped the communities to prepare proposals for community infrastructure and social service projects. Up to December 2008, 2,146 projects had been started, 55 per cent of them roads, 16 per cent multipurpose buildings and 11 per cent water supply.

SOs also built community capacity in organisational management and development, budgeting, accounting and micro-finance. At the end of the year the communities are expected to be able to manage their VOs and the VOs are expected to be able to undertake village development with technical and financial resources provided by the Gemi Diriya Foundation.

Gemi Diriya Foundation monitored this process carefully, and took remedial action to overcome these shortcomings. By 2007 instead of using NGOs to mobilise and educate communities joining the programme, Gemi Diriya started to engage CPs to do this work. During this time the community must form the Village Organisation and register it as a company with the Registrar of Companies and prepare the village plan.

Challenges and Responses

A very significant challenge initially was to insulate the programme from political interference. There could have been political interference in the selection of staff for the Gemi Diriya Foundation, selection of areas where the programme is implemented, selection of beneficiaries, and formulation of procedures to allow for political patronage in infrastructure development.

The establishment of Gemi Diriya Foundation as an independent body to implement the programme was the strategy used by the programme to avoid political interference.

This strategy has worked well. An effort by the Minister in charge initially to interfere in staff recruitment was resisted. Gemi Diriya Foundation received support for the stand it took from the highest echelons in government and it did not recur even after changes in the government. The selection of areas was done in a very systematic and transparent way. This did not leave room for interference by politicians at the local level. History of village institutions has been marked by their decline due to their politicisation. To face this challenge Gemi Diriya broad based the People's Company by making it a requirement that at least 80 per cent of the families in the village must become shareholders of it. At the same time, to prevent rural elites capturing power in the Company the acquisition of shares by one family is limited to not more than 10 per cent of the issued share capital.

Another very significant challenge was to change the attitudes of rural communities which had become accustomed to dependency as a result of government and NGO programmes that gave hand outs. Gemi Diriya was advocating self-reliance both for the individual community members and the community as a whole. Understanding and practice of the core values of the Gemi Diriya programme enshrined in the TGRs were essential the programme's success. However, in the household survey nearly 45 per cent of respondents indicated that they did not know the TGRs.

Resources

Most of the financial resources for Phase I of the Gemi Diriya programme came from the grant of $51 million from the World Bank and the allocation of $11 million from the GOSL. However, the total expenditures through December 2008 was $37.9 million. Of this $33.63 million was from IDA and the remaining $4.28 came from GOSL. 61 per cent of this was utilised for Village Development Fund and another 28 per cent for social mobilisation and organisational development. The Foundation also provided funds for infrastructure subprojects.

Of the funds for livelihood improvement, 5 per cent is to be given as one time grants to the poorest families and 10 per cent as loans for skill development for youth. Funds allocated for Livelihood Support disbursed by the VSCO. By December 2008 VSCO had released $13.09 million as

96,938 income generating loans and had received $1.22 million as interest income. This Fund will grow over time with the accrual of interest on loans.

Community resources are mobilised primarily through compulsory saving. Members who want to benefit from the Gemi Diriya programme must become members of the Small Groups and save at least $0.01 per day which they give to the Treasurer of their Small Group at its weekly meeting. Financial resources mobilised in this manner are available for members of the Small Groups to obtain emergency loans. As at the end of 2008, there were 145,124 members in 22,039 Small Groups who had saved $680,000 million as compulsory savings.

A few village communities have received funds from the decentralised budget of Provincial Council members and Members of Parliament.

Community resources are also mobilised through voluntary savings. Members who wish to save over and above the compulsory savings requirement can save with the Clusters and receive interest on their savings. These savings are collected by the Treasurers of the Small Groups and handed over to the Treasurers of the Clusters who deposit them in banks as Fixed Deposits to earn interest for the members. They had saved $1.15 million as voluntary savings by December 2008.

The time members spend on working for the Gemi Diriya programme voluntarily is also a resource mobilised by the programme. An important contribution in this regard is serving in different capacities in various bodies such as the Small Groups, Clusters, VSCO, Company and its sub-committees. The strengthening of community members in the various skills needed to perform these tasks is social capital that has been built up by the programme. A specialised aspect of this social capital is the CPs and the CPLTCs. The specialists available at the Hub Offices of Gemi Diriya and the Divisional Secretariats are also resources available for community members to implement their sub-projects.

Regulatory/Legal Structure for Participation

Unlike in regular projects a single implementing agency does not implement the entire programme. Gemi Diriya Foundation is the overall implementing agency while village institutions implement the programme at the village level. When discussing the institutional structure of the Gemi Diriya programme, it is necessary to distinguish between these two parts of the organisational structure.

The Gemi Diriya Foundation has been registered with the Registrar of Companies as an independent organisation under the Ministry of Nation Building & Estate Infrastructure. The World Bank recognises it as the agency responsible to implement this programme. The funding from the World Bank and the GOSL comes to it from the Treasury through this Ministry. Its Board of Directors is representative of the government and private sectors and is in overall charge of the programme implementation and the administration is headed by a Chief Executive Officer (CEO). Additional Project Directors and a Finance Controller are in charge of the main management functions at the Head Office.

The Foundation works at the District level through District offices in the seven Districts and at the DS division level through 33 Hub offices in 54 DS divisions. District offices are the link between the Foundation and the Hub offices. The Hub office is the lowest level to which the Foundation extends itself and maintains links with village institutions which are linked with the Foundation through these Hub offices and District offices. The Field Operations Unit of the Hub office is responsible for its work at the community level. The District and Hub offices are maintained by the Foundation and their staff are employees of the Foundation.

While the Foundation has a conventional top-down organisational structure described above, the organisational structure in the Gemi Diriya villages resembles a bottom-up structure that promotes the widest possible participation.

The base level organisation in which most of the members of the community participate is the Small Group consisting of 5-7 members and has a Chairperson, Secretary and Treasurer. Every village community that joins the Gemi Diriya programme must organise itself into Small Groups to enable face-to-face interaction, build trust and promote mutual self-help. They form the base of the village institutional structure. Unlike with most NGOs, the Foundation did not undertake the task of mobilising and organising the communities into Small Groups but outsourced it.

The Chairpersons and Treasurers from 5 – 6 Small Groups form the next higher level organisation,—the Cluster. These Clusters also have their Chairpersons, Secretaries and Treasurers. The Cluster Chairpersons and Treasurers form the Village Savings & Credit Committee (VSCC) which also includes two representatives from the Board of Directors of the People's Company of the village. It is the decision-making body in the Village Savings

& Credit Organisation (VSCO). Although VSCC is a part of VSCO, while the VSCC is a part of the bottom-up process, any member of the community can become a member of the VSCO by becoming a shareholder in the village People's Company.

The Village Organisation (VO) is a company registered with the Registrar of Companies. It is the only legal entity among the village institutions and disburses funds received from the Foundation. Members of the community who are members of Small Groups can become shareholders in the Company but in order to broad base it, no family can own more than 10% of the shares. There are no direct links between Small Groups, VSCO and the VO except that members of VSCO and shareholders of the Company are the same people who are the members of Small Groups.

Stakeholder Accountability

As Gemi Diriya does not conform to the normal "project" format and the model it has implemented devolves power to the community, accountability is practiced differently from regular projects. Accountability is usually to the higher level in the implementation hierarchy but in Gemi Diriya there is accountability both ways.

The Board of Directors and Committees of the People's Company are accountable to its shareholders who constitute the General Assembly. The Board of Directors must:

- inform the General Assembly the details of all the activities undertaken by it;
- place before it details of all spending, procurement, etc., for its approval; and
- seek its approval for all the rules, plans, etc.

Village institutions display information to the community on Village Information and Display Boards that are located in places where people gather. Small Groups, Clusters, VSCO, People's Company and its sub-committees maintain Minutes Book, Books of Accounts and other records that are available to any member of the community for inspection.

At the DS division and District levels, the Hub and District offices are accountable to the Foundation as well as to the communities. Community representatives participate in the evaluating the performance of these offices.

At the national level the Gemi Diriya Foundation is accountable to the GOSL and the World Bank through the Ministry of Nation Building and Estate Infrastructure Development. The CEO of the Foundation reports to its Board. Representatives of the Federations of VOs are invited quarterly to report to the Board on progress at their level and discuss challenges they face.

Outcomes of Gemi Diriya Project

Effectiveness

The World Bank decision to fund Phase II is an indication of the success of Gemi Diriya.

Its effectiveness must be judged on how successfully the Gemi Diriya model has taken root in the communities. According to the Mid-Term Review, "These broad indicators may be suggesting a process that is underway that is not immediately translated to substantial gains in income, but rather, strengthening the foundations of communities and their capacity to collectively address common issues and a set of public services."

Participatory procedures in which especially the poor, women and youth are involved are a core objective of Gemi Diriya. Many of these expectations have been realised and nearly three-fourths of the households had participated in the formulation of the Village Development Plan. However, its findings indicate that more than half the households felt that they had little or no control over decision making. It is encouraging to note that 32 per cent said that they had more control over decisions affecting their lives than before the Gemi Diriya intervention.

SOs were expected to play a critical role in introducing the Gemi Diriya model, values and procedures.

According to the MTR "The main objective of this sub-component (i.e., village level institutions) is to develop self-reliant, self-managed and sustainable peoples' organizations for community development and livelihood improvement in rural areas. Some SOs and VFs were not well versed in the approach that the GDP was promoting. This affected the community and the quality and performance of the VOs where these SOs worked."

A quantitative target set for its Phase I is the number of villages to be covered. This Phase aimed to cover 1,000 village communities during its four years. At end of the first phase the programme had set up VOs in 1,036 village communities thus fulfilling this target.

Efficiency

It is not possible to assess the efficiency of this programme simply on the basis of inputs and outputs because the programme mission aims to achieve qualitative goals that are not time bound. Therefore a significant proportion of the resources have been invested in building up social capital that would bring long-term benefits. Of the expenditure on Project Management a fair proportion could be considered to be directly or indirectly incurred for the same objective.

The VOs and Federations of VOs help members of the communities to obtain inputs on more favourable terms, find markets for their products and negotiates to obtain better prices for them.

Innovation

The most significant innovation made by Gemi Diriya is the trust the programme has placed in rural communities that is manifested by the devolution of responsibility, resources and authority to them. Gemi Diriya Foundation provides funds direct to them and they have the authority to decide how to utilise those funds within broad guidelines set by the Foundation. This is real empowerment of the people, especially the poor, women and youth. Developing CPs who could undertake social mobilisation and organisational development at the community level is also an innovation that has reduced the dependence of communities on external human resources.

Another innovation is the provision made by Gemi Diriya to sustain and improve the processes and benefits of the programme after it withdraws. Hub Offices play an important role during the initial period of implementation but their functions are taken over by Federations of VOs that are being formed at District level. The scaling up of operations through Federations and networking have helped the VOs to mainstream their activities through links with the private sector.

Unexpected Outcomes

The unexpected outcomes have been positive. The most important of them is the recognition that the Gemi Diriya approach has received from the government. In the initial stages of implementation, much displeasure was expressed by politicians about being left out of the loop that transferred funds to the communities. Also the power that VOs were given to decide on contracts deprived the local politicians of funds they could have distributed to their supporters.

The decision by the government to adopt the Gemi Diriya approach and methods to its countrywide programmes of Samurdhi and Gama Neguma is a very significant unexpected outcome. This would bring about a more unified approach to rural development-poverty alleviation programmes in the country.

Another unexpected outcome is the emergence of CPs and the establishment of CPLTCs. The idea came from members of the communities in VISHLI themselves. It is now well established and there were 1,332 CPs as of December 2008.

Lessons Learned

A key operational lesson learned is that the Gemi Diriya model can be implemented and replicated successfully.

A complementary lesson is that the success of the model has been ensured by a carefully worked out implementation methodology. The programme invested in developing 14 detailed community operational manuals on the different aspects of the model to enable community members to understand their role and procedures they should follow to achieve development for themselves and their community. This process of community education and mobilisation was facilitated by SOs engaged for that purpose. When the programme observed that SOs were failing in this task, it supported the development of CPs. That was an initiative that emerged from the communities themselves.

Other lessons include:

- a new leadership can emerge if women and children are particularly involved.
- Financial support should be given in the form of loans rather than hand outs to all but the poorest of the poor.
- It is important to prevent political interference in the beginning of the programme; political backing may be useful after some time as long politicians do not use the programme to appease their constituents.

- Transparency, methodological fairness and participation of beneficiaries lended the programme credibility.

Gemi Diriya and Sustainability

Degree of Sustainability

Gemi Diriya has built in safeguards to ensure the sustainability of the VOs and the benefits communities gain through them. An important achievement in that respect is the building up of social capital, i.e., enabling communities to manage institutions. Initially, this was done through social mobilization to educate the communities on the benefits of working collectively. Subsequently several training courses were conducted to provide the community with the required skills to manage their institutions and undertake development. The emergence of CPs and the establishment of NCPLTC and District CPLTCs is an outcome of this process.

Gemi Diriya has recognised that ideology is necessary but not sufficient to sustain what it has initiated. It has, therefore, backed it up with institutions in which most of the members in the communities can participate in deciding how community resources are utilised. Detailed procedures are laid out in Community Operations Manuals for the good governance of these institutions. A system of accountability ensures that good governance is practiced. The People's Company which is the apex institution in each community comes under the strict surveillance of the Registrar of Companies. These measures are designed to avoid the malpractices that caused other rural institutions to fail.

In order to gain more favourable terms of trade with commercial enterprises in the private and government sectors, Gemi Diriya has networked VOs with each other. As a further step in that direction VOs have been federated at the District level to transact business on a larger scale.

Partisan politics have played an important role in the breakdown of village institutions in the past. Gemi Diriya has avoided this by incorporating measures that prevent political capture of the programme.

The VOs pay their staff moderate allowances which helps to minimise the management costs. In the long run it might become necessary to pay them higher salaries; it is expected that the VOs will meet that cost. The MTR found "90 per cent of the VOs are generating revenue from interest on loans, profits from operations, in excess of operating costs." The following data on the income and expenditure of five typical VOs from different Districts illustrate that for most VOs revenues exceed expenditure.

Leadership plays a vital role in the performance of village institutions. Gemi Diriya uses several methods o prevent local officials from replacing the Gemi Diriya leadership. The VOs in Gemi Diriya villages are led by members of the community who are inspired by its TGRs and are committed to serve the community. This leadership is voluntary and tends to be drawn from among the women and youth in these communities and is better equipped to sustain the VOs. To avoid a few people having to carry this responsibility all the time and enable more to participate in leadership, office-bearers must be changed periodically but to maintain continuity, only a portion of the leadership is changed at any one time.

Achieving Greater Sustainability

Although Gemi Diriya has been introduced to 1,036 village communities during Phase I which ended in mid-2008 different communities are implementing it at varying levels of success. This is due to:

- varying degrees of competence and commitment of SOs and CPs;
- not all the communities were equally committed to the Gemi Diriya process that emphasised self-reliance;
- the leadership in some communities did not fully understand the Gemi Diriya approach and was not committed to it.

In process oriented programmes like Gemi Diriya there would always be VOs that lag behind. Part of the strategy to help them catch up with others has been to be link hem up with more successful communities that could help them.

Most VOs are too small to face challenges on their own; they are therefore strengthened by bringing several of them together. This is being done by forming Federations.

Challenges Ahead

With greater convergence of Samurdhi, Gama Neguma and Gama Neguma Community Development and Livelihood Improvement Project (Gemi Diriya renamed in Phase II to distinguish it from the national programme by the same name) there is a risk of political interference. The main safeguard is that World Bank funding will depend on a strict adherence to the Gemi Diriya principles and procedures. At present these are protected by the CEO and the Chairman of the Board. More independence and a stronger role for the Board of the Gemi Diriya Foundation would help the programme to be insulated better from political interference, however, there is a strong possibility that the Foundation would be dissolved by the end of Phase II. This would be a major challenge for what Gemi Diriya has so far implemented successfully.

As its livelihood component becomes more successful and the programme is extended to more villages, it needs to pay more attention to developing its commercial strength. The attempt by Gemi Diriya to give the VOs an ideology-based corporate character needs to be strengthened through continuous education and training. In the future, VOs and Federations must undertake this cost; it will be a challenge to make them realise the importance of this.

There will be a need to find more markets as well as add value to rural products through processing. This will present challenges in introducing new technology, quality consciousness and marketing that will require strengthening of commercial skills of VOs and the Federations. It will also be necessary to develop a commercial outlook among producers to raise productivity and quality at different levels to gain the full benefit from the new opportunities.

Replication and Scaling Up

Replication

Replication of Gemi Diriya has taken place in Sri Lanka. After the institutional model to be used for Gemi Diriya was pilot tested as VSHLI between 1999 and 2004 Gemi Diriya programme Phase I expanded very rapidly between 2004 and 2008. In the five years of pilot testing it expanded from 3 to only 27 villages but in the next four years Gemi Diriya added another 1,009 communities. It will also be replicated in other countries since projects in India and Bangladesh plan to use the Gemi Diriya approach.

Potential for replication

The need for what Gemi Diriya is achieving is there in every developing country. As the Gemi Diriya model is community driven, theoretically it is possible to implement it in any community. However, it is a very resource (human and financial) intensive model and requires a considerable amount of resources and an effective implementation system to implement it successfully.

Where conditions are very different, the model would have to be modified suitably for communities to adopt it successfully. It is not a model that could be simply transplanted from one community to another quite different community.

Scaling up

The success that Gemi Diriya has demonstrated has persuaded the government to adopt this approach for its flagship rural development programme; Gemi Diriya has been renamed accordingly as the 'Gama Neguma Community Development and Livelihood Improvement Project'. Even the long standing poverty alleviation programme, Samurdhi, is adopting some of the Gemi Diriya strategies. Samurdhi Authority has been entrusted to implement this programme in 50 villages under Phase II. Both of these programmes are implemented countrywide. Staff from these two programmes is being trained in Gemi Diriya approach as the government is intending to bring about convergence of these three important rural development-poverty alleviation programmes.

Necessary changes in policies and institutions

Even within the Gemi Diriya communities, the People's Company is the only legal entity. Apart from being accountable to its shareholders it is accountable to the Registrar of Companies also. There are no legal provisions to regulate the conduct of the Small Groups, Clusters and VSCOs which are crucial to the savings and credit activities of community members. Their strength as well as their vulnerability is that they are self-regulating. Given good leadership and commitment they would function well but in the absence of such leadership and commitment, they could become inactive. There is a need for a mechanism to supervise, regulate and support them. Considering how ineffective governmental systems could be, some independent body might be better for it. The Federations play this role to some extent but it might be better for that body to be independent.

References

Alkire, S. (2002). Dimensions of human development. *World Development* Vol. 30 (2): 181 – 205.

Asian Development Bank ADB RETA (2002). Regional Technical Assistance for the coastal and marine resources management and poverty reduction in South Asia – 5974. Situation analysis report - Sri Lanka component. Asian Development Bank and IUCN Sri Lanka.

Carney, D. (editor). (1998). *Sustainable Rural Livelihoods*. Department for International Development, UK.

Narayan, D., Chambers, R., Shah, M. and Petesch, P. (2000). *Voices of the poor: crying out for change*. World Bank, Washington, D.C., USA.

Senaratna, S. (2003). Community participation in research: Research undertaken in Sri Lanka 2002. Sustainable Coastal Livelihoods (SCL) Project Report, IMM Ltd, Exeter, UK.

Skutsch, M. (1990) Social forestry in integrated rural development planning, Sri Lanka. RWEDP, FAO, Bangkok, Thailand.

White, S. and Pettit, J. (2004). Participatory approaches and the measurement of human well-being. WIDER Research Paper No. 2004/57

4

Philippine Rural Reconstruction Movement

The Philippine Rural Reconstruction Movement (PRRM), is a non-governmental organization and institution formed in 1952 in order to assist the poor members of society in the Philippines. As a movement, it was initiated by upper and middle class group of individuals based on the experiences gained from the rural reconstruction and development done in China during the beginning of the 1900s. After World War II, among its tasks had been the establishment of cooperatives in rural communities. It was the inspiration of the founding of the Federation of Free Farmers in 1953, as well as the birthing of organizations similar to PRRM in other countries such as Thailand, Colombia, India, and Guatemala Its main office is currently based in Quezon City., which became possible through Dr. Yen's establishment of another related organization during the 1960s, namely the International Institute of Rural Reconstruction (IIRR).

Over the past five decades, PRRM has made a number of major contributions to Philippine rural development. It pioneered a whole era or rural development and local democracy in the country. PRRM was the first NGO to send its workers to the villages to implement its integrated, fourfold program of education, livelihood, health, and self-governance. PRRM pioneered the establishment of an elected barrio government. Today's Barangay Council can be claimed by PRRM as one of its contributions to grassroots democracy. PRRM inspired the formation of similar national movements in Colombia, Guatemala, Ghana, India and Thailand.

Vision and Mission of PRRM

The PRRM envisions a world of equity and sustainability, where society is free of ignorance, poverty, disease, and powerlessness; and where development takes place within the environment's carrying capacity .

Other than that, the PRRM also plans and implements integrated and community-based resource management . The visions and missions of the PRRM aim to bring the welfare and living standards of the people of the Philippines to a significantly better level.

Values of PRRM

The PRRM believes in several values . Firstly, PRRM believes in justice and equity, which means that the poor should be treated with a preferential bias since they would have already been faced with much inequality in the past. PRRM also wishes to promote gender inequality and this would be shown in the projects done by PRRM.

Secondly, the PRRM believes that one key ingredient for authentic development would nonetheless be unity and peace. It is especially essential for the Philippines as it is a vibrant nation with a diversity of culture and religious beliefs. The variances and differences should be overcome so that the Filipinos can achieve their goals as one united nation, and this will eventually lead to development for the country.

The PRRM also believes that nationalism, a reflection of a common ideology, is the key to authentic development. The people of the Philippines need to truly believe in their capacity in achieving what they want. Indeed, special attention to utilizing and developing the indigenous efforts is essential in promoting self reliance.

Furthermore, PRRM believes that all development must take into consideration the protection of the environment. This will ensure that the environment will not be heavily strained on and that the future generations can continue to benefit from the Mother Earth.

With regards to culture, PRRM believes that the Filipino people have a vibrant and beautiful culture which they truly enjoy sharing with others.

Last but not least, PRRM also believes that development is for the people and by the people. Genuine people's participation at every stage of development is the essence of community empowerment.

Goals of PRRM

Among its present-day roles is the promotion of sustainable agriculture, technologies in the fishing business and farming, agroforestry, planning and implementation of managing resources in communities, the fight against ignorance through education, the fight against proverty through livelihood training, the fight against diseases through health education, improvement in access to justice, restoration of cohesion and connection among and between communities, creation of livelihood, environmental stewardship, awareness of public policies, and the dissemination of information to other Philippine and Asian non-governmental organizations.

A core objective of the Philippine Rural Reconstruction Movement is to build up the Conrado Benitez Institute for Sustainability (CBIS), which functions as the educational, research and technical troubleshooting wing of the PRRM. By focusing on education for sustainability through providing educational courses which cover topics such as sustainable local economy, agriculture, coastal resource management, new and renewable energy, and gender issues, CBIS aims to inculcate sustainability into the future generation. In addition, the PRRM intends to advocate issues related to environment and sustainable development, economic development, social development and the rights of women, children and youth, and governance and citizen's participation.

Other long term goals also include the creation of an organization information database and the implementation of a "report card" system. The former acts as the basis for monitoring the ongoing projects and operations and the aim is to boost the efficiency of the different operations by at least 25% . While for the latter allows progress and accomplishments of ongoing projects to be recorded and reported. The PRRM aims to achieve workflow streamlining, publication exposure and quality, improved staff training and management accountability.

Historical Background

In the 1900s, the Philippine Rural Reconstruction Movement was founded and inspired by its then leader Dr. Y.C. James "Jimmy" Yen (also known as Yan Yangchu), a national of China. It was brought the Philippines, specifically in Nueva Ecija and then also in Rizal province, by Filipinos such as Conrado Benitez, a person connected to the University of the Philippines, with the vision to empowering and developing rural communities and the aim of providing training on self-government and on how such communities can sustain itself globally, nationally, and locally.

Apart from Conrado Benitez, original members of PRRM's Board of Trustees also included Salvador Araneta, Cornelio Balmaceda, Cecilio Putong, Juan Salcedo, Jr., Asuncion A. Perez, Gil Puyat, Paul R. Parrette, and Albino Z. Sycip. Apart from Benitez, Sycip, Putong and Salcedo, Jr., PRRM's original incorporators also included Esteban E. Abada, Eulogio Rodriguez, Jr., Roland Renne, Juan Cojuangco, Oscar B. Arellano, and Jose S. Camus.

In 1970, former Philippine Secretary of Health and Senator Dr. Juan Flavier, conveyed his experiences while working with and for PRRM by writing his book entitled Doctor to the Barrios.

In 2009, PRRM became a partner of the Ayala Foundation USA, with the task of building potable water facilities within chosen Philippine barangays.

Integrating Climate Change Adaptation and Disaster Risk Reduction into Local Development Planning

PRRM uses a multi-stakeholder approach to promote climate change adaptation and disaster risk reduction in the local development planning processes.

Communities in the Philippines are feeling the brunt of climate change through decreased agricultural production, unpredictable seasons and weather patterns, sea level rise, and increasing intensity of typhoons.

Scientists and professionals have linked these effects to the predicated impacts of climate change but do so in highly technical terms citing melting ice caps and concentrations of greenhouse gases, which at the community level in a tropical country can be difficult to relate to. Most of activities to address climate change in the Philippines have been research based. Only a few examples can be cited of community based climate change adaptation projects.

PRRM used an approach that was inclusive and transparent to all concerned sectors, contacting all relevant sectors before the project began to describe the activities and the potential involvement of relevant stakeholders. Community based workshops were then held with 5 barangays (villages) located on San Miguel island, Tabaco City, Albay, to analyze the vulnerabilities and capacities and to assist the communities in their formulation and prioritization of issues and potential solutions. These were then presented at a validation workshop with all key stakeholders present. In this way all felt that they had a stake producing resilient communities. In one case commitments were made to support the initiatives proposed that helped maximize local resources and reduce dependency on external aid.

This localized approach is in turn being utilized to update the national policies and systems to incorporate DRR within the context of the Hyogo Framework for Action.

Location

The practice took place in San Miguel Island, Tabaco City, Province of Albay, Philippines as shown in Map 6 below.

The City of Tabaco is one of three cities in the Province of Albay. It is located on the eastern coast of Albay province with an area of 11,714 hectares. Its territory occupies a large part of the mainland, which extends from San Miguel Island located a few kilometers to the east, within the Lagonoy gulf, the Municipality of Malinao to the north, the Municipality of Malilipot to the south and the City of Ligao to the southwest.

The city is composed of 47 barangays (villages), 21 urban barangays and 26 rural barangays. There are 5 island barangays,—those of San Miguel Island (Rawis, Sagurong, Visita, Agñas and Hacienda), 9 coastal, 18 lowland and 15 upland barangays.

The City of Tabaco's land (generally flat terrain with small hills (maximum 13m above sea level) and seascape is overshadowed by the active volcano Mount Mayon, which rises over 2,462 meters above sea level.

Socioeconomic Profile

The province of Albay had a total population of 1,190,823 in the year 2007 and the City of Tabaco accounted for almost 10% of this total population. Tabaco had the second highest population in the whole province. The City is projected to have a total population of 131,685 for the year 2012. This means that there will be 2% growth within a five year period from 2008 to 2012. With Tabaco's land area of 117 sq. km., it has a density of 1,054 persons per sq. km., which is higher than the provincial average of 478 persons per sq. km. in 2007. The majority of the population is urban and found on the western side of Tabaco. The urban part of Tabaco which has an area of 18 sq. km. is denser than its rural portion. It has a density of 3578 persons per sq. km. while the rural area, which has a total land area 98.8 sq. km., has a density of 569 persons per sq. km. Based on the 2008 CBMS survey the labor force of Tabaco is 56% of the total population while the total dependency ratio is 60%.

There are 24,850 households with 121,752 population in Tabaco City. Males make up 61,655 or 51% while females are slightly lower in numbers with 60,097 or 49%. 30% of the households of the city belong to absolute or subsistence poverty threshold and 48% belong to the poor. The absolute or food poor are those households whose total income is not enough to buy food requirements for its members. The poor are those households whose total income is not enough to cover food and other essentials for their members.

San Miguel Island in Lagonoy Gulf east of Bicol is endowed with vast coral reefs, seagrass/algal beds, and mangroves where inhabitants rely on fisheries for food and income. The island's economy is basically capture based fisheries, in particular, it is reef resource-dependent as shown by the dominance of reef fish and invertebrates in the composition of catch from the island. Fishing and other activities by humans, directly or indirectly stress these habitats and, are therefore a prime concern for management. The population of San Miguel Island totals about 13,500.

About half of the population (48%) live in housing made of strong materials (concrete, brick, stone, wood, galvanized iron), while 35% live in housing made of light materials (bamboo, sawali, cogon, nipa). Most vulnerable are those living in makeshift housing or who are squatters; the share of households in this group ranges from 0.6 to 6.2%

All households share a source of water, either dug/shallow well (3 barangays), river/stream/spring (1 barangay) or deep well.

Less than half of the total households have sanitary toilet facilities:

Eight per cent of children aged 0-5 years old are malnourished. With the assistance of the City and Provincial governments the Barangays are implementing supplemental feeding programs in an effort to reduce this percentage.

The island got electricity in 2008, but still not all areas are covered. It is expected that by the end of 2009 all areas will have access to electricity thereby facilitating home-based livelihoods, and school work being carried on beyond dusk.

The island has elementary and high schools but no college. For the latter, students have to travel to and from the city (approximately 30 minutes boat ride). For the available schools on the island most of the teachers commute each day from the mainland. This means that when the sea is rough, there are no classes or they are delayed.

There is also a high drop-out rate of children from school – especially high school. A recent survey by the Tabaco City Government and the Department of Education found that the main reason children did not attend school was the lack of supplies. In response the city government has allocated funds for the provision of supplies.

Economic Data

Fishing, farming and handicraft making are the primary sources of income for the five Barangays in San Miguel Island. The unemployment rate on the island is 13.4%, with barangay Rawis contributing over half of the total number of unemployed. Share of the population below the poverty line is quite nigh in all barangays ranging from 70 to 85%. The situation is worst in Rawis.

The main environmental issues include deforestation and destructive fishing practices. Apart from Barangay Agnas that has local policy restricting the cutting of trees for family use only, all other areas suffer from forest denudation, especially Barangay Hacienda that has the largest land area of all 5 barangays. Extensive deforestation also extends to mangroves-a vital buffer between land and sea and an important nursery habitat for many marine species. Very few mangroves remain on the island today with most having been cut for charcoal making for cooking. Coral reefs around the island have also been impacted by the practice of dynamite fishing. An attempt to alleviate this situation was the implementation of a fish sanctuary zone in Barangay Sagurong, established in the 1990's by the Bicol University Tabaco Campus (BUTC) and bans all fishing activities in this area protecting the reefs and breeding grounds of the fish.

The main programs implemented are Health assistance, Credit programs, Education/Scholarship programs, Supplemental feeding programs, Housing programs and Skills/Livelihood training programs. Most programmes are implemented by Private/NGO and City Government (CBMS).

Needs Addressed/Situation Analysis

The Philippines ranks as the world's fourth most disaster-prone country. In the last quarter of 2006, the country was hit by three destructive typhoons and a volcanic eruption which displaced most of the communities in the province of Albay.

Typhoons provide the greatest natural (climate related) hazard risk to the City. Climate related disasters have also been increasing over the previous decades within the Philippines generally and in Tabaco City as well.

Efforts need to be taken to reduce vulnerabilities to these hazards and increase capacities to cope.

Households and communities are more impoverished than ever after disasters occur. There is an urgent need to restore their lost livelihoods and assets as well as rebuild their ravaged natural habitat and transform them into disaster-resilient and self-sustaining communities.

Government goals to reduce poverty and improve health and education are unlikely to be achieved unless efforts are unified to address disaster and climate risks.

In partnership with Local Government Units (LGUs) and other key stakeholders, the PRRM developed a program addressing the lack of enabling policy and institutional framework to systematically integrate disaster risk reduction and climate change into local development planning. This integration will facilitate the transformation of these communities from their current state of vulnerability into sustainable communities that are resilient to natural disasters and climate change.

Focus of the Practice

In general, this project aims to build awareness and capacity of key stakeholders to integrate and mainstream disaster risk reduction and climate change adaptation into the local development planning and budgeting process.

Specifically, this collaborative action research project aims to raise awareness of the key stakeholders, the LGU, the private sector, people's organization and local communities on disaster risk reduction and climate change adaptation to foster a culture of safety and resilience. It builds key stakeholders', individual, community and institutional capacities in participatory risk and vulnerability assessment and DRR and CCA planning for integration into local development planning. Finally it disseminates the results of action research for adoption and replication by other LGU, DCCs and other organizations in similar coastal ecosystems.

The action research project adopts a participatory, community-based, multi-stakeholder approach to disaster risk reduction (DRR) and climate change adaptation (CCA) assessment and planning involving the key stakeholders. Project activities are undertaken in coordination with the LGU, relevant government agencies, the people's organizations and the target coastal communities and other groups and individuals in San Miguel Island.

The main tool used during this project was a training/workshop that incorporated participatory research tools. The training module consisted of the following sessions:

1) Climate Change Adaptation Orientation
2) Disaster Risk Reduction Orientation
3) Vulnerability and Capacity Assessment
4) Indigenous Systems for Early Warning and responses Mechanisms
5) Issue Identification and Prioritization of responses to the risk of disasters
6) Mainstreaming climate change adaptation and disaster risk reduction into the local development policy, planning and budgeting processes

The use of participatory research tools and techniques such as mapping, diagramming, ranking, etc. makes use of local/traditional knowledge of the communities in disaster risk reduction and climate change adaptation. This local knowledge is combined with scientific data and information generated from various government agencies in order to produce a coastal development plan that reduces their vulnerability to natural disasters such as tropical cyclones, droughts, and the adverse impacts of climate change.

Scale of the Practice

The practice aimed to train 25-30 key community members in each of the 5 barangays on San Miguel Island. In total 154 community members (direct beneficiaries) attended the training which through participatory approaches analyzed their areas of vulnerability and capacity and prioritized effective solutions for climate and disaster risk reduction. These were then presented at a validation workshop with barangay, city and provincial stakeholders in attendance (49 in total) to guide incorporation of suggested measures into local development planning.

The actual practice (series of community trainings together with the validation workshop cost around $11,000. The projected cost of proposed solutions incorporated into local development plans and budget reached over $213,000 (the majority of which were expenses for upgrading water supply systems).

Duration of the Practice

The practice lasted for 12 months.The community action plans were incorporated in 2008 for effect in 2009. The follow up showed that although many of the plans were implemented, those that were not are included in the plans for 2010. CDRR initiatives will be incorporated into all future development plans at the barangay and city level.

Institutional Structure

As PRRM began in 1952, it demonstrated the effectiveness of involving local communities in development planning. This demonstration prompted the Philippine Congress to enact the Barrio Council Act in 1954 which paved the way for the election of barrio (village) officials.

The City Disaster Coordinating Council (CDCC) of Tabaco is the local support unit of the National Disaster Coordinating Council (NDCC). Its task is to facilitate the coordination of the public and the private sectors within the city in times of calamities and natural disasters.

The City Social Welfare and Development Office (CSWDO) has identified locations (with respect to the specified natural disaster) to be used as evacuation centers in cases of Mayon volcano eruption or typhoons and floods.

The Tabaco City Disaster Management Plan follows the guidance given by the NDCC which is governed by the following legislation:

Presidential Decree (PD) 1566, "Strengthening the Philippine Disaster Control, Capability and Establishing the National Program on Community Disaster Preparedness", issued on 11 June 1978, established the authority, units concerned, and process required to manage disasters with emphasis on emergency response rather than risk reduction. An analysis of the Philippine Disaster Management System (PDMS) shows that the commitment to respond to disasters as reflected in the calamity fund appropriations from 1991 to 2007 is overwhelmed by the cost of damage brought by the fury of natural hazards. The legislation and characteristics of the PDMS were designed in a time before disaster management evolved into a longer-term outlook of disaster risk reduction and more recently with regards to climate change issues. The National Disaster Coordinating Council (NDCC) has adopted the Community Based Disaster Risk Management (CBDRM) as a model to engage communities in disaster risk reduction, but the capacities of the local disaster coordinating councils are uneven. This is contained in a Strategic National Action Plan on CBDRM 2007 – 2011. For over a decade now, various groups, including PRRM through the DRRNetPhils, have been advocating for a new disaster risk management law due to the various gaps, limitations and reactive posture of Presidential Decree 1566. The proposed DRRM Bill encourages the government to shift its focus to disaster prevention and risk reduction by putting more emphasis on strengthening the communities' and people's capacity to anticipate, cope with and recover from disasters, as an integral part of proactive development programs.

Practice Development and Operations

Initiation, Planning and Design

PRRM has been working with the communities in Tabaco City and San Miguel Island especially since 1999. People's Organizations were formed around the concerns of health, livelihood and the environment (fisheries) with the support of 2 externally funded projects.

When the area was heavily impacted by Typhoon Reming in 2006, there was a realization (by the PO's and PRRM alike) that sustainable development initiatives were being hampered by disasters, especially climate related disasters (that are projected to increase in intensity due to climate change) and there was a need for risk resiliency to be incorporated into community programs.

An area profile was developed through these discussions, courtesy calls were made to the relevant stakeholders and secondary data was gathered to localize the intiative.

Focus on the Poor

The practice targeted the poor since it benefitted the residents of San Miguel

Island most of whom subsist on fishing and farming and live below the poverty threshold.

The practice assisted the community members to identify their own vulnerabilities and capacities towards climate related disasters. By integrating the prioritized outputs from the workshop (the community participants prioritized their own issues and devised workable solutions) into their local development plans they could assess what they could absorb with their available resources and what could not. The results were then presented to the other key stakeholders including the City and Provincial governments at the validation workshop before commitments were gained for assistance and incorporation into City and Provincial Development Plans. This approach ensured that a bottom-up approach was employed and that the needs reflected the genuine concerns of the poor and most vulnerable (as they were the ones who crafted the solutions to their own needs.

Throughout the practice indigenous knowledge was maximised and all issues and solutions came from the participants through participatory capacity and vulnernability analyses. The following participatory tools were used during the community trainings/workshops:

- Community Organizing & Preparation
- Community Involvement in the final design of the workshop through discussions during courtesy calls
- Climate Change Impacts through focus group discussion
- Hazard Mapping
- Historical Profiling of Disasters
- Participatory Capacity and Vulnerability Analysis
- Issue Prioritization through ranking exercises
- Solution Identification
- Stakeholder validation where community members assisted in the small group discussions

Participants who have a direct role in disaster risk management were selected by the communities for the trainings and workshops. They included Health Workers, Police, Conflict Resolution Workers, Nutrition Staff, Day Care Workers, Youth Council, and Officials. Participants also represented different social groups: women, men, youth, elderly, farmers and fishers.

Participation

Through its Good Governance Framework based on sustainable development PRRM is mainstreaming climate change adaptation & disaster risk reduction at the grassroots level.

The national level advocacy of PRRM is based on its grassroots experience (a bottom up approach recognising the capacities and needs of the communities in PRRM's covered areas. An example of this was the training conducted in San Miguel Island, Tabaco City, Albay, where climate and disaster risk reduction measures using local knowledge and building on existing capacities to overcome vulnerabilities was integrated into local development planning as a measure of sustainability– first with the concerned barangays of the island, then what could not be covered locally was taken up into the city and provincial level planning.

The communities were consulted prior to the beginning of the practice to assess whether this was something that was needed and would benefit the community. The community then assisted in the module development through focus group discussions as to the main issues facing the community, especially the poor who are most vulnerable to disasters. Participants the trainings were selected by the communities they included Barangay (Village) sectors, Health Workers, Police, Conflict Resolution Workers, Nutrition Staff, Day Care Workers, Youth Council, and Officials. These community sectors are all active in emergency management. Workshop groupings were defined by the above sectors to identify sectoral issues for equal participation and analysis by the different sectors. The participants represented different social groups: women, men, youth (represented by the youth leader in some barangays), elderly, farmers and fishers.

Practice in Operation

Courtesy calls and an area visit took place during the last week of January 2008. The information gained during this time together with commitments of support to the project from the various agencies assisted in the areas of analysis research and secondary data gathering, together with validating the initial stakeholders analysis completed Mid-November 2007.

During the period of February and March, further research and data gathering was conducted on existing disaster management processes locally within Albay and also at a National and International level. This knowledge was combined with the experience of the project supervisors:

The training module development included adapting 4 existing types of modules (Climate Change Adaptation, Disaster Risk Reduction, Participatory Coastal Resource Assessment, & Local Development Planning) into one 3-day training adapted, into the local context.

Community training/workshops were conducted on "Integrating Disaster Risk Reduction and Climate Change Adaptation into Local Development Planning" in five barangays/villages in San Miguel Island, Tabaco City, Albay. These 5 communities were Barangays Hacienda, Agñas, Sagurong, Visita and Rawis. Each workshop aimed to increase the skills, knowledge and attitudes of local communities in adapting to climate change and responding to disasters; and to build awareness and capacities of these communities in disaster risk reduction and climate change adaptation.

After these training/workshops the participants were able to describe the basic concepts relevant to climate change, describe the relationship among hazard, vulnerability and disasters and the impact of climate change in this relationship, describe the different aspects of disaster risk reduction and link these to climate change adaptation and sustainable development work, and to establish mechanisms for integrating their recommendations into local development plans.

The first of 5 scheduled community workshops was held in Barangay Hacienda in the village warehouse on May 5-7, 2008 with 25 community members. The general impression from participant evaluations was positive with requests for further trainings on adaptation and risk reduction solutions.

Challenges and Responses

Some delays in implementation were unavoidable due to unavoidable circumstances such as bad weather making access to the island impossible. In these instances community leaders were contacted directly to reschedule the activity.

The major challenge to any CDRR work is that benefits can only be seen in future disasters that have minimized impact in terms of damages; it does not have any tangible profits in the present. Orientations provided by the practice and experiences shared of the increasing vulnerabilities and reduced capacity to cope, helped elicit more support for the work.

Although this projects acted as a catalyst for the prioritization of many CDRR measures/projects (over $213,000 worth), there are still outstanding projects to be carried through to 2010.

Resources

The series of community trainings together with the validation workshop cost around $11,000. ProVention Consortium granted $5000, PRRM provided $4000 and the Tabaco City Government contributed $2000. The estimated cost of proposed solutions incorporated into local development plans and budget reached over $213,000 (the majority of which were expenses for upgrading water supply systems).

Regulatory/Legal Structure for Participation

The practice drew upon 2 major structures as described above—the decentralization of roles and responsibilities to local government and the national disaster management structure. Principles of participation are embedded within these regulations but due to lack of resources and support during the devolvement process these are not maximized.

The Climate Change Act of 2009 was signed recently by President Arroyo. The main content of RA 9729 is the creation of Climate Change Commission, headed by no less than the president of the Philippines, which will mainstream climate change concepts in policy and development plans at all level of the government, as well as receive funds and endowments to address this problem. The law also provides for the formulation of the Framework Program on Climate Change and National Climate Change Action Plan, aims that have already been mentioned in previous legislations.

In 1991, President Aquino created the Inter-Agency Committee on Climate Change (IACCC) under the Environmental Management Bureau of the Department of Environment and Natural Resources (DENR) through Presidential Order No. 220. The stated aim of the committee is to "harness and synergize the various activities being undertaken by the national government and civil society in response to the crisis posed by growing the problem of climate change".

In 1992, the Philippines signed the United Nations Framework Convention on Climate Change and agreed to the mandate that it "should protect the climate system for the benefit of present and future generations of humankind, on the basis of equity and in accordance with their common but differentiated responsibilities and respective capabilities."

Philippine Disaster Management System

The organization of the *NDCC* is mandated by the Presidential Declaration of June 11, 1978 (PD. 1566) that calls for the strengthening of the Philippine Disaster Control Capability. The salient provisions of PD1566 are: State policy on self-reliance among local officials and their constituents in responding to disasters or emergencies, Organization of disaster coordinating councils from the national down to the municipal level, Statement of duties and responsibilities of the *NDCC*, *RDCC* and Local DCCs, Preparation of the National Calamities and Disaster Preparedness Plan by *OCD* and implementing plans by *NDCC* member-agencies, Conduct of periodic drills and exercises, Authority of the government units to program their funds for disaster preparedness activities in addition to the 2% calamity fund as provided for in PD 474.

The Disaster Preparedness Plan was originally drafted in 1970 and amended since then. Under the Plan, the *NDCC* exercises control, through the *OCD*, over all emergency operations, from the regional down to the barangay level. The plan also states the responsibilities of the government agencies and organizations involved in disaster mitigation, from the national level to the regional, provincial/municipal and barangay level. All member agencies of the *NDCC* are required by the Plan to organize reaction teams in their main offices as well as in the bureau. Aside from this common function, each agency is assigned specific tasks.

The Office of the Civil Defense (*OCD*) was created in January 1973 as part of an entire government reorganization. The *OCD* has a key role in natural disaster management. Its Administrator acts as Executive Officer of the *NDCC*. The *OCD* has significant coordinating functions at all levels and monitors the overall implementation of Presidential Decree 1566 (June 11, 1978).

Since its inception, the *OCD* has become the main coordinating body for all disaster related activities of the government and private sector.

The Secretary of Defense convenes the Council, whose members are representatives of 14 government departments (National Defense, Public Works and Highways, Transportation and Communication, Social Welfare and Development, Agriculture, Education, Culture and Sports, Finance, Labor and Employment, Justice, Trade and Industry, Local Government, Health, Environment and Natural Resources, Budget and Management, and the Philippine Information Agency), the Office of the President, the Armed Forces and the Philippine National Red Cross. The executive officer is the Administrator of the Office of the Civil Defense.

The primary function of the *NDCC* is to advise the President on the status of the national disaster preparedness program, disaster operations and rehabilitation efforts undertaken by government and the private sector. The Office of the Civil Defense is the operations center and secretariat of the Council. The mandate of the *NDCC* is to manage the operations center and secretariat of the Council. The mandate of the *NDCC* is officially stated to be:

Prepare a National Disaster and Calamities Preparedness Plan, organize disaster coordinating councils down to the municipal level, develop self-reliance among local government units in the management of disasters, advise the President on the status of the national disaster preparedness program and rehabilitation efforts.

Disaster Coordinating Councils (DCCs) have been established at the regional, provincial, municipal, city and barangay levels. They are charged with providing services in three phases: pre-disaster; during disaster; and post-disaster. Among these services are communications and warning; emergency transportation; evacuation, rescue and engineering; health; fire; police; relief and rehabilitation; and public information.

On receiving information of an impending disaster the *NDCC* is mobilized and information is sent down through the network to the regional provincial, municipal, city and barangay level disaster coordinating councils.

The BDCC's relay information house to house to prepare for the disaster. Immediately after they are also responsible for collecting damage assessments to send back up through the chain to the *NDCC*.

Although the PDMS is backed by legislation that advocates for a decentralized approach the system still tends to be top-down in its implementation and is still more reactive than proactive in mitigating the impacts of the numerous hazards that frequent the Philippines. The legislation and characteristics of the PDMS were designed in a time before disaster management evolved into a longer-term outlook of disaster risk reduction and more recently with regards to climate change issues.

At present, the major source of funding for disaster recovery efforts are the National Calamity Fund (NCF) and Local Calamity Fund (LCF). From 2006 to 2008 alone, the NCF totaled to about US$33 M. 5% of the annual local budget of the Local Government Units (LGUs) is set aside for the LCF. For the same period, the total LCF registered US$ 51 M. The NCF and LCF can only be used for relief, response, recovery and rehabilitation post disaster, with some allowance for imminent preparedness once a warning of the approach of a hazard has been issued. This is a reactive mechanism.

Pre-event disaster management is accomplished by pooling government resources before catastrophe occurs. The financial and insurance markets play a key role in preparing for the impact of extreme natural events and help in spreading the risks therefore lessening the burden for the government.

For the Philippines, it is clear that there is much further market maturity that has to be developed for catastrophe risk insurance mechanisms, but the national government is increasingly providing resources at the sub-national government levels toward responding to localized disasters.

Updating of PD1566 which was brought into law over 30 years ago providing the mechanism for the NCF and LCF and reactive approach to disaster management is on-going at present to cover the international paradigm shift to a more proactive disaster risk reduction approach, which will provide an enabling policy environment for the development of risk transfer mechanisms. An initiative for regional mechanism for inter-country cooperation and cross-insurance together with the neighboring countries may be an initial platform for cooperation and the development of a regional catastrophe risk insurance mechanism.

Stakeholder Accountability

Throughout the project implementation, the project team submitted a mid-term and final narrative and financial report to the funding agency: ProVention Consortium. The Mayor was informed of the progress on a regular basis (coinciding with project implementation visits to the area) and a final financial report was submitted at the end of the project for reimbursement as per LGU protocol.

With regards to monitoring the plans and activities: the barangay officials held meetings twice a month to discuss community concerns and planned activities. Once a month the barangay captains discussed these with the city government.

The PO's have been empowered through strengthening activities to monitor the transparency and accountability of the elected officials, most recently through activities such as the community based monitoring system

(CBMS). With regards to barangay development planning, the barangay council sets the plans and budgets after consulting the concerned sectors of the community. All levels of government are obligated to meet the targets set within the local development plans and is monitored by the next tier up e.g. Barangay by City, City by Provincial, Provincial by National. Besides this there are also special bodies within government where CSOs can participate to monitor and advise on the progress of activities. Similar to this are the Regional Development Councils that monitor development activities within a cluster of provinces.

Outcomes of CDRR

Effectiveness

The significant outcomes of the practice were as follows:

- Stakeholder's gained better understanding of the importance of integrating climate/disaster risk reduction (CDRR) into the city development planning (CDP) process;
- The results/outcomes of the community training workshops conducted in the five barangays in San Miguel Island were validated/agreed upon and supported by the other key stakeholders – not part of the initial community based training;
- Ways of integrating these into the decision making processes at the city and barangay levels were identified;
- A plan of action on integrating CDRR into the city development planning and budgeting processes was crafted;
- To confirm the above commitments a Memorandum of Understanding was signed by the City Government of Tabaco; Albay Provincial Government; PRRM & Other Donor Partners
- During the validation workshop, a Memorandum of Understanding (MOU) was signed by the City Government of Tabaco; Albay Provincial Government; PRRM & Other Donor Partners) which identified ten priority projects for the year 2009.
- At the barangay level, the 5 communities of San Miguel Island have had the increased capacity to enact about 70% of their action plans, most notably in the areas of resolution writing for policy enactment, waste management, tree planting, and organic farming.

- At the City level most of the outputs from the validation workshop have been incorporated into the 2009 City Development Plan.
- The project also drew local media support.
- Requests for replicating the project have been received by PRRM to cover the remaining 13 coastal communities of Tabaco City, together with selected areas at the Provincial level. Other disaster affected areas of the country have also made requests for replication. All these requests have come from the respective local government units which highlights the recognition of the need to integrate CDRR into local development plans to enhance community resilience.

Efficiency

Without the participation and support of the community and the City Government of Tabaco this practice could not have achieved the outcomes listed above. The practice relied on participatory techniques to elicit indigenous knowledge on CDRR for enhancement and support for the initiatives proposed.

45% of the funding of this initiative came from the ProVention Consortium (external donor), 45% from the City Government, and 10% from PRRM. However the solutions incorporated into the local development planning process rose to $213,000 a nineteen times benefit increase. So although participatory approaches are costly in terms of time, in this regard it increased efficiency for delivery of CDRR measures and projects.

Innovation

The particular features that have made this practice different and innovative is it relied solely on the participation of the stakeholders and their local knowledge and capacities. It also relied upon the solutions being incorporated into local plans with local resources or provisions for local resource mobilization to address the needs raised by the practice.

Unexpected Outcomes

Activities not included within the 2009 plans are considered priority for 2010 plans. CDRR initiatives will be an annual inclusion into local (barangay and city) development plans as an outcome of this project.

At an international level, the project drew interest from Oxfam Hong Kong who arranged, with the assistance of PRRM, study tours to the island for Hong Kong high school and college students for them to learn from and share experiences of CDRR initiatives.

Tabaco City has been chosen as one of the pilot sites chosen for local adaptation of the vulnerability and capacity assessment of the Philippines Second National Communication on climate Change, expected to be submitted to the UNFCCC in the first quarter of 2010.

Key Operational Lessons Learned

Based on the outcomes of the practice, the next steps to pursue, will be the following:

Expand and strengthen linkages existing linkages with Civil Society Organizations (CSOs), government, academe, the corporate sector and potential donor partners and explore areas of collaboration with them towards the integration of climate and disaster risk reduction into their respective policies and programs (including formal and informal education programs).

Disseminate results with PRRM area of interventions and partner LGUs for project replication.

Forge strong partnerships with supportive LGUs towards the development and implementation of demonstration projects on climate change adaptation and disaster risk reduction.

Build a strong working relationship with the local mass media (i.e., print, radio) to increase public awareness and catalyze local action with prepared media kit readily available for quick dissemination of information and other materials.

Develop information, education and communication (EIC) materials in the local language for dissemination to local communities and other stakeholders.

Degree of Sustainability

With the communities selected above, peoples' organizations have already been formed through community organizing and community development techniques. This is key before any project implementation as it ensures the trust and participation of the group. If this was to be replicated in other communities time should be allotted at the beginning or introductory phase of the project for these activities. There is no short cut or sustainability will be compromised. Once the community organization is formed then it is ideal to include other stakeholders (to be identified during a community mapping exercise as part of a vulnerability and capacity assessment) as soon as possible to gain wider support for the initiative.

The main challenge with CDRR projects is the concept of long-term preparedness measures. People know emergency response and are comfortable in their role and to expand that role into long-term preparedness (being proactive rather than reactive) takes some adjustment. Hence it is important to link with on-going development (sustainable development) projects in the area to emphasize the importance and relevance to disaster work with regards to the bigger picture. It also helps to integrate the work into the local development planning process to ensure continued support (especially financial) at the local level thereby reducing dependency on external/foreign agencies and increasing local capacities. With commitments to continue integrating CDRR initiatives in local development plans on an annual basis the process adopted for this project can be deemed sustainable – not only in the short term but also for long-term sustainable development.

Achieving Greater Sustainability

At present there is no enabling policy environment at the national level guiding implementation and resource allocation at a local level for community based CDRR. A revised DRRM Bill is being lobbied for at the national level. It does not seek to create a new policy, but rather to expand the coverage of the outdated Philippine law on disaster related concerns such as Presidential Decree 1566 which created the National Disaster Coordinating Council or NDCC and local DCC's.

With the Philippines as one of the most disaster-prone countries (natural and human-induced), there is a need to push for this policy that is responsive to the needs of the citizens in addressing the root causes of the problem.

DRRM Bill of 2009

The DRRM Bill proposes for the strengthening and expansion of the functions of agencies covered by PD 1566.

Aside from disaster response, programs on disaster preparedness and disaster risk reduction and management must also be strengthened and expanded.

Government policies should not only focus on short-term preparedness, relief operations and rehabilitation of affected communities, but rather to build long-term preparedness that aim to reduce disaster related risks and build the resiliency of communities to disasters.

Calamities cannot be avoided but its effects can be prepared for and mitigated. Risks can be reduced by implementing programs that will strengthen the preparedness of communities and the people.

It includes the following vital support factors that are lacking in the present policy:

- Focuses on vulnerability reduction—environmental protection, sustainable livelihood, health and nutrition, rights and participation of women, children and youth, elderly, differently-abled and other vulnerable and disadvantaged groups, safe locations, safe building construction, etc.
- Agencies and institutions tasked with responsibility of safeguarding environmental protection, health and well-being, sustainable livelihoods, social protection and the regulation of public and private infrastructure have access to and are equipped with the skills, information, competence, strategies necessary for effective risk assessments and planning, vulnerability reduction, emergency response, and rehabilitation
- Recognizes the need to strengthen capacities at a local level
- Promotes a Community-Based Disaster-Risk Management approach (CB-DRM)
- Integration of the DRM Framework into the development planning and budgeting processes
- Risk assessment be made mandatory as part of all development planning, and planning for public and private projects
- Incorporation of climate risk assessments in the disaster risk assessments
- Declaration of Policies are based on the Hyogo Framework of Action, Community Based Disaster Risk Management and the Strategic National Action Plan for an updated DRR/M perspective
- *Increased budget allocation to contribute towards resiliency and disaster risk reduction*—National government line agencies shall allot

5% of their annual budget; legislators shall allot 5% of their PDAF while LGUs shall allot 5% of their development fund for the implementation of DRR measures with the goal of contributing to disaster resilience by investing on participation of major stakeholders, environmental protection, health and well-being, sustainable livelihoods, social protection, safer settlements and infrastructure especially in communities highly at risk to disasters

- *Multi-stakeholder approach*
- *Permanent DRM Offices at the local level, together with local DRM Councils (*LDRMCs): to produce Local Disaster Risk Management Plans with corresponding budget
- *A National DRM Coordinating Council* (NDRMCC) that will produce and monitor a NDRM Framework and Plan that integrates local and national development plans.
- *The secretariat of the NDRMCC* will be an Authority, that is an independent and autonomous arm of the national government for DRR

Challenges Ahead

Although legislation is in the process of being updated (Climate Change Act, DRRM Bill) to incorporate a risk reduction framework, it will only be effective if it is combined with bottom-up consultations taking into consideration the real needs of the local communities and particularly the most vulnerable as well as monitoring of eventual implementation.

An Adequate Timeframe should be Allocated

To develop the hazard maps to pinpoint areas/sectors of highest vulnerability and research into the localized impacts of climate change to devise the most appropriate strategies for risk reduction. However, this needs to be balanced with the practical measures needed at present to address the underlying conditions of vulnerabilities and existing additional stress factor of climate change impact being felt today.

Awareness Raising

A participatory approach to raising awareness and conducting community based vulnerability and capacity assessments related to CDRR takes time. However it is essential for building trust, awareness, inclusion and local ownership of the project. All sectors need to be reached and content of information needs to be adapted to reach the different audiences e.g. on consultation with a city councillor he did not want to know about ppm's of greenhouse gases in the atmosphere or melting ice caps as he felt that removed the issue from a point of direct concern. Once the link was made in a way that was directly relatable to the issues faced by his constituents he fully supported the activities. This is also very important in raising political will to sustain the strategies for CDRR as a long-term view point is needed. There is a need to demonstrate projects with immediate benefits while incorporating longer term projects.

Resources

This can create a dependance on external resources and the question then becomes one of sustainability. However if the projects are undertaken in a multi-sectoral approach involving all stakeholders, and can be incorporated into local development plans that maximises local resources and capacities (as in the case of San Miguel Island), then once the initial input of external funding has completed the pilot/demonstration project it can be handed over. However this does need political will for follow-through.

The main distinctive feature of this project, was in raising awareness of the communities with regards to climate change and assisting them assess their own vulnerabilities and capacities. From this came *their own* prioritized needs and solutions to be incorporated in local development plans. The main risk that could impede replication of this process would be in areas resistant to a bottom-up approach.

However, most of the solutions proposed could be contained already in the prescribed budget lines of the development plans so the threat that new legal, financial, institutional and regulatory mechanisms is minimized.

Risk Transfer

At present in the Philippines the only insurance that is readily available and accessed is for health. Mechanisms to protect crops and homes in view of CDRR needs to be researched and implemented in a way that it reduces vulnerabilites and increases capacities to cope especially after an extreme climate event.

In summary: Natural and human-induced disasters continue to undermine our development efforts and divert resources to disaster response. The resulting economic and social impact is a very serious concern. The allocated budget for disaster response is insufficient to cope with the increasing costs of disaster, and capacities to cope are being challenged: there is a need to take a proactive approach to protect lives and livelihoods; and to enhance the capacity to manage and thereby increasing resiliency to climate and disaster related risks.

Replication and Scaling Up

Replication

Requests for replicating the project have been received by PRRM to cover the remaining 13 coastal communities of Tabaco City, together with selected areas at the Provincial level. Other disaster affected areas of the country have also made requests for replication e.g. Alaminos City in Pangasinan. All these requests have come from the respective local government units which highlights the recognition of the need to integrate CDRR into local development plans to enhance community resilience.

Further Intiatives by Partners

The City of Tabaco is now in the process of updating its City Development Plan and Land Use Plan, into which it is incorporating aspects from the community trainings in terms of hazard mapping, vulnerability and capacity analysis, together with drafting an Ordinance on Solid Waste Management and Environmental Code to be enacted by the Sangguniang Panlungsod. The province is also providing capacity building in terms of CDRR.

Potential for Replication

The practice was designed specifically for coastal, island communities, however the content could easily be modified for other ecosystems that are vulnerable and impoverished.

The practice did rely upon an existing People's Organization present in the area. If the practice was to be replicated in other areas without PO's, further time would need to be added to the preparatory stage of the practice to gain local knowledge for incorporation into the design and to gain the trust and openness to share and participate by the beneficiaries.

Scaling up

This practice concentrated at the barangay level initially then scaled up to the city and provincial level and is being used to inform national level advocacy to produce an enabling policy environment. However, without this through PRRM's networks of federations this practice could become widely accepted and adopted if time and financial implications are taken into consideration. The timeframe for the practice would have to be extended for wide scale use for it to retain its participatory nature and build on the beneficiaries existing capacities for risk resiliency.

Necessary Changes in Policies and Institutions

Climate and Disaster Risk Reduction as a concept is gaining wide recognition in the country, however in practice there are only pockets of initiatives, including those (such as this practice) that incorporate a community based and participatory approach.

There are moves to enhance the existing disaster management law and there is also a climate change bill being crafted. However all policies from land use planning, building codes, development plans etc need to be viewed with CDRR integrated into their updates.

References

Aldaba, Rafaelita M. and Caesar B. Cororaton. (November 2002). "Trade Liberalization and Pollution: Evidence from the Philippines". EEPSEA publications.

Annan, K., (1999). *Facing the humanitarian challenge: Towards a culture of prevention*. Paper read at the 54th session of the United Nations General Assembly, New York.

CBMS Survey, (2008). "Community Based Monitoring System". Tabaco City Government.

CPDO, (2009). "City Land Use Plan", City Planning and Development Office (CPDO). Tabaco City Government.

Eric Schwartz, (2006). *A Needless Toll of Natural Disasters. Boston Globe*, March 23.

Tongzon, Jose L. (2005). "Trade Policy in the Philippines: Treading a cautious path". ASEAN Economic Bulletin, April 1.

5

Participatory Rural Development in Europe

The scope for participation in rural development is set by the economic functions of rural areas and these have changed considerably in recent years. On the one hand, there has been an inexorable decline in primary sector employment and traditional rural industries have been squeezed. On the other hand, new industrial and service activities have emerged, although not necessarily in those regions suffering the most from rural decline. These changes in economic functions have led to a rethink in the philosophy of rural development towards approaches in which local people are cast as key agents in the development process.

Forces of Change Affecting Rural Areas

All the EU countries have suffered losses of primary sector employment over several decades. There are now few regions in the EU where agriculture contributes more than 10% of the regional value added and these are concentrated in Greece, Portugal and Ireland. Forces of mechanisation have widely affected not only agriculture, but forestry, fishing and mining too; and expansion of production has encountered problems of over-exploitation and over-supply. At the same time, processing and manufacturing activities once closely linked to the primary sector (such as farm machinery manufacture, food processing, the leather industry, timber processing, etc.) have undergone significant economic and geographical concentration and face growing competition from outside the EU. Many service activities traditionally found in rural centres have also experienced intensified competition from urban centres. The consequence of all these developments has been the loss of much localised employment from rural areas and regions.

At the same time, new economic functions have emerged for rural areas. Indeed, new firm formation rates and employment growth have been higher in small towns and rural areas than in large urban centres. In France, for example, 52% of all industrial jobs in the period 1976-85 were created in rural areas. In Italy, between 1971 and 1981, 63% of the non-agricultural jobs created by private firms were situated in rural areas. The situation varies greatly from one country to another and from one region to another. In some cases growth is due to the decentralisation of productive activities, but very often it is due to indigenous industrialisation. In any case, research done in southern European countries shows that industry in rural areas has increased productivity considerably. Furthermore, in more central regions, certain service activities have also relocated to rural areas, thereby accentuating an employment pattern already heavily weighted towards the service sector.

Certain characteristics of rural areas may be identified to account for these new roles. These include:

- a relatively low-wage and non-unionised workforce;
- reduction in migration flows from rural to urban areas, as a result of both the urban production crisis and better accessibility, helping to stabilise rural labour supply;
- a small-scale business structure and a culture of entrepreneurship which provides conditions for rapid economic adjustment;
- state support for agriculture, which has been capitalised in land values, giving rural landowners sources of collateral to invest in new businesses, and which provides support systems designed to encourage farmers and rural landowners to diversify;
- greater accessibility for rural areas as a result of improvements in telecommunications and transportation systems;
- the favouring of rural locations by some of the new-wave technologies, particularly biotechnology and information technology;
- the high priority given to non-material and positional goods by influential and affluent sections of society, who place increasing value

on the opportunities rural areas provide for living space, recreation, the enjoyment of amenity and wildlife, and a wholesome and pleasant environment.

These characteristics are not uniformly present. No longer so subject to the imperatives of a single sector, the development trajectories of rural areas are diverging, leading to a more differentiated countryside across Europe. This is heightened by the increasing competition within and between regions to attract or resist external forces of change. Certain areas are seen to offer comparative social, locational and environmental advantages to the technologies and processes of flexible production and have benefited from the decentralisation of economic activity. These areas, in part through their attractiveness to the professional and managerial classes, have a good skills base and local business services. Other areas—particularly ones with poor communications infrastructure with difficult or unattractive environmental conditions, or with a weak skills base—continue to suffer from rural decline.

In the European Commission's assessment of the socio-economic challenges facing rural areas, specific comparison was drawn between:

- rural areas under 'pressure of modern life', which commonly means those within easy access of large urban areas, enjoy a relatively favourable economic performance;
- rural regions in decline, which tend to experience high rates of unemployment and out-migration;
- 'very marginal areas', where rural decline is even more marked and the potential for economic diversification is highly limited. This last group is characterised most notably by mountainous and island regions on Europe's periphery.

Exogenous Model of Rural Development

The classical formulation of the rural development problem was founded in an understand'ding of urbanisation and industrialisation as mutually reinforcing and unilinear processes whereby capital and labour were increasingly concentrated in cities. Within the modernist development trajectory, the function of rural areas, stripped of other economic activities, was to provide food for the expanding cities. The notion of balanced or articulated development was embodied in the achievement of a spatially polarised but nationally integrated geography in which cities, functioning at the core of specialised regional economies, concentrated the bulk of population and commercial and industrial activity, while rural areas became dominated by a technically progressive, market-orientated agriculture. The spatial category of rural was often viewed as a residual category and became equated with the sectoral category of agriculture.

The 'problem' of rural development followed from this classification and was seen to arise in those regions and countries where too many people remained on the land, thus restricting the transfer of profit and labour needed to fuel urban and industrial growth, as well as inhibiting the development of a competitive and efficient agriculture. It was widely believed that such stagnant regions needed to be connected to dynamic centres and expanding sectors. It was never clear, however, what the eventual equilibrium between urban centres and their rural hinterlands would be. Even areas of highly commercialised agriculture seemed destined to steadily lose population because of the tendency towards diminishing returns within agriculture. Thus even the most developed and prosperous rural areas were locked into an unequal exchange relationship with urban-industrial growth poles.

Classically, therefore, the development problems of rural areas and regions were diagnosed as those of marginality. As a concept, marginality has a number of dimensions—economic, social, cultural and political—although in discussions about rural development marginality is often understood in geographical terms to be synonymous with peripherality or remoteness. In this sense it has long been recognised that people living in rural areas have suffered problems of physical exclusion from urban-based services and jobs. Low productivity in the primary sector has compounded such difficulties, condemning those who live and work in rural areas to a low standard of living.

Peripherality, though, was always a metaphor for other types of distance too. Rural areas were distant technically, socio-economically and culturally from the main (urban) centres of activity. In all of these respects they were either backward or lagged behind. From a regional perspective, the ideal model depicted dynamic centres as being locked into dynamic regions. Steps could be taken to encourage the transfer of progressive models, technologies and practices from dynamic sectors and regions. However, it was only through overcoming peripherality that rural 'back-waters' could be reconnected to the main currents of economic and social modernisation. Within this fundamentally exogenous perspective on rural development, the basic policy response was a combination of subsidising the improvement of agricultural production to enhance farm incomes, and the encouragement of labour and capital mobility.

The state-sponsored modernisation of rural services and of agricultural practices and technologies has been a constant feature of post-war rural development. Policies to encourage labour and capital mobility, though, have fluctuated. The first phase in European policy was one of consolidating farm structures (i.e. land reform in southern Italy and Greece, and plot consolidation and enlargement programmes in Belgium, France, West Germany, Spain, and the Netherlands) linked to land improvement schemes (including drainage and irrigation) and the development of farm-oriented infrastructure. The aim was to establish commercial units able to mechanise and absorb other 'productivist' technologies and to reduce the agrarian population particularly through the elimination of small and marginal holdings. Although this strategy was intended to strengthen the economic and social structure of rural areas, the aim was closer integration into regional, national and international markets. Participation in these wider fora, it was thought, would ultimately determine rural development patterns.

However, it became apparent that such measures could not stabilise rural economies and rural populations; indeed, they seemed to intensify the flow of labour out of agriculture and often out of the rural areas altogether. A second phase of rural development therefore emphasised the attraction of new types of employment into rural areas. Manufacturing firms were encouraged to relocate from urban areas or to set up branch plants. As well as financial and fiscal inducements, development agencies concentrated on providing infrastructural support, including improvements in transportation and communication links and the provision of serviced factory sites and premises. Most European countries adopted this approach, but it was particularly strongly pursued in France, Ireland, Italy and the UK. In some regions the emphasis was on the development of tourism as well as, or instead of, manufacturing, particularly around the Mediterranean, but also in remote and mountainous areas across central and northern Europe.

By the late 1970s the exogenous model of rural development was falling into disrepute. The continued intensification and industrialisation of agriculture came up against the saturation of domestic markets, against ecological limits (with rising problems of agricultural pollution and ecological degradation) and against a greatly diminished capacity in the urban sector to absorb the surplus rural population. Moreover, the recession of the early 1980s resulted in the closure of many branch plants and a growing sense that rural regions that had attracted a great deal of such inward investment were highly vulnerable to fluctuations in the world economy. Areas that had experienced rapid expansion of tourism also came to realise its seasonal and cyclical fluctuations as well as the destructive impact on local cultures and environments of mass tourism. Terms such as 'branch plant economy' and 'development without growth' were coined to highlight the incorporation of such regions within the global business logic of firms governed elsewhere; a logic working against any self-governing and self-sustaining regional economic development.

Exogenous approaches to rural development thus came under criticism for promoting:

- *dependent development*, reliant on continued subsidies and the policy decisions of distant agencies or boardrooms;
- *distorted development*, which boosted single sectors, selected settlements and certain types of business (e.g. progressive farmers) but left others behind and neglected the non-economic aspects of rural life;
- *destructive development*, that erased the cultural and environmental differences of rural areas;
- *dictated development* devised by external experts and planners.

Endogenous Approaches

These difficulties encouraged the exploration in the 1980s of so-called endogenous approaches to rural development based on the assumption that the specific resources of an area—natural, human and cultural—hold the key to its sustainable development. Endogenous development ideas drew on three separate sources.

First there was the recognition that out of the economic restructuring of the 1970s and 1980s certain rural regions, with previously unrecognised internal dynamism, had emerged as leading economic regions. The Third Italy was the most celebrated example but successful rural regions could be identified across Western Europe, including, for example, East Anglia, Bavaria and South Jutland. The question arose of what was the key to success for these regions and whether it could be replicated elsewhere. Picchi (1994) cites the following elements as critical to development 'from within' in the

Emilia-Romagna region of Italy: the importance of the agricultural sector for the provision of capital and labour needed in non-agricultural enterprises; the ability of this labour to engage in new economic activities; the cultural orientation towards self-employment; an extensive network of small- and medium-sized enterprises; and a dense system of interdependencies between economic sectors and units. He also identifies a set of political-institutional arrangements which have helped strengthen endogenous development patterns. These include a rich network of services provided by local administrations for economic sectors, economic planning mechanisms and a stable climate for industrial development.

The second source of endogenous development ideas was regionalist movements and agencies seeking to overcome previous policy failures and to promote forms of local development less dependent on external capital. The emphasis shifted to rural diversification, to bottom-up rather than top-down approaches, to support for indigenous businesses, to the encouragement of local initiative and enterprise and, where these were weak, to the provision of suitable training. Prominent examples of this kind of approach can be found in the activities of development agencies particularly in peripheral regions of Europe, for example in the Irish Gaeltacht, in the local contract plans drawn up in the fragile zones in France, in the Scottish Highlands and Islands, in rural Wales and in mountain community projects in Italy.

The third source of endogenous development ideas was from the debate about rural sustainability. Increasingly, the environmental and natural resources of rural areas have come to be valued, and forms of development favoured that benefit from and enhance those resources. The sustainability concept seeks to bridge not only the conventional divide between economic development and environmental protection but also embraces the viability of localities and communities on which the maintenance of both the environment and economic activity ultimately depends. Thus there has been a growing awareness that a conserved countryside must be socially viable and is therefore dependent on the vitality of rural communities.

In general, ideas of endogenous development in Europe and North America have been informed by 'alternative development' approaches and theories formulated in the Third World. The failure of official aid programmes based on notions of community development (i.e. the involvement of local people in development projects) to tackle rural poverty in the South led to a major rethink amongst development agencies and rural development workers which had begun in the 1970s. Increasingly it came to bc seen that it was not just a question of the design and targeting of development projects but the failure to address the structural causes of poverty and to incorporate marginal groups. Many influential ideas emerged from this reassessment of the fundamental aims of development assistance—such as the notions of 'putting people first' 'development from below', 'popular participation in decision-making for development', and 'sustainable livelihoods.

There is a tension running through the 'alternative development' literature, however, between advocates of what might be termed integrationist and self-reliance perspectives. The former perspective is well represented by work done in this field for the World Bank. Here development is conventionally defined as "financially induced growth and change" that will perforce integrate local people into market economies. The role of participatory rural development is seen as being to strengthen the terms on which they are integrated. The philosophy is defined as "giving people more opportunities to participate effectively in development activities". This can be achieved through "tailoring the design and implementation of projects to the needs and capabilities of people who are supposed to benefit from them".

Advocates of the self-reliance perspective on the other hand challenge the very desirability of integrating under-privileged groups into external market relations, arguing that it leads inevitably to dependency and reinforces processes of proletarianisation and marginalisation. They question whether local people can ever really participate in an increasingly globalised economy on their own terms. This perspective draws on the insights of rural sociologists into the ways in which peasant societies maintain their solidarity and routinely resist the imposition of external authority. Many poor communities are seen not to be interested in 'development' and operate their own co-operative structures of self-help. From this perspective, the very notion of external development assistance is problematic, especially when it is observed that "government support for community participation in social development results not in an increase but in a diminution of community involvement". The only appropriate response is the empowerment of marginal and poor communities by giving them control over the resources needed to manage their own livelihoods.

Rural development initiatives and theorising in the North have borrowed eclectically from the Southern experience despite the different political and economic contexts. In that all social groups and regions in the North are to some extent integrated into external market relations, autochthonous or self-sufficient local development is a utopian ideal. It has been argued that:

> rural areas are subject to both localising and globalising tendencies. This is why the exogenous/endogenous distinction presents a false dichotomy. Most forms of development in capitalist societies involve the welding of local with extra-local labour and resources. The crucial question is how local circuits of production, consumption and meaning articulate with extra-local circuits

From this point of view the key issue is the interplay between local and external forces in the control of development processes. Effective rural development strategies must seek to build up the economic and political institutions at the local and regional levels which help to ensure favourable terms of trade with the external world.

Nevertheless, notions of self-reliance have gained considerable currency amongst two groups in the North—radical greens and development activists working with particularly marginalised groups. The former have elaborated the 'small is beautiful' thinking of Shumacher into the field of community economics. The intention is to reassert local control over economic activities. Douthwaite argues that sustainability requires communities to have control over their economies to protect themselves from the forces of globalisation and restructuring. This means local production primarily for local needs and appropriate control over energy production and distribution, finance and food production.

Development activists working with marginalised groups have also promoted notions of self-reliance. A feature of community development in peripheral regions such as the West of Ireland, the Scottish Highlands and Islands and the mountainous areas of Italy has been the promotion of community enterprises and community ownership and management of natural resources, through the formation of craft, fish farming, tourism and agricultural cooperatives. Advocates of cooperatives argue that not only can they mobilise and effectively exploit under-utilised natural and human resources, but they can also ensure that resulting benefits are retained locally and distributed on an equitable basis. There are those, though, who are pessimistic about the ability of cooperatives generally to compete effectively against private enterprise.

Arguments for Participation in Rural Development

Participation in rural development is now generally assumed to be a good if not vital thing. The assumption is that more participation is better than less and that past development strategies failed through its absence. There is, however, surprisingly little written about *why* participation is so important.

The increasing interest in participatory forms of rural development can be seen in the context of the wider shift in models of development from exogenous to endogenous approaches. Previously, development policies—intended to overcome what was seen as the intrinsic backwardness of rural areas—had focused on improving their physical facilities and material resources. The emphasis was on investment to restructure and boost productivity in the primary sector, the financing of infrastructural projects and the encouragement of inward investment. Places on the receiving end were seen merely as the locations in which externally-driven economic forces were played out with little consideration of the potential for indigenous development. However, during the 1980s, both academic research and the assumptions underpinning development policies began to shift as the human and cultural resources of localities came to be seen as neglected factors in understanding the geography of economic development in Europe's rural regions.

As a result, the dominant top-down development paradigm has been replaced with a more bottom-up perspective which focuses on territory, diversity and the optimisation of local resources. A territorial approach is one that seeks to enhance the particular strengths of a rural locality by developing the potential of local actors—individuals, businesses, communities and voluntary organisations—and its cultural and natural assets. It entails recognising and accommodating the integrity of local areas—the interdependencies of environment, economy and society within a locality.

It is argued that such a system develops:

> through adaptive change rather than by linear progress... it is dynamic and its parts interact by influencing each other. It is not possible to effect change in one element of the system in isolation without affecting the other parts. Consequently the system as a whole has to be understood in order to identify and help bring about desired changes

Recognition of such interdependencies, which are seen to underlie the correlation between vibrant local cultures and strong local economies (Asby and Midmore, 1996), has fuelled calls for a more *integrated* approach to rural policy, one that combines economic, social and environmental objectives. This approach requires a sensitivity to the diversity of rural circumstances rather than a single, universal notion of 'the rural':

> Basic dimensions of rurality must be respected such as the small size of communities the low density of activities and facilities, the limited capacity of human and financial resources, the strong social networks and the slower and less regular pace of change. These dimensions result, in turn, in distinctive needs from one rural community to another. The most likely place to obtain an appreciation of these needs is from the rural community itself.

Participation is a central feature of such endogenous development, in terms of both *what* it is seeking to achieve and *how* that is achieved. As a means to an end, participation involves harnessing local people's resources and support as an input into a programme on the assumption that this will improve its effectiveness and efficiency. The measures taken are then more likely to address local needs and to be better adapted to local circumstances, and the external resources applied can better complement and help mobilise local resources. The efficiency of the participation will be judged by the material outcomes of the programme. Such promotion of local participation as a means to achieve developmental goals is often referred to as community development. However, participation can also serve as an end in itself, with the overall purpose being to strengthen the capacity of local people to participate, whether in the economic or political sphere or both, as the only sure way of overcoming their dependency or marginality. This involves a fundamental reinterpretation of what development is about. It is reasoned that

> development is not simply a question of undertaking projects, nor of achieving objectives specified in narrow economic terms. Development is also a process, by which is meant the creation of social products such as upgraded local leadership, a culture of enterprise and innovative action, or the enhanced capacity of people to act in concert, purposefully and effectively so as to cope with the threats and opportunities they face.

There is thus an increasing emphasis on the need for 'capacity-building' and organisational support for grassroots action. According to Mannion, two factors should be taken into account in order to ensure representative local participation and make operational the bottom-up approach to development:

- the extent to which local people have the capacity and skills to contribute to the development of their own area;
- the opportunities they are given to express themselves through meaningful involvement in the development process.

But what do we mean by *capacity building*? At its most basic, it means "strengthening the knowledge, skills and attitudes of people so that they can establish and sustain their area's development". Capacity building therefore includes: the individuals and groups living in the target area, and the institutions that support them. Shorthall and Shucksmith refer to capacity building as "a gradual and complex process aimed at upgrading the local physical and human resource bases"—a type of investment, in other words. For them, the term applies to the capacity of an entire local population, rather than just individuals, to contribute to local development, and it can be enhanced through improving skills, encouraging new forms of organisation, stimulating new forms of linkages between groups and public agencies, and by enabling individuals and organisations to be more flexible and adaptable to changing situations.

Implicitly or explicitly, the promotion of local participation is a challenge to established structures of political representation and how these are embodied within government. On the one hand, the instrumental notion of participation implies that existing structures of functional representation, usually organised on an indirect, national and sectoral basis, are inadequate to convey the needs of particular areas or social groups. The dominant type of functional representation for rural areas relates to the agricultural sector, and the promotion of participatory rural development recognises the requirement for other types of representation to reflect the actual diversity and multifunctionality of rural areas.

On the other hand, the promotion of local participation as an end in itself carries a more fundamental challenge to formal democratic structures. This is not always acknowledged which is one reason why such initiatives often fail. What drives them is captured partly in the notion of subsidiarity with its implication that decisions should be taken at the lowest possible level. Subsidiarity, however, is about choosing the most appropriate tier of government at which to take particular decisions, while participation involves the establishment of informal structures and procedures that are additional to, and in many cases separate from, local government. This may reflect the weakness or insensitivity of the formal local structures of elected representatives, officials and councils. In some instances the promotion of local participation may help to reinvigorate those structures but in others the intention may be deliberately to by-pass them. A number of commentators have pointed to the complicity of national governments and the European Commission seeking to shape local structures to their own ends. More generally, the official emphasis on community-based solutions has been associated with the curtailment by the state of many local services. Even so, the emergence of new modes of informal and voluntary participation outwith existing state structures is seen by some commentators as part of a process of local democratic evolution towards more direct, inclusive and cooperative forms of political expression.

Participatory Strategies

Fundamentally, therefore, participation raises the issue of power and its redistribution. Local groups cannot gain control without others losing some. Participatory strategies can be distinguished according to how much or how little control they concede. In principle, the pursuit of participation as a development objective should involve a greater transfer of power than when it is used as a means of development planning or implementation.

The most celebrated model of different levels of community participation is that proposed by Sherry Arnstein who studied citizen involvement in planning in the USA. The lower steps though, are essentially non-participative and, characterised as *'manipulation'* and *'therapy'*, are little more than public relations exercises. The next step, *'informing'*, represents the most important first step to legitimate participation, but typically the flow of information is one way without opportunity for feedback. *'Consultation'* is the next step and might, for example, involve attitude surveys, neighbourhood meetings or public enquiries. Arnstein was sceptical about the practical merits of this level of participation, suspecting that the tendency was for consultation to be used merely as a window dressing ritual. *'Placation'* comes next on the ladder of participation and this involves the co-option of hand-picked local 'worthies' onto committees to advise on plans or projects, but the right to judge the legitimacy or feasibility of the advice is retained by the power-holders or 'officials'. At the next stage of participation, that of *'partnership'*, power is redistributed through negotiation between local citizens and power-holders, and planning and decision-making responsibilities are shared through, for example, joint committees. *'Delegated power'* represents the next step. Here citizens hold a clear majority of seats on committees with delegated powers to make decisions.

It may not be possible, however, to involve the whole community in the planning and execution of local development projects. As Moseley and Cherrett point out, "the scale of such involvement is too massive and the public in any case is made up of many different people with different interests, priorities and resources". Moreover, only a few people have the time, resources and inclination to commit themselves to lengthy involvement. There is therefore another dimension to the redistribution of power besides that between state agencies and local communities, namely the way in which participatory structures and procedures affect the power relations within communities and localities.

The approach adopted to this issue reflects different models of community development. distinguishes two dominant models:

- *the consensus model.* "The emphasis is on all the people within a particular area working together and taking actions to improve the 'whole' community. Although disparities of income and access to other resources may be recognised, the underlying assumption is that the similarity of interests is powerful enough to form the basis for building consensus".
- *the conflict model.* This sees local inequalities as an expression of the structural causes of poverty and marginalisation. While the model equally emphasises "bringing people together to discuss their problems and organise collectively in search of solutions, its focus is more directly on the poor and disadvantaged and 'empowering' those who are outside the power structure".

Most rural development projects rest implicitly or explicitly on the consensus model, assuming a certain social cohesiveness or homogeneity and a solidarity of interest arising from the problems and difficulties of living in a particular locality. Actual community structures vary considerably, however, and so such assumptions will be more or less applicable in different contexts. However, for many people the consensus model represents an ideal to strive for whatever the underlying social reality.

Given that it is usually not practically possible to involve all members of a community in running a local development programme, the tendency often is to operate through the community's social and political leadership. This may be the best way to achieve practical results. It is non-provocative and avoids stirring up local conflicts or tensions. Critics of the consensus model argue, however, that such an approach reinforces existing power structures that oppress or marginalise the poor and other disadvantaged groups. An analysis of 'whole-community' development initiatives in rural Ireland observed that they "tend to be dominated by a small group of enthusiasts, adept at assembling the illusion of consensus that allows the interests of some to masquerade as the interests of all".

An overview of the rural projects included in the European Union's Third Anti-poverty Programme concluded that:

> It would be naive to think that more decision-making power devolved to local levels would, of itself, help to counter exclusion. This is because localities are 'negotiating arenas' where there can be sharp gradations of power, and the social composition of local organisations can be a factor in creating or maintaining exclusion. The counter process must be one of deliberate interventions to improve the capacity of excluded people to function collectively and effectively in their own interests.

Intervention should therefore focus on advocacy of and support for the underprivileged, including siding with them in their struggles with locally dominant forces, whether these be landowners, large farmers, middle class residents, corporate interests or state agencies.

However, promoting the participation of the poorest sections of communities can present particular difficulties. The Irish experience with anti-poverty programmes is instructive as these have been specifically based on the conflict model of community development, combining a local development brief with a particular emphasis on assisting the poor and most disadvantaged, and have accumulated experience over a twenty year period. Under the First European Anti-poverty Programme, the approach adopted by the project teams brought them into direct confrontation with local power-holders, including the Catholic church and prominent business people, but, in their efforts to involve the poor, all the projects "found eventually that they worked largely with people who had sufficient resources to enable them to become involved in group work and who were not living from crisis to crisis as the poorest appeared to be. The Second Anti-poverty Programme sought to broaden the participation of the poor through such measures as establishing resource centres, holding public meetings, publishing newsletters and building confidence through training initiatives. The rural projects in the Third Anti-poverty Programme built on this experience but, while the overall level of participation achieved was high, it was still found difficult to involve the poorest in management structures. Reviewing these successive episodes Curtin finds that "the evidence is inconclusive as to whether community efforts to alleviate rural poverty should be focused on the most disadvantaged or whether the gains to the poor are ultimately greater when emphasis is placed on involving the 'whole' community and increasing the resource base and opportunities for all".

An intermediate approach between the conflict and consensual models is one that recognises the different sectional groups within a locality but does not intervene in a partisan way. Thus Moseley and Cherrett, propose identifying and encouraging as wide a range as possible of interest groups covering all aspects of local political, economic, social and cultural life, and focusing their interest and attention on the elements and stages of the proposed project or plan which have most significance and importance to them.

The case is made that "those who don't have much at stake may be happy to be informed or consulted. Others will want to be involved in decisions and possibly action to carry them out".

Effective participation, then, is most likely "when each of the key interests—the stakeholders—is satisfied with the level of participation at which they are involved". The notion of stakeholder includes not only those who will be affected by any project, but also those who control the information, skills and resources required, and who may help or hinder progress. Stakeholders need not necessarily be equally affected by a scheme and therefore need not necessarily require an equal say. While such an approach may optimise the opportunities for participation, it does not look at what is behind different levels of involvement. It therefore may overlook the causes and consequences of social exclusion.

Achieving participation is about pursuing appropriate means as well as a clear strategy. From their investigations of Third World rural development projects, Oakley and Marsden pinpoint two important features which characterise those projects that seek effective participation:

- where project activities to bring about participation are an end in themselves and the project is designed and staffed to this purpose;
- these activities are seen as an essential and necessary foundation to activities of a more economic nature.

Flowing from these two features, Oakley and Marsden go on to list those elements that might form part of an effective participatory strategy. These are listed in Table 1.

Table 1. Important elements in an approach to effective participation

(a)	the process nature of such project work, in which it is difficult to establish fixed, quantifiable parameters;
(b)	the disaggregation of the rural poor and the identification of discrete socio-economic groups as the basic unit of development;
(c)	the notion of bottom-up with the absence of any pre-determined models and the emphasis upon the emergence spontaneously of a relevant approach from below;
(d)	the principle of self-reliance and the need to reduce development based upon dependence;
(e)	the issue of local control of the development project activities by the groups concerned;
(f)	the importance of collective action by the group to tackle the problems which they confront

Organisational Structures for Participation

Various organisational structures have been tried for promoting participation in rural development. The following are the most common. They are not mutually exclusive and occur in a variety of combinations.

Animateurs

Animateurs work with communities by providing support and advice to local people, businesses and groups to enable them to participate in developing projects to meet local needs. Their role is to help these actors identify key problems and opportunities, articulate their concerns, and formulate appropriate solutions. Through arousing enthusiasm and interest, and imparting particular skills and resources, the participatory practices that animateurs seek to promote can be sustained beyond the life of an individual project, and thus have longer term benefits for an area.

The Community Network or Forum

A community network or community forum can be established to bring together on a regular basis a locality's key political, professional and economic leaders, along with local activists and interest group personnel. The purpose is to exchange information on the locality's main social or economic issues and to debate development strategies or projects to be pursued. The membership should be representative of the area. To be effective, discussions and decisions also need to be taken forward to avoid the sessions becoming merely 'a talking shop'.

Cooperatives and Community Enterprises

Co-operatives and community enterprises involve the more formal cooperation of local people working together to run practical ventures such as businesses, community services, local employment schemes and the like. Co-operatives are *de facto* non-profit businesses which draw their capital from local savings, with those local people who subscribe their capital or labour becoming shareholders. Such arrangements may require substantial technical, legal and administrative support.

Rural Development Partnerships

Institutional partnerships are an increasingly common feature of area-based rural development programmes. They bring together agencies and organisations with responsibilities for an area in order to coordinate their actions. The thinking is that "a synergistic effect is created by a range of bodies working together which in turn generates more strategic and effective regeneration than if these bodies acted independently of one another". They may be led by local authorities or other localised state or quasi-state agencies. The involvement of community organisations in local partnerships is increasingly seen as a key element. Community involvement can be fostered by means of

Village appraisals

Village appraisals are another means by which participation in rural development can be extended. They are a type of 'stock-taking' exercise in which the resources and facilities available to a rural community are audited and the households comprising the community are surveyed about their circumstances and opinions to clarify local problems and needs. Village appraisals usually represent a 'do-it-yourself' exercise with community members having a voice in what types of questions are asked in surveys and in analysing the information and drawing up priorities for action. Because of this participatory ethos, village appraisals are considered to be both a means of community development but also an end in themselves.

direct community representation on main partnership boards or committees or through local animateurs acting as a channel between local communities and 'the partnership'. However, detailed research into the operation of partnerships in the UK found that such mechanisms "appear to have achieved only limited results, especially in involving and empowering the most excluded groups and communities".

Tools for Participation

Moseley and Cherrett identify the following as the key tools for promoting participation in rural development projects and programmes:

- *Public meetings* are a useful way of publicising projects and providing open debate;
- *Adult education and training* play a determinant role in the active involvement of local people, most particularly in the implementation of development projects;
- *Village appraisals* are self-administered community surveys for local people to formally identify their common problems and opportunities and the action needed to tackle them;
- *Exhibitions and fairs* can be means for bringing projects to public attention and eliciting popular responses;
- *Media and telecommunications* provide for widespread and regular dissemination of information and debate about development projects and programmes.

Social Exclusion of Marginalised Groups

Endogenous approaches to rural development emphasise the importance of the human and cultural resources of a local area in the formulation, implementation and outcome of development initiatives. The effectiveness of such initiatives depends upon the involvement of the different sections of local society. Some sections, though, enjoy many fewer opportunities than others. If problems of need are to be tackled then such excluded groups must be equipped to share more fully in the benefits of social and economic development. Otherwise, an area cannot achieve its full potential and problems of need will persist.

Conceptualising Disadvantage

There is now a considerable literature within rural studies and in social policy studies more generally about the most appropriate way in which disadvantage might be conceptualised. Poverty, usually taken to denote levels of financial need, is no longer the sole focus. The term deprivation has often been used as an alternative, to refer to a complex of problems beyond financial need, including difficulties of access to basic services. However, the subjectivism of that term has moved commentators to refer instead to the marginalisation or exclusion of certain social groups by the broader society.

Mernagh and Commins define social exclusion as follows:

> Social exclusion can be described as a process whereby certain categories of people and the environments in which they live are excluded from the opportunities, status, power and privileges accorded to others in contemporary society. This exclusion leads to multiple forms of inequality, and not just poverty of material resources, for such people and places.

The following are the broad groupings of factors that structure rural living and are the primary mechanisms by which opportunities and access to resources—advantage and disadvantage—are determined:

1. *Labour market,* including levels of engagement with the labour market (rates of part-time and full-time employment); the structure of local labour markets (levels of unskilled, skilled, managerial and professional employment); training and education opportunities; and access to employment for different groups (for example, men, women, the young).
2. *Housing market,* including the structure of local housing markets; the supply of accommodation suited to levels and nature of local demand; and differential access to the housing market.
3. *Service access,* including the provision and accessibility of education at primary, secondary and tertiary levels; training opportunities for the acquisition of labour market skills; healthcare facilities such as primary health care; transport facilities; and community services.
4. *Social and community life,* including levels of local social cohesion; the existence of supportive social networks based on kith and kinship relations; access to community groups and organisations; and tolerance of different cultures within a locality.

A number of case studies and comparative analyses conducted in various European regions attest to the salience of these factors in people's circumstances and opportunities. Social exclusion may thus be conceptualised as the denial of access to labour or housing markets or services or social and community life—in short, the basic facilities enjoyed by the majority in society and regarded as essential by that society in order to fulfil human potential. The concept extends to cover opportunities for participation in civil society in its fullest sense, including, for example, denial of political representation of specific interests.

The Heterogeneity of Marginalisation

The key point about the experience of marginalisation or social exclusion is that different social groups and individuals experience it in different ways. It cannot be conceptualised as homogenous with universally applicable causes and effects. Whilst similar factors may be implicated in the production of exclusion, the severity and interplay of these factors must be seen as specific to individuals and groups. The identification of these factors has to be recognised as a pre-condition for development strategies. This is necessary because successful strategies to overcome exclusion rely on tackling the causes of that exclusion as much as the symptoms of it.

The territorial, physical and economic diversity of the European Union's rural areas is matched by the diversity of lived experiences of the people of these areas. There are vast differences in people's experiences, for example, between rural Andalucia and Friesland or between the Highlands of Scotland and Bavaria. Diversity of lived experience is also tangible *within* regions, for example, between the landowner and the landless or between the unqualified local youth and the commuting professional. In consequence, different people experience different things as good or bad in different places. Recognising this diversity is important, in view of the tensions that exist between the equitable distribution of resources and the imperative to target scarce financial resources most effectively. It has implications for the identification of need, the method of involvement and the applicability of procedures for monitoring outcomes. The conceptualisation of social exclusion as a heterogeneous and geographically varied experience, though, is critical to the evolution of rural development initiatives that are inclusive of the people in specific places and relevant to their particular needs.

First, the heterogeneity of marginalisation and exclusion will be explored with reference to the experiences of specific groups often defined as marginalised. Using the framework suggested above, the exclusion of different groups through the mechanisms operating in the labour and housing markets, service access and social and community life will all be explored.

Alternatively, the different factors that contribute to social exclusion (agricultural decline, social service provision, the operation of the housing market and so on) might be analysed in terms of their impacts on different social groups (the young, the elderly, etc.), as exemplified in a recent study of poverty in rural Ireland. By examining social exclusion with reference to the experiences of particular groups across the European Union, the intention is to show how particular groups might share the label of exclusion, but how this might be manifest in very different ways in different places. The emerging picture is thus rather complex, in terms of material and cultural experiences, which serves to reinforce the point that strategies to deal with exclusion have to be carefully targeted at both people and places.

Women

It could be argued that the conceptualisation of women as a marginalised group is problematic, when they constitute half the population. However, the position of women across the European Union provides a useful entry into discussions of marginalisation. Many of the factors that might cause marginalisation in labour and housing markets, difficulties in terms of access to services and in terms of their roles in community and social life are problematic for many social groups but most keenly felt by women. Furthermore, it is essential for the effective delivery of policies directed at reducing marginalisation that the experience of women in different areas is noted. This is because policy mechanisms are often directed at the dominant group in a deprived region, often male heads of households or those working in a particular sector. The invisibility of women means that rural development policies are often not directed at their specific needs.

The invisibility of women's work often results in their *de facto* marginalisation. Their contribution to both formal and informal labour markets is usually undervalued by official statistics. In areas dominated by family farming, their diverse contributions are treated as subordinate family labour and generally go unremunerated and unrecorded. Even in areas dominated by large estates, where labourers' wives and daughters have always been engaged in work in the fields and their contribution is essential to the economic viability of the household, it is still undervalued, gaining lower wages and often being omitted from official counts of employment.

The negative social image of women's involvement in agriculture contributes further to their marginalisation. In addition, many women bear a double burden of both paid employment and unpaid work within the home, a reflection of the way processes of marginalisation operate within strongly patriarchal societies.

Women are also marginalised through factors in the sphere of social and community life. Again, the impact of these processes is also felt by other social groups, but again, the experience for many women is instructive. In many European cultures, community and social life is dominated by activities undertaken by women, either because their lower levels of engagement with the labour market gives them greater opportunity to facilitate social activities, or because of the pressure of social expectations about their 'natural' role. Certainly, as Seymour and Short note in terms of women's participation in church activities, they are likely to predominate in unpaid and voluntary positions within an organisation that provides an important focus for rural communities. However, this inclusion can be oppressive. First, the participation of women in voluntary and unpaid social activities can often reinforce rural gender relations which work to uphold patriarchal values which ultimately work against women's interests. Second, as Hughes notes, participation in community and social life is often undertaken more as a duty than a joy, with reluctance compounding social isolation for those unwilling to undertake voluntary activities. The operation of such dominant forces should be recognised, particularly when policy mechanisms seek to rely on the availability of women in unpaid or voluntary capacities.

Lone Parents

We noted above how the operation of factors associated with the labour and housing markets, services and community life might all lead to social exclusion or marginalisation for different groups. The experience of lone parents in rural areas, the majority of whom are women, illustrates how this complex of factors operates in the production of this marginalisation.

There has been little research to date on the experiences of lone parents in rural areas. This reflects both the social invisibility of the subject as well as the demographic fact that the majority of lone parents live in urban area. The research material that does exist on rural lone parents demonstrates extreme levels of marginalisation and exclusion from social and economic life for many.

The interplay and interdependence of factors which structure marginalisation makes the identification of causal factors problematic. Difficulties in access to the labour market are generally taken as highly significant. The issue is primarily one of access to employment, hindered by difficulties in finding affordable, reliable childcare which in rural areas can be particularly difficult, as research by Stone indicates. Access to housing markets is also a problem; lone mothers unable to find employment which they can combine with family responsibilities are often faced with limited access to housing due to a lack of financial resources. This is compounded by the paucity in many areas of suitable housing in both the private and public rented sectors. In addition, lack of financial resources makes transportation a problem; if a lone parent cannot afford to run a car, this can make access to education, health and community services difficult.

Research by a voluntary organisation in Norfolk in the UK provides a good example of how this complex of problems operates:

> One of our clients has three small children under 8, one in a pushchair and two just starting school. She has had to move away from where she grew up because of a violent partner. She did not know the area and when she was offered a house to rent in a small village, she accepted virtually the first thing she saw as she was desperate — very soon after she moved in she realised her mistake. She had to walk one and a half miles [c. 3km] along unmade roads to the school bus stop and one and half miles back again every day twice a day with two small children walking and one in a pushchair. Often when we rang her she was in tears totally frustrated at having to placate grizzling, cold children on her own.

Ethnic Minorities

The experience of the various ethnic minority groups across the European Union is instructive for this account of social exclusion and marginalisation. Some are confined to urban areas while others do find acceptance in rural areas. But for others, living in a rural area compounds existing problems of xenophobia and the knock-on effects of racism experienced in the labour and housing markets, and in access to services and community life.

The experience of migrant workers in rural Spain illustrates the mechanisms by which members of ethnic minorities become excluded from material and social opportunities. Much of the Mediterranean coast of Spain is characterised by intensive small-scale agriculture geared towards the production of export crops, accounting for around 60% of the agricultural exports of Spain. This is a low wage labour market, characterised in more recent years by a lack of indigenous labour willing to accept the wages and working conditions offered by farmers. Farms are coming to depend increasingly on migrant workers, mainly people from North Africa and South America, who now constitute a significant proportion of the agricultural labour force employed in parts of Almeria, Murcia, Valencia, Castellon and around Tarragona. Due to many employers' unwillingness to conform to labour legislation enacted in the early 1990s, many of these migrant workers are employed illegally in the informal economy. Such employment tends to be irregular, unprotected by health and safety legislation, characterised by long hours and difficult working conditions. These employment practices are often compounded for migrants by rudimentary or inadequate housing conditions and difficult access to health services. For many members of ethnic minority groups, economic marginalisation is added to by racism and discrimination causing social exclusion.

The situation on the Mediterranean littoral of Spain is repeated in other southern European countries. An estimated 1 million non-EU immigrants in Italy are irregular workers, employed mainly in the heavy and worst-paid jobs, particularly in agriculture, construction or catering.

One ethnic group that is often identified as suffering some of the greatest problems of marginalisation are gypsies. An estimated 2-3 million gypsies live within the European Union, with about double that number on the EU's eastern border. Increasingly, gypsies are bearing the brunt of rising nationalism and xenophobia. Many local, regional and national authorities do not accept them as citizens with rights to pursue their traditional lifestyles. They suffer increasing harassment and enforced displacement, and are one of the most socially excluded groups in the EU.

Cultural processes, as well as economic ones, can lead to social exclusion in rural areas. Rural areas are significant spaces for the construction of national identity. In expressing the dominant national or regional culture, rural ideologies leave little room for ethnic minority or immigrant cultures. As European cities have come to play host to a variety of cultures, so rural areas have come to be portrayed as places of racial purity where the nation's true cultural roots reside. Ethnic minority groups feel excluded from the countryside. This exclusion extends from direct experiences of racism encountered by those who move into rural areas, through to the lack of recognition of the contribution of ethnic minority groups to the national cultural heritage.

The experiences of what some might term indigenous minorities is also pertinent here. In certain parts of the European Union—Brittany, Galicia and Wales for example—a local linguistic minority feels marginalised through the in-migration of a dominant majority language group. So, for example, Welsh-speakers in rural Wales have experienced cultural and linguistic marginalisation due to the in-migration of significant numbers of English speakers.

The Elderly

Europe's rural areas tend to have a higher proportion of older people than the national average, reflecting lower birth rates and higher levels of out-migration from rural areas by young people and people of family-rearing age. These processes are compounded by the fact that in general demographic terms, Europe's population is ageing. Thus the problems of exclusion felt by many elderly people in the 1990s are likely to be shared by a higher proportion of rural residents in the 2020s, purely on demographic factors. For this reason, it is important to assess the social exclusion and marginalisation of older people.

The social exclusion and marginalisation of the elderly in many areas is a reflection primarily of poverty through a lack of access to economic resources. The rural poor are more likely to be elderly than the urban poor. A recent study of deprivation in rural areas in England and Wales found that seven out of ten households living in poverty were made up of elderly household member. Furthermore, because of differential mortality rates between men and women, a high proportion of those households will contain a single elderly woman. This pattern is replicated across many countries of the European Union.

They are the consequence of the interplay of factors relating to the housing and labour markets, access to services and social life. Like many lone parents, the elderly's experience of exclusion is often attributable to the *interplay* of factors, rather than any single primary cause. Much research does emphasise, however, the importance of access problems in structuring this marginalisation.

The elderly are often marginalised most acutely because of problems of access to services. This limits the use they can make of services that enable them to participate fully in social life and reap the benefits of living in economies with highly developed welfare systems. Research conducted in Ireland illustrates many of the problems elderly people face in rural areas. For example, many people face a fundamental problem of access to health services. Provision in rural areas may be adequate for those with transportation of some kind, but for the 'rural transport poor', a group which includes many elderly who cannot drive, do not have access to their own transport or who are badly served by limited public transport facilities, access to basic health care services can be extremely difficult. For many elderly, the problems of difficult access to health services are compounded by low levels of community-based care and assistance, either from health care providers or from family members due to the effects of out-migration. As O'Shea notes, changes in family formation, an increase in the labour force participation rate of women, and the consequences of prolonged and on-going emigration has tended to reduce the pool of potential carers in rural areas, a process that seems set to continue given the salience of current migration and labour market trends. This process is repeated in parts of north-east Italy, Portugal and Spain.

A specific problem for the elderly, compounding experiences of marginalisation, is the gap between lived experience and expectations. Many of those who now call 'the elderly' grew up in the years of economic depression in the 1930s and social turmoil of the Second World War and post-war years, living through hardships with the promise of an easier old age through the availability of a supportive family structure and provision of the modern welfare system. With the disruption to family life caused by the out-migration of younger people, and the decline of health and transport services through the restructuring of many welfare systems, many rural elderly seem sorely disappointed that their expectations of a secure old age remain unfulfilled.

Young Unemployed People

The problems of young people living in rural areas are often overlooked. Broad demographic indicators show a tendency, across Europe's rural areas, for out-migration amongst younger people, in search of employment opportunities and perhaps a more adventurous life-style in major towns and cities. This is a long-term historic trend, little affected by counterurbanisation processes mentioned above.

International comparative research undertaken as part of the European Commission's Poverty 3 programme provides some key indications of the nature of social exclusion and marginalisation experienced by young people in rural areas. The most stark fact to emerge is the very limited number of options facing young people: to remain unemployed or to emigrate. Furthermore, it is important to recognise that the unemployment faced by rural youth sits within a wider European context where high levels of unemployment are already a concern. Common features of unemployment across the European Union include the simple fact of too few jobs for too many applicants, the inability of many unemployed people to compete for job vacancies because of a lack of qualifications or appropriate skills, and the fact that both the long-term unemployed and first-time job seekers are often the least favoured by employers. Furthermore, unemployment is often linked to wider social issues such as discrimination against minority groups and the effects of living in an area of high unemployment where inadequate income is linked to a loss of confidence in the local economic system, disillusionment, poor self-esteem, social isolation and involuntary migration. All these factors apply to rural as well as to urban areas, but the experience of rural unemployment is compounded for many young people because of the local effects of adjustments in the agricultural sector (a traditional employer), peripherality of many regions and the costs associated with spatial exclusion such as the problems of access to education and training facilities.

For many rural residents in Europe, the lack of employment opportunities for younger people is perceived to be the most serious problem facing rural communities. For example, research conducted into poverty in Scotland indicated that although many respondents recognised that limited work options were a fact of life for those living in peripheral regions, appreciation of this fact did little to ameliorate people's frustration at the lack of local labour market opportunities and dismay at some of the consequences for the wider community of the out-migration of young people1. Furthermore, the out-migration of those more able to make use of limited labour market opportunities makes the position of those left behind even more stark. This group of young rural unemployed face exclusion in terms of labour market participation which has a knock-on effect in terms of their ability to compete in the housing market, their ability to access certain services (particularly education and training) and more generally their ability to participate fully in social life.

Strategies for the Reduction of Social Exclusion

This brief overview of the experiences of marginalisation and exclusion for different groups in Europe's rural areas has explored some of the principal factors structuring that exclusion, and shown how some of these factors operate in practice. Three points lead on from this discussion.

First, would wish to emphasise again the importance of recognising, on the one hand the diversity of experiences of social exclusion, and on the other the commonality of causative factors producing this exclusion. Recognition of the diversity of lived experience should not be taken as indicative of some sort of inherent difficulty in tackling the issue, but rather as a *sine qua non* for the formulation of effective rural development policy to tackle the problems of exclusion. Marginalisation and social exclusion affect groups in different ways; policy needs to be sufficiently flexible to address this diversity of experience. Furthermore, it needs to address the causes of this exclusion as well as its consequences.

The emphasis of much of the literature is on the locality as the locus for marginalisation and the focus for policy. The strategy suggested here is that a more people-orientated policy approach requires, as a first principle, research into living conditions and experiences.

Third, and to return to the central theme of participation in rural development, there is still less in terms of public debate and literature as to the most appropriate mechanisms for enabling full participation in rural development strategies by those who are socially excluded. Further research is needed in this area. As the European Union takes steps towards greater integration, it should be remembered that political and economic stability rest on inclusion and participation rather than exclusion and marginalisation.

Cultural Identities and Social and Economic Development

Endogenous development favours economic activity based on place-specific resources. For rural areas which may be poorly endowed with physical capital (equipment and infrastructure) and have low population densities, the focus is increasingly on the environmental and cultural resources with which they are often richly endowed. Cultural products and services have thus become a feature of local and regional development. It is argued that, by raising consciousness of local cultural identity, participation could be stimulated in forms of social and economic development that would be fixed in the locality. Regionalist movements have supported economic and political strategies to valorise regional cultural identities, including 'minority' languages. At the same time, the rise internationally of 'green' and ethical consumerist concerns has encouraged forms of development that respect and value local differences, such as ethnic craft products and cultural tourism.

What term the 'culture economy' approach in rural development, then, is an admixture of: the economic theory of competitive advantage and international trade; the marketing concept of niche markets; and a response to the critique of exogenous development and the notion of modernity as a 'cultural melting pot'. It is also a manifestation both of localist agendas, as rural regions and regionalist movements explore new opportunities to re-integrate peripheral areas or minority cultures, and of European agendas, such as the EU's 'Unity in Diversity' cultural policy. In terms of development theory, the approach can be located in the logic of economic growth within consumer capitalism in which a cultural system is seen as a means to create space-specific resources for economic exploitation. Alternatively, the approach can be seen as a reaction to modernism and its homogenising, centralising and disruptive changes.

The culture economy approach has considerable potential to promote a participative form of rural development. First, the approach allocates a central role to the local community. It is often the unit in the design and implementation of projects, whether in the pursuit of 'soft' (social) development or 'hard' economic development. The local level thereby assumes some control, and captures the direct benefits, of development activity. Second, the cultural approach entails the creation (or re-discovery) of a territorial identity and serves to promote the area in wider policy and commercial circles. In those cases where the cultural identity is founded on the reconstruction of an existing regional or ethnic identity then a further participative rationale can be added in the empowerment of an historically repressed or marginalised cultural system—such as Gaelic, Breton or Lap—which may continue to have potent symbolic and quality of life meaning for the indigenous population, and perhaps for visitors and incomers too. A further important element of the culture economy rhetoric is the raising of local consciousness of territorial identity so as to cultivate a general commitment to the area within local businesses and individuals and to raise confidence in the ability of the area to regenerate itself.

Although similar issues to do with the employment of cultural resources in local social/economic development may arise in the context of urban regeneration, the notion is particularly germane to rural development. Faced with geographical and economic peripheralisation, attributed to historical factors and external forces (mobile capital, political and economic polarisation, etc.), rural areas are increasingly paying attention to *territorial* resources as a means of exerting control over development. It is also the case that in these rural areas the raw material for culture economies is still tangible and often conveys a strong sense of 'authenticity'; for example, a peripheral area may still contain speakers of the regional language, traditional foods, remnants of craft skills, important historical or archaeological sites and the native flora and fauna. Finally the type and scale of economic activity generated, involving specialised and niche markets, tend to be more related to the capacity of rural areas and their small-scale enterprise structure.

It begins with cultural tourism—perhaps the most readily identifiable form of the culture economy. This is followed by a consideration of how the culture economy operates more directly at the community level. It deals with the special case of linguistic economies in which regional languages are employed as a resource of rural development. Running through all these dimensions is the argument that the culture economy has to be seen not only as a straightforward economic means (resources to generate local economic activity) but also as a socio-cultural end. In other words, the type of activity initiated in the culture economy approach plays an important and direct role in cultivating the socio-cultural well-being of an area.

Cultural Identity and Participation in Tourism Activity

Cultural identity has come to manifest itself in tourism in a number of forms: cultural (ethno-) tourism, literary/art tourism, green tourism and regional cuisines. They are all 'upmarket' forms of tourism, having in common the potential for higher added-value than the mass tourism of the 'bucket and spade' and 'Costas' varieties. There may be geographical benefits too in switching pressures from over-developed coastal areas to rural hinterlands needing an economic stimulus. Cultural tourism, though, defines itself in terms of, and sees its benefits deriving from, its limited scale and the potential for local control of the nature and economic benefit of the activity.

Cultural tourism in rural development has evolved two interconnected rationales. The first relates to the exploitation of place-specific resources in order to generate locally-tied economic activity. These economic benefits may occur through employment opportunities where local people have unique qualifications, such as the ability to speak a local language, in-depth local knowledge to act as guides and local craft skills. The argument used by Comunn na Gaidhlig in support of their approach to Gaelic development in Scotland is that cultural tourism can generate higher status jobs for local people. In contrast to the conventionally low-paid, unskilled, seasonal employment characteristic of mass tourism, cultural tourism is said to provide opportunities for creative artists, naturalists, linguists, crafts people, local historians, etc. This ties in with the generation of local jobs in regional cultural development beyond the tourist sector (especially in arts, crafts, television, film and conservation).

The other rationale is that of social development. Until comparatively recently, the view of cultural theorists and regionalists was that tourism represented a threat to the viability of local cultural systems, bringing with it international consumerism and the threat of cultural homogenisation—what Ritzer referred to as McDonaldisation. However, the new approach argues that this may no longer automatically be the case and that a tourism sector and an indigenous culture are not mutually exclusive. Furthermore, tourism, as an explicit recognition of the worth of a local culture, can play a role in building community self-confidence which, in turn, can drive its rejuvenation.

The market available for exploitation by local tourism initiatives is an expression of a demand to experience certain values that are associated with rurality and that contrast with modernity and the urban model. These can be any combination of 'pace of life' (community, conviviality), the natural environment, ethnic or wholesome cuisines and folklore practices and artefacts. The tourist may be seeking an experience that is metaphysical (for example, participating in a religious festival), or romantic (visiting places that are remote or idyllic), aesthetic (visiting localities associated with certain artists or authors), gastronomic (regional cuisines and wines) or educational (places of historical or wildlife interest).

This puts the locality—the 'producers'/guardians—in control because the product/service, by definition, is tied to the particular locality which means that each locality has a comparative advantage: although 'new' tourism activity can be initiated elsewhere, this is not the same threat as the capital mobility that endogenous development seeks to counter.

The territory can also exercise control and local populations have been observed to exhibit a range of strategies in their engagement with tourist activity. At one end of the spectrum are examples of where a product/service is 'manufactured' for the tourist, leaving the 'authentic' local culture free from being overwhelmed or even commodified by the culture of the tourists. Back places, concealed from the tourists, can be set aside where locals can be themselves. At the other end of the spectrum, local people will engage actively with visitors, and share the modern facilities provided, and view this engagement as a healthy input into the social and cultural vibrancy of the area. Furthermore, where such tourist activity is based on local participation in its design and implementation, then these local voices will often wish to limit the scale of the activity so as to minimise any social disruption.

Not only is it controllable, but cultural tourism can also function to raise community self-confidence. This sort of tourism activity can rejuvenate local cultural awareness leading to a re-assessment of the local culture as something of worth. If visitors are prepared to travel to the territory and pay to experience its cultural, historical and environmental resources, then this can feed back to cultivate a local community's feeling of self-worth and connectedness to a wider world. The need not to feel 'stuck in a backwater' is a major psychological concern. This is an important factor given that a major cause of the socio-economic decline of many rural areas was the systematic undermining of regional cultures by the institutions associated with the process of nation-state building. For rural localities to be able to generate endogenous, sustainable, socio-economic development requires that they put this process into reverse and begin to believe in their innate capacities and resources to hold people, innovation and capital to the territory. The ultimate objective is to use cultural tourism to bring about a change in local people's consciousness so that 'the local' is no longer seen as intrinsically inferior.

Culture Economy at the Community Level

In endogenous development, the local community—village, township, commune, etc.—is seen as an important, if not the key, locus through which to animate popular participation in development activity. According to this view, it is at the community level that people's voices are best articulated and 'soft' development promoted. The inference is that community level activity ensures that development rests on a foundation of participative democracy.

The culture economy at the community level emphasises the 'soft' development approach but not to the total exclusion of direct economic effects. For example, the culture economy can generate resources upon which community enterprises may be built and, more generally, community resources can support regional tourism. But central to the notion of a culture economy is that direct economic outcome does not necessarily have to be demonstrated in order for the approach to be valid.

'Soft' development is about regenerating the socio-cultural vibrancy of a locality so that local people feel good about their area. Through a raised awareness of its history and cultural resources, their feelings of belonging and commitment to the local area are affirmed and reinforced. One of the most effective means to achieve this is to create, or assist, organisations and individuals whose primary focus is the community-level. Local cultural activity thereby becomes a vehicle for locally-controlled change. If development can be imagined through the analogy of 'unfurling' rather than 'growth/competition, then the role of the culture economy approach becomes one of promoting a participatory form of cultural creativity. This is in direct contrast with the sort of 'cultural policy' that elevates national or cosmopolitan cultural resources over those of the locality.

Just as the approach can be used to celebrate place and belonging, so it can also be used to express the identity of minority or repressed socio-cultural groups. As Clinton and Glen comment:

> artistic products are by their nature intended to be highly visible and can in turn confer visibility on those who create them; community arts can help challenge inequalities and oppressions as experienced through ageism, ableism, sexism, homophobia and racism by explicit targetingand positive action through engaging with a variety of communities of interest and identity

Linguistic Communities and Participatory Rural Development

Language can be a key marker of a cultural system. The idea explored is that a regional language can be both an objective of development policy/ action and a resource to drive economic development.

The conservation of languages is primarily a manifestation of regionalist agendas. The explicit assumption is that it is possible to reverse the historical trend that has seen some languages grow at the expense of others as a result of systematic state action or local economic restructuring (e.g. the decline of traditional sectors). That assumption rests on the notion that the dynamics of language competition in a region or nation will be played out within key social 'domains', such as the home, the church, education, public administration and business. Thus, a regional language will lose status if it is displaced as the medium of (local) communication in, for example, the business domain. The history of many regional languages has been a retreat to the domains of 'home, field and church' in the face of competition from the state language that eventually assumes complete domination of public, business and media domains. As a result, the regional language comes to be seen as inferior, and lacking utility in modern life so that many local people (especially the young and ambitious) will choose to abandon it.

Regions where there is a regional language issue can respond in two ways: they may argue that a regional language should be maintained for its function as a cultural marker; and they may promote the language as an agent for territorial economic development.

The first of these is based on the notion that a language has an intrinsic value which may be considerable for local people. It is an ethical issue whether to maintain a language as a living thing through policy intervention. Language maintenance becomes a mechanism for people 'to know who they are', a medium for their 'world view' and its connections to place and history, and how they relate to others outside of the cultural group.

Thus, it can be argued that policy aimed directly at promoting the learning and use of a regional language can play a role in participative rural development. The concept of language domains has also been linked to socio-economic groups as, for example, in the identification of the agricultural sector as the 'natural guardians' of a language (Hughes *et al,* 1996). In this case, an argument can be made that cultural development could be assisted through policy aimed at these key socio-economic groups.

A 'language planning' approach can be justified as participatory in 'redressing historical injustice' and enabling a group to retain a cultural marker that has major symbolic value for the speakers, learners and others sympathetic to the language. In the discourse of the Celtic languages, advocates often claim that their linguistic-cultural system contains within it meanings of development/world view that are particular to the Celtic peoples (invoking a spiritual dimension, the elevation of a folk creativity such as through the poetic form, an environmental ethic, etc.). During the construction of a cultural basis for a local rural development initiative in the Highlands and Islands of Scotland in 1990, these notions were made explicit.

The sense of belonging to a particular territory and culture underpins the other approach which attempts to re-introduce a regional language into the domains of business, public administration and the media. By raising awareness and the visibility of a language, the rootedness of local entrepreneurs, professionals, school leavers and local people in general to their home territory (or their adopted home territory) can be enhanced. The belief is that the resulting sense of commitment to the territory will help to resist forces behind the outmigration of people and businesses.

The approach extends into attempts to create language-based employment. This has happened in Wales with, for example, the expansion of Welsh language radio and television and the private production companies that serve the S4C channel, and it has begun to happen with Gaelic in Scotland. In addition to direct employment in these cultural production companies and the associated service sector, income can be generated through export markets for products such as regional language films.

The employment potential is much broader than just the cultural especially if large organisations in the public or private sectors can be encouraged or obliged to adopt the regional language. They may also require legislation in order to re-establish 'language status' in terms of its legal status in contracts and in terms of the language policy of significant organisations. Regions have also tried to extend the use of their languages into the private business sector in general through linguistic/enterprise development agencies. For most companies, this means the development of a bilingual operation.

This model, in particular, is being promoted in various European regions (and supported through EU rural development programmes such as LEADER and other policies relating to cultural diversity and Information Technology). Although a regional society would remain bi/multilingual in ability, there would be an ethos that privileged the regional language. The indigenous population (together with incomers who expressed a preparedness to learn the language) would thus have their indigenous language skills valorised. This is, in fact, the regionalist version of the nation-state development model in which one particular language is privileged for internal communication and where the ability to operate within that language confers on the individual crucial capital. Thus, for example, in regions that are pursuing a bilingual policy, such as Wales, local people who are able to speak the regional language gain privileged access to local employment opportunities (especially in public administration, education and the media). Indeed, the role of the public sector could be seen to be a crucial foundation for the linguistic economy model.

Whether the causal relationship between economic growth in the industrialism/consumer capitalism model and the demise of a regional language can work in reverse is as yet to be proved. The relationship between this approach and the 'alternative value set' that some have suggested lies at the heart of the linguistic-cultural model is even more problematic. But even if these doubts are set aside, this study of participation in rural development has to note the further problem—that of social exclusion. The regionalist argument is that dominant 'colonialist' powers have historically been very ethnocentric, systematically repressing regional cultures, and that local people should now be allowed to resurrect their cultural systems as something that is important to them.

However, none of these regions is culturally homogenous. They will include both indigenous people and incomers who do not speak the language and who chose not to learn it. If local jobs are created that discriminate in favour of those with the appropriate language skills, the issue has to be faced that some local people may become economically excluded. Thus, the linguistic model may have the capacity to replace one form of exclusion with another. But, at the end of the day, the approach hinges not on policy intervention but, rather, on popular support for the notion that affairs be conducted in the language.

General Reflections on the Cultural Identity Approach

The cultural identity approach, as discussed above, can operate in two modes, both of which attempt to counteract the centripetal forces that over time leave certain rural areas socio-economically disadvantaged. First, cultural markers (folklore traditions, festivals, languages, cuisines etc.) can be seen essentially as commodities. Their support and promotion can be seen as a beneficial form of economic activity in that the activity and the benefits derived are tied to the local territory. Primarily, this means that leakage of economic benefit and demographic out-migration can be reduced as local jobs are secured, opportunities for local enterprises increased and higher status employment opportunities created. The cultural identities involved in any particular case may reflect, authentically, the lives and world views of local people, but not necessarily; they may be 'staged' for the visitor or customer. In other words, the perceptions of the consumer in constructing the identity are just as important. However, this increased external interest in, and valuation of, regional cultures can work to raise the consciousness of local people.

The other mode is more akin to cultural engineering (including language planning). The argument here is that the rejuvenation of a regional cultural system as a living entity will indirectly result in social and economic benefits. The difference from the first mode is that the primary focus is on the 'authentic' but modernising culture and the intervention needed in order to ensure its rejuvenation and continuation, so that local people can, once again, choose to live their lives through the forms and values of their indigenous culture. Exponents of this mode argue that participation would be enabled as the innate, historically-frustrated, need is satisfied.

Here, the discussion enters the area of development ethics. In the context of the Third World, there has recently emerged a critique of the bottom-up/cultural approach for perpetuating what to the liberal mind seem unacceptable repressive practices, particularly regarding the role and status traditionally ascribed to women. In the case of the rural areas of the European Union, one might assume that the value choice is less extreme as these local systems have been penetrated by modern values and cultural forms. However, to the advocates of regional identity in this second mode, there remains the feeling that they are engaged in a fight to renegotiate their right to live according to their cultural system. Regionalists argue that the indigenous culture, albeit open to outside influences, is still a 'natural/ authentic' system and that cultures, just like species, have a right to exist if local people choose for this to be so. Smith and Maffesoli among others have analysed this as the expression of a basic need within human society to organise itself into identity groups whose scale is smaller than the modern nation state and whose rationale can call upon resources that appear to have more meaning than those of the nation state. Without a re-assertion of this territorial culture, the suggestion is that the historical decline of peripheral areas will continue.

The promotion of a regional culture enables people to have a sense of belonging and ownership. It creates resources that can be employed to regenerate local social and economic vibrancy. This is not a matter of autonomous, nor even purely endogenous, development. It is remarkable the extent to which practitioners involved in cultural initiatives are Eurocentric in their thinking. Furthermore, in relation to the language issue, the model is a bilingual one in which the regional language cultivates a local identity and this sits within broader spheres of identity that transcend the locality.

However, and especially in a study of participative development, attention has to be paid to the internal heterogeneity of these rural areas. Despite the enlightened rhetoric of the regionalist—that they are relativist rather than ethnocentrist (i.e. that they are different from, not better than, other cultures) and that they emphasise culture rather than race (thus, allowing for incomers to elect to join the group rather than having to have been born into it)—there remains the issue of those local people who would choose not to subscribe to the revived culture.

Relevant EU Policies

Evolution of EU Policies for Rural Development

In the past, the main means of support for rural areas of the European Union was the Common Agricultural Policy (CAP) and this still remains the case. However, whereas in the 1970s the CAP accounted for some three-quarters of total Community spending, and in the 1980s about two-thirds, by the mid-1990s it was down to about a half. Although often justified on social grounds, the bulk of this aid has been spent on maintaining commodity prices. The distribution of the aid within the farming community has been quite regressive: the main beneficiaries have not been the smaller farmers and poorer regions but the larger farmers and more prosperous agricultural regions.

Parallel policies have developed specifically to address rural disadvantage. They have been geographically targeted, reflecting concerns over regional inequalities, and until recently have commanded very much smaller shares of the Community's budget. Apart from Italy, the original member states were felt to have relatively homogenous regional economic structures, and regional inequalities were not an issue for the early European Community. Matters changed after Britain's accession in 1973. Initially, the

British Government saw regional assistance as a counterweight to CAP spending, and in 1975 the European Regional Development Fund (ERDF) and the Less Favoured Areas (LFA) programme were set up. Directive 75/268, under which Less Favoured Areas are designated, authorised financial compensation for farmers operating in mountains, hilly terrain and other 'less favoured areas' to "ensure the continuation of farming, thereby maintaining a minimum population level, or conserving the countryside". The programme operates through direct income aids to farmers based on their livestock numbers. In 1979, the possibilities of support were broadened through the introduction of integrated development programmes which formally recognised that the overall economic fabric of LFAs and not just their farming sectors was vulnerable. In 1985 the Integrated Mediterranean Programmes were introduced partly to offset what was seen as a northern bias in the CAP and partly in response to the fears of France, Greece and Italy over the likely glut in Mediterranean produce following the accession of Portugal and Spain.

Table 1. Objectives and Principles of the EU Structural Funds

Objectives	
Objective 1	Regions where development is lagging behind and where GDP is less that 75% of the EU average
Objective 2	Regions seriously affected by industrial decline
Objective 3	Combatting long-term unemployment
Objective 4	Facilitating the entry of young people into the labour market
Objective 5	Concerned with (a) the adjustment of agricultural structures and (b) the development of rural areas
Objective 6	Regions with very sparse populations (of less than 8 inhabitants per square kilometre)
Principles	
1. Concentration of resources on areas of greatest need	
2. Programme approach rather than one-off projects	
3. Improved co-ordination between instruments and agencies	
4. Partnership between Commission, national and regional interests	
4. Additionality in the provision of resources	
6. Monitoring and evaluation given a high priority	

The Single European Act of 1987 confirmed the principle of cohesion and the importance of a Community regional policy to flank the efforts to complete the Single Market. Along with mounting pressures to reform the CAP, it provided the impetus for the development of a more prominent and coherent regional policy and for the formulation for the first time of a rural policy.

It emphasised the diversity of circumstances in rural Europe, the need for integration of policy, and the need for a shift from sectoral to territorial approaches. This thinking was embodied in subsequent Community initiatives, particularly Objective 5b of the Structural Funds and the LEADER programmes.

New Regulations agreed in 1988 doubled the resources available under the Structural Funds and brought together the three formerly separate Funds (the European Regional Development Fund, the European Social Fund, and the European Agricultural Guarantee and Guidance Fund) in order to target resources more effectively. Five overall objectives were drawn up, along with a set of principles to govern the administration of the Funds. The main effect for rural areas was to channel extra monies to support development programmes extending over several years in 'less developed' regions with per capita GDP below 75% of the EC average (often embracing wide stretches of countryside, especially along the Mediterranean and Atlantic peripheries) and to designated 'rural areas', with high (but declining) levels of agricultural employment, low average incomes, and the need for alternative work. The Less Favoured Areas support was drawn into the new Objective 5a, combining together the horizontal measures for the improvement of agricultural structures. The LEADER Programme was also established to create new development structures in rural areas incorporating local community organisations, private interests and public agencies.

Major reform of the CAP was agreed in 1992 essentially as a response to world market pressures. The reform involved a shift of support from market-based means to direct payments to farmers, partly decoupled from production levels. Efforts to modulate the payments so that large farmers would benefit less and small farmers would benefit more did not succeed.

In 1994 a significant expansion of the Structural Funds took place out of a commitment to increase the proportion of the Community's budget devoted to regional development at the expense of that devoted to the CAP. Both the budget and the geographical coverage of Objective 1 and 5b programmes were significantly expanded. Also a new Objective (6) was added to provide support for the northern regions of Sweden and Finland.

The support was to be similar to Objective 1 for which these regions were ineligible (on the GDP criterion) and was justified instead on the sparsity of their populations (the criterion of designation being less than 8 inhabitants per square kilometre). The Structural Funds now account for a third of the total Community budget.

The promotion of participation in development projects and programmes was a feature of these initiatives.

In *The Future of Rural Society*, the Commission reasoned that:

> External intervention has little prospect of success without the support of local communities. Moreover, the involvement of local and regional authorities and other social, local and regional economic interest groups in the identification of problems and the quest for solutions limits the number of errors of diagnosis that are all too common when planning is carried out from the outside.

The Commission envisaged the creation in rural regions of "a network of rural development agencies (or agents) to play a stimulating, mobilising and co-ordinating role". The next two sections examine how these aims have been achieved in the Objective 5b and LEADER Programmes.

Participation in the Regional Funds for Rural Development

It is Objective 5b of the Structural Funds that has proved most significant in developing a new style of rural policy for Europe. Objective 5b programmes have been administered through two 'programming periods'. The first ran from 1989 to 1993 and the second is currently running from 1994 to 1999. Areas eligible for designation for Objective 5b funds are those that exhibit low population densities, high rates of emigration, job losses, overdependence on and vulnerability to decline in the agricultural sector and the disappearance of enterprises and services. The regions covered by the first programming period had a combined population of 16.6 million inhabitants; the overall financial allocation was ECU 2,978 million at current prices. For the second programming period, the scale of Objective 5b was expanded to total ECU 6,667 million and to include 73 different programmes that together contain over 28 million people.

Objective 5b policy was designed to be flexible and regionalised so as to accommodate the wide-ranging socio-economic characteristics of Europe's rural regions. The policy is intended not only to allow affected rural regions to adapt better to changes resulting from the reforms of the

Common Agricultural Policy, but also to strengthen social and economic cohesion across the Union as a whole.

Participation is encouraged in two respects. Firstly, the Structural Fund rules require that each Objective 5b area be administered as a partnership. Partnerships draw together the European Commission, Member State governments and sub-national actors. This requirement in part reflects a shift towards a more bottom up approach to formulating and implementing rural development programmes. A Programme Monitoring Committee has to be established for each area comprising representatives of the partnership bodies, to collectively agree the administration of the funds at the local level. Local partnership arrangements have also been stimulated through the requirement that Objective 5b funds are matched with funds from other sources, public, private or non-profit. These various partnership requirements, in the main, encourage the participation of local organisations, key interest groups and economic and professional elites.

The first round of Objective 5b programmes was evaluated for the Commission by consultants in 1994. The Commission felt that "despite the modesty of the resources allocated, Objective 5b can at this stage be considered to have been an acknowledged success and to have given a fresh impetus to development in vulnerable rural areas". It went on to claim that in many Member States, Objective 5b had "heralded the launch of a genuine and multisectoral rural development policy, bringing together all the partners concerned in capitalising on the potential of the rural areas".

Objective 5b has been an innovative policy that requires new administrative linkages and arrangements and new ways of making decisions. The novelty of the scheme, however, "created considerable initial difficulties for the different administrations involved and these, inevitably, led to delays in starting which France Luxembourg (1); Netherlands (5); United Kingdom (11) had a cumulative effect as the programme unfolded". Considerable efforts have been required at all levels of government, from the Commission, through Member State governments and to the local level in co-ordination, consultation and the development of collaborative working arrangements. The distinct administrative traditions within the Member States were challenged by the new Structural Fund arrangements. The detailed requirements for planning, monitoring and co-financing of projects all contributed to significant delays which limited the effectiveness of the funds.

The consultants found that partnership was considered to be "a strong and positive feature" in most of the programmes. Some serious problems were encountered in specific cases where the principle of partnership was found to have "only shallow roots and failed to involve all the levels of the administration". Several local authorities in France and Spain had complained of inadequate or non-existent consultation. Overall, however, the detailed evaluation confirmed the extent to which "local participation at a grass-roots level improves the quality of the programme and facilitates effective implementation, including the participation of private funds". The role of local animateurs was highlighted as a significant contributor to the success of participation and of the programmes more widely. The consultants concluded that

> a very important factor affecting success is the generation of local interest by project promoters. Local animateurs and committed project officers can serve as a link between the initiation of ideas and their implementation and can greatly improve the rhythm of development of the programme and its quality. This is a novel approach that demands more time and resources. However, ultimately they result in far more effectiveness

Participation in Leader

The *Leader* (Liaisons Entre Actions de Développement de l'Economie Rurale) programme was introduced as an Initiative of the European Commission in 1991. Arising out of the reform of the Structural Funds to target more directly *territories*, rather than *sectors*, in need of assistance, LEADER represented a venture by the EU into rural participatory development at the local level. The scale of the new territorial programmes was at the sub-regional level (smaller than the NUTS 3 level and less than 100,000 population) and confined to Objective 1 and 5b areas (subsequently extended to include Objective 6). In 1996, a five-year successor (LEADER II) programme was introduced, with the number of participating initiatives rising from 217 to, at the last count, over 800.

The essential elements of the LEADER programme are:

- to explore innovative approaches to rural development (and that could be transferable to other areas);
- through essentially low cost projects;
- organised around a locally-controlled organisation;

- to animate the participation of local people and organisations in development projects in the social, economic, cultural and environmental fields;
- funded by a block grant from the EU but requiring matching funding from local/regional/national public and private bodies.

Each initiative begins with a Local Action Group (an existing structure or newly-formed for the purpose) writing a development plan for the area based on local consultation. The LAG has to be structured around "leading figures in the local economy and society" but can be located in the public or private sector, or any mixture of the two. The plan, which must reflect the role of cultural and environmental resources in local rural development, has to demonstrate a compatibility with existing Structural Fund programmes for the region and conform to project categories set by the Commission. For LEADER I, these were: vocational training; rural tourism; local agricultural and fishery products; SMEs; and 'technical support'. For LEADER II, categories were reformulated as: acquiring skills; innovation programmes (as for the list for LEADER I categories, plus environmental conservation); transnational co-operation; and participation in pan-EU information exchange networks.

The LEADER approach is wedded to the principle of local participation although the meaning of this is a function of the structure and ethos of each local group and of the implementation style adopted for each plan. Participation, then, varies with context.

From the experience of the 'pilot' first phase, LEADER has demonstrated a capacity to allow local groups to operate at locally-determined points along an 'ethos continuum'. At one end of this continuum are the groups that put the major emphasis on strategic development projects *by the group itself.* Conceptually, this is the ethos of 'enabling the territory' as an entity. All LEADER initiatives must construct a territorial identity for themselves but the extent to which they go on to cultivate a 'corporate identity' under which local products and services (food products, tourism, etc.) can be joint-marketed is a function of each group. In this mode, an initiative attempts to enable the territory as an entity and so enable the component enterprises, associations, communities and individuals to participate more fully in social and economic activity. Most commonly, this manifests in the territorial promotion of tourism but can also be applied to agricultural and craft products. In some cases, a strong territorial identity has been necessary in order to broaden and deepen the participation by, and commitment of, local people and organisations to the LEADER initiative. In certain other cases (e.g. LEADER in Brittany, France), the territorial identity has been a crucial tool where the LEADER group has assumed for itself a lobbying role in relation to regional and national policy as it affects the local area.

At the other end of the ethos continuum is the animation of grassroots ideas and projects. Within this, the LEADER programme has demonstrated yet further flexibility. The ethos of some groups has dictated an emphasis on the village community as the unit of participation and, therefore, the use of village appraisals/village action plans co-ordinated by community or communal associations. Other techniques used by LEADER groups include the employment of residents as local animateurs, and the employment of field officers with either territorial or sectoral remits.

Evaluations of LEADER indicate that there is a high degree of participation at the grass roots level but, again, the means vary according to context. An approach used by one initiative was to advertise the LEADER programme as extensively as possible and then to respond to whatever project ideas arose. Although this adheres most closely to the 'bottom-up' principle, it can raise questions of equity in that access to LEADER funds can become a function of who gets to hear about them first and of the differential ability to respond with the appropriate sorts of project ideas. The village appraisal approach used by many LEADER groups addresses this issue but only at the expense of confining action to those projects enjoying majority support.

The need to target directly locally disadvantaged groups has in some cases been identified as a priority in the LEADER plan or has been addressed by the LEADER group acting in strategic mode, for example, in tackling official bodies to explore the possibility of re-designing policy delivery to meet the specific characteristics and needs of the LEADER territory (as, for example, in the case of services for the unemployed, government training provision, 'minority' language groups).

There is also variety in the mechanisms available for local participation in decisions about LEADER design and implementation. Some groups are located primarily within a local authority structure and so can appeal to a model of representative democracy. Other groups allow people from the community to become members of the decision-making structure. Many groups formalise local participation through a committee/working group format (made up of individuals, local businesses, the local voluntary sector, representatives of quangos, etc.), conforming more to a model of participative democracy. There are cases, too, where formal democratic procedures within the LEADER organisation itself are absent, relying either on utilitarianism (ends rather than means focus) or a demonstration of accountability through an openness in their *modus operandi*.

One explanation for the variation in the structures of participation comes from the national political ethos. Thus, Scottish (UK) initiatives were strongly influenced by the pervading contractualisation and privatisation culture of the 1990s that had brought local (private sector) development companies acting as agents under contract to the regional rural development quango. In Brittany (France), on the other hand, LEADER initiatives were firmly controlled by local authority structures within the French local-regional-state political and planning system. There was also an element of opportunism involved with those bodies more fully briefed about EU opportunities being better able to respond with an application that had a good chance of succeeding.

Thus, LEADER has enabled both local and national contexts to influence the meaning of participation. There are those who suggest, however, that the variety and indeterminacy of LEADER are too 'anarchic' and would benefit from an element of standardisation in definitions and ideas of 'best practice'. The contrary view to this is that participatory rural development is more about dynamic learning in context, whereby each locality cultivates its own perspective and methods.

Further Reform

Overall, of the EU policies relating to rural development, the CAP is notable for its lack of emphasis upon participation. Despite successive reforms, the CAP continues to be oriented to agricultural support, primarily through commodity price support or area payments to farmers. Policies to stimulate more integrated forms of rural development have been developed since the late 1980s which have sought to increase the participation of local and sub-national actors in the formulation of development programmes. The mid-1990s have seen new developments in European rural policy as the EU moves towards the millennium and seeks to accommodate new Member

States from the east. For example, in November 1996, the 'Cork Declaration' was issued following a large conference involving over 300 delegates from across the Union with expertise in rural development convened by the Agriculture Commissioner, Franz Fischler. The Declaration laid out a set of principles to inform future rural policy including the desire to encourage participation in the formulation and delivery of rural policy. Subsequently, in July 1997, the Commission published its proposals for reform of the CAP and the Structural Funds in the run up to enlargement. The proposals for CAP reform represent a continuation of the reforms of 1992, with the gradual expansion of a bottom-up approach to integrated rural development. For the Structural Funds, it is recommended that the six existing objectives be concentrated into three new objectives, with none *specifically* devoted to rural areas but with the new Objective 2 applying to those urban and rural regions confronted with major economic and social restructuring needs. Successive reforms take place as each programmatic phase of the Structural Funds nears its end. These time constraints tend to serve as an important limitation on the scope for EU programmes to foster truly participatory forms of rural development.

References

Amin, A. (1993) The regional development potential of inward investment in the less favoured regions of the European Community. *Paper presented at the Conference on Cohesion and Conflict in the Single Market, Newcastle upon Tyne.*

Blakely, E.J. (1989) *Planning Local Economic Development.* Newbury Park CA, Sage.

Cloke, P.T. (ed) (1988) *Policies and Plans for Rural People: An International Perspective.* London, Unwin Hyman.

Goldsmith, M. (1993) :The Europeanisation of local government", *Urban Studies* 30, 4/5: 683-699.

Moseley, M. and Cherrett, T. (no date) *Involving People in Local Development*, (LEADER Dossiers series, Brussels: European Commission.

Reid, D. (1996) *Participation in Local Decision-Making; Examples of Local Action.* Scottish Natural Heritage.

6

Decentralization and People's Participation in Rural Development

International donor agencies acknowledged decentralization as a platform to improve citizen participation and service delivery. Decentralization is a source for bottom up participatory development, thus improving local governance resulting poverty reduction in rural areas. The whole purpose of development is being redefned so as to bring people to the central stage. Participatory Rural Development (PRD) also called by someone as community driven development or community participatory development is an approach for more accountable governmental and increase poor people participation. Decentralization is widely used concept now a days and policy makers applied this concept for the promotion of the development. It has increasingly been promoted as major component of the poverty alleviating strategies.

Most of the developing nations are still struggling for efcient use of their resources. In order to overcome physical and administrative constraints of the development, it is necessary to transfer the power from the central government to local authorities. Distribution of power from improves the management of resources and community participation which is considered key to sustainable development. Donor organizations, nations and international development institutions sig-nifcantly shifed their attention from urban-industrial development and focus on rural participatory development. According to Kliksberg, decentralization and agriculture growth are alternate and appropriate tools to achieve such development.

> The states must to look human development as its ultimate goal, that's always leads towards strengthen the democracy and increase social welfare. Working in teams with private enterprise and other non governmental organizations leads towards organizations and development of civil society.

The growing progress in decentralization in state management, an acceptable and generalized process at the international and international level, has many implications in term of participation as well as management efciency. Tis shif was considered as background to the evolution from centralized (development from above) to decentralize and now a day's developing societies considered as most appropriate development strategy.

THE CONCEPT OF DECENTRALIZATION

Developing societies advocate decentralization as source of development and empowerment since their independence. Decentralization has three main phases of popularity. According to Conyers, In late 1950's and early 1960's, the interest in decentralization was interlinked with the transition to independence and then afliated desire for creating democratic structures when colonial rules was imposed for control. Colonial system was an uneven approach to decentralize services where services were distributed on the basis on caste system. Tis result was that basic services are not available to marginalized groups.

In 1970's, the concept of decentralization was advocated as an easy way to take relieve from unresponsive centralized planning. The countries emphasized to decentralize their hierarchical structure in efort to make service delivery to public more efcient and giving local administrator's more responsibility to extend service delivery and ultimately a means to increase popular participation in development. Similarly in 1970's, due to economic and fscal crisis, rising prices of oil, decreasing level of exports forced societies to use their own resources efectively and the only way they found were decentralization, thus many countries in Africa, Asia and South America pursued decentralization.

The concept of decentralization varies from program to program. It depends upon goals and objectives of the program. Developing countries in Pacifc and Asia have so for interpreted and implemented decentralization as being the source to delegate and transfer power for planning, implementation, evaluation and participation in decision making. Similarly transfer of administrative authority from the central government and it connected departments to feld organizations, local government or non-governmental organization.

Liberal and democrats in west and developing countries have diferent opinions for decentralization. According to the liberal democratic tradition in west, decentralization government is perceived as the institutional vehicle for political stability, training in leadership, political education, equality, responsiveness and liberty. While developing countries perceives this term in broader context. It has positive connotations as well as emotional overtones', particularly when it is used for achieving important goals and objectives of concern programs such as people participation, local democracy, transfer of decision power to people, need based relevant development, co-ordination, integration and de-bureaucratic setup.

Grifn, a fundamental politician and economist, advocate decentralization but stress that

> It is agreeable that in many countries power to local government is more rigorous, exclusive and applied more mercifully against the poor than at the central government. Tus it cannot be said that more decentralization leads towards greater democracy, nly power to poor cannot solve most of the problems but its all depend on the situation, measures and requirement for which devolution had taken place. Sometimes decentralization is considered just to improve the fnancial condition of the country and sometime to improve governmental institution structures.

Experiences of decentralization from developing countries demonstrate that decentralization bring about minority dominance by a few powerful rich local leaders and the case become worst if such leaders were chosen to lead the respective councils. Sometimes these elite lead on the basis of their heredity or some other favors. Such types of problems in decentralization have long lasting impacts and cannot be dismissed lightly.

Modalities of Decentralization

According to the Brain Smith, who is considered one of the fullest account of decentralization to date, the term "Decentralization", got diferent meanings in diferent era's and felds and academics are not agree on proper use of this term. Tus decentralization can be referred as the transfer of authority to the linked lower hierarchy, whether the lowers tier related to local government or to some big organization. In contrast, Morgan, a management scientist emphasis the decentralization as an organizational principle for divisionalised organization, but normative values for decentralization are diferent. Tere is functional, deconcentration/devolution dichotomy, political elite power administrative decisions and tetorrial decentralization. According to Guzman, decentralization refers to the systemic sharing and dispersal of state government power. It's about delegation of authority to local level institutions, involving all the stockholders to come together as close as possible to problem area thus allow multi-sector decision making.

Administrative Decentralization or Deconcentration

Deconcentration refers to the simple dilution of centrality by distributing various elements of political and administrative activity to non-central ofces. With deconcentration (also known as 'administrative decentralization), strong centralizing tendencies coexist with particular forms of bureaucratic decentralization. It is a means of increasing central control. Many writers, for example Heager, are critical of the deconcentration approach to decentralization. He considers, deconcentration as a method for the central government to increase its power by more efectively curbing liberties".

Manor is also critical of deconcentration when he says indeed, it is ofen used as a device used by the government for better control over lower level. But sometimes a greater degree of deconcentration is achieved through feld administration by transferring them power to plan, decide and implement with in the boundaries set by central ministries. The power of feld administrators, as Smith stresses, is 'bureaucratic rather than political.

Functional Decentralization or Delegation

Functional decentralization is also deconcentration to parasitical agencies with some fnancial and administrative separation from the main bureaucratic hierarchies. Delegation implies the lending of central authority, responsibility, and resources for exercising administrative and substantive functions to subordinate units or organizations in the centre. Although these organizations and agencies have been decentralized, they really serve to reinforce centralization and decision-making at the higher levels. The relative autonomy of these agencies, and their bureaucratic way of assuming certain functions and responsibilities, have given rise to serious problems of coordination and control. Delegation of function represents a more extensive decentralization than administrative deconcentration.

Political/ Democratic Decentralization or Devolution

Transfer of resources, activities and power to decide for local development and division of tasks from the central government to lower authorities is called devolution. In devolution the lower authorities work as an autonomous body, independent from central government. Devolution implies more permanent and inter-governmental transfers, from national to local governments, of political as well as administrative and technical functions, answerable to the local community as a whole. The local government may challenge the central government's mandate, as asserted by Mrs. Tatcher, when she states that: "the hard lef power was entrenched in three institutions: the Labor Party, local government and the trade unions.

The transfer of power to geographic units of local government that lie outside the formal command structure of the central government'. Tus devolution represents the concept of separateness, diversity of structures within the political system as a whole.

Privatization

It connotes the transfer of responsibility and resources for certain governmental functions to the private sector. Trough privatization, governments divest themselves of responsibilities either by transferring them to voluntary organizations or by allowing them to be performed by private business. It is a recent fash-ionable policy prescription and political philosophy for national development. It is claimed to have many virtues. It could relieve government of its fscal burdens, rationalize its role in development and improve the administration of programmes appropriate to the public sector. Its advocates argue that decentralization mean passing power from central government to private frms and democratization by increasing choice for 'customers' who receive services.

The defnition of decentralization as transferring authorities and power to the lower authorities from central authorities including planning, decision making and administrative control, opens up questions about the market provision (deregulation, privatization) of services since the market can be regarded as a centrally regulated, but with decentralized allocation mechanism.

The public choice approach and the emergence of the 'New Development Administration school stresses deregulation, privatization, minimal government and popular participation. It is this approach that opened up a debate between Slater and Rondinelli in the journal of 'Development and Change'. Rondinelli produced a political economy model, which combined public choice and public policy approaches and added privatization as the form of decentralization, which marked a shif from his earlier work of ranking deconcentration and devolution as the prime decentralization methods. Tis directly contradicts another of his statements: especially the poor must be allowed to participate and decide about their own needs and demands' and 'have rights to work for local as well as national development'. Terefore, privatization can be found in this context, implicit in the concept of de-bureaucratization.

Nature of Participatory Rural Development

Form past few decades developing countries making great eforts to improve the lives of the deprived communities. Awareness towards education and maternal health improve signifcantly. Now there is low infant death rate and life expectancy improved by more than ffy percent. Almost in more than half population, children started their schooling. Similarly, there is signifcant improvement in provision of clean drinking water to rural areas. Average per capita income of the developing countries rose to almost double.

Over the past few decades new approaches to development have been adopted. The human element has lately acquired a new signifcance. Getting over their earlier obsession with economic growth, planners now readily appreciate that it is the involvement of people in the development process that ensures sustainable development. While programs difer substantially in design, objectives and target communities, a common organizing principal is clearly discernible.

It is the belief and principle of participatory development, according to Keith R. Emrich that development must begin in the very lowest tier or level. Tere must be real opportunities for participative decision making for the target groups and those decisions must relate to their future development.

According to the advocates of Participatory Rural Development (PRD), Aim of the Participatory development is to accomplishing following three functions including:

1. Communities should indentify and implement projects for themselves for need based development.
2. Improve the capacity of the local peoples to organize themselves as community.
3. Enable community organization to work together for common purpose.

Peoples' Participation

Ultimate and practical way of democracy is to consolidate with the local people and encourage them to participate in development activities. Motivating them to participate, organize them in groups and communities and involve them in decision making is only way which refects basic desire of people. In developing world, participation of communities in development process is considered as a basic element for good governance resulting accountability of government and beneft to poor peoples.

Participation has been defned in narrow and broad terms. In its narrow connotations, participation is defned as the active engagement of citizens with public institutions, an activity which falls into three well-defned modes: voting, election campaigning and contacting or pressuring either individually or through group activity, including non-violent protests. Excluded in this defnition are attitudes towards participation and participation in rural development eforts. In its broad terms, participation is a "collective sustained activity for the purpose of achieving some common objectives, especially a more equitable distribution of the benefts of development".

Political participation has been an issue in development management from the beginning, but its signif-cance has increased principally because it has become part of ofcial rhetoric. Individual full participation in making societal choices and decisions is a natural outcome of the endowment of individual dignity because it contributes to individual self- development. Responsibility for the governing of one's own conduct develops one's dignity. In particular full individual participation within the local institutions contributes to the creation of community solidarity because everyone feels involved in what is going on relative to their welfare. Although there are diferent ways to defne participation, the dominant perspective is to treat it pragmatically and to view it as a strategy to improve the development process.

Participation was considered and defned in terms of politics during late 1960's. It was only considered as people participation in vote casting, become a member of party and volunteer in some association. But with modernization in world, involvement of public is considered important for development. In the mean time, autonomous public organizations provided the channels for active community participation. Political parties are forced to consider public as asset and their demand should be given privilege.

"During implementation, individuals and groups have diferent motives and interests that might be conficting and they compete to secure limited available resources. Limited resources and scarce funds leads towards poor development and sufer government-people interaction". Similarly according to Lele "self confdence and self-reliance gained by rural community during planning and implementation of the projects is very important to keep development process efectively". An infuential statement by learning group of World Bank regarding participation is as under "Participation is an activity in which development process is shared, infuenced and controlled by stakeholders and two factors which afect them are decision and resources".

Dimensions of Participation

Participation is a very broad concept, and when the term is used in the context of development activities the question is how to operationalise that participation? The clear answer to this question demands familiarity with i) what (activities), ii) who (elites /ordinary people), and iii. How (the way /method of peoples' involvement) dimensions of participation. The 'what' dimension of participation consists of the various activities where people may participate? It implies the involvement of people in goal setting, planning, formulating, implementing and evaluating of development projects. According to Cohen and Uphof (1980), people's participation includes a participation in decision-making and participation in Program implementation and evaluation.

The second dimension is a focus on who participates in a truly participatory approach those entire afected have to play a role at all stages of the development process. Cohen and Uphof identifed two groups of participants, residents and leaders, as particularly important in participation in development. The World Bank approach to the 'who' dimension of partici-pation calls for the participation of 'stakeholders'. The Bank defnes stakeholders as the parties who either affect or are afected by development actions, which either have no power or lack information thus excluded from developmental process.

The third dimension of participation is its organizational imperatives. The commentators and practitioners in development pleaded for participation through local organizations. The democratic, accountable and responsive organizations and associations including village councils, progressive unions, farmer's societies, traders associations and multi-purpose co-operatives, may be efective in participatory development.

The focus of 'how' dimension of participation is also on the degree or level of participation—the degree of empowerment. Latter indicates participation of the highest intensity. Each level of participation is characterized by a diferent relationship between the implementing agency and the benefciaries. Information sharing participation refers to a process where the agency informs intended benefciaries about the project, and so fows of information and control are both in downward direction. In a process involving consultation information fows are more equal, with the agency ofen making use of local knowledge; however control is still from the top down. In decision-making participation benefciaries have some control over the process. Finally where participation has advanced to the stage of the benefciaries initiating action both information and control fows are primarily upward, from the benefciary group to the agency, but the donor agency retains some degree of control. According to World Bank, following are the measures which should be taken to improve the participation. Tese measures involve six mechanisms whose infuence on stakeholders is from bottom to up. Teses includes following

1. Methods for information sharing among community and government
2. For better understanding consultation mechanism should be preferred
3. Appraisal Mechanism
4. Participatory decision making methods
5. Collective action for better development
6. Community empowering methods.

Arnstein long ago considered peoples' participation as a categorical term for people power. According to her, it denotes nothing less than a redistribution of power that enables have-nots to share in the benefts of society.

Participatory Approaches to Rural Development

Tere are many obstacles to expand the citizen participation in rural areas.

Tere are many approaches for participatory development but all have to face the same challenges. The concept of participation in the process of community development is far from new. Indeed, it was part of the rhetoric of the New Deal in the 1930s. It has become the dominating ideology in contemporary thinking in both non-governmental organization (NGO) and governmental / inter-governmental agencies.

There are two main traditional approaches to rural participation:

(1) community development programmes which were aimed at preparing the rural population to collaborate with government development plans; and

(2) the establishment of formal organizations (cooperatives, farmers associations etc) which were to provide the structure through which the rural people could have some contact with, and voice in, development programmes.

Community Development Approach to Rural Participation

The approach was based on development of capacity and self-reliance among community to participate for better development. Tere are good reasons for the close association of participation with a community development approach. First the aim to meet basic needs obviously requires the participation of all in benefts. Second, participation in implementation improves efciency through the mobilization of local resources. 'Tird, the development of a community's capacity to plan and implement change will require greater intensity and scope of participation as the project proceeds. But Oakley and Marsden concede that the strategies developed had no meaningful impact on poor people and local community participation in development and the local elites continued to make and implement decisions in their own interests under the cover of a participatory organizational structure.

Partnership Approach to Rural Participation

A second general approach to participation can be distinguished from fostering people's organizations or promoting community-based activities. Tis approach attempts to create participatory partnerships rural development authority and governmental authorities for local development. Oakley and Mars-don have labeled this a collaboration approach to rural participation where governmental or non-governmental organizations remain the primary driving force. Because decentralization programmes are an attempt to transfer specifcally defned aspects of authority and control to District Councils or other local representative bodies. But many constraints, particularly ones of fnancial accountability and aid administration, make this a difcult task. In any case, as observers have noted, representative bodies remain just that:

"Participation becomes the prerogative of a privileged few who now fnd themselves included in a widening but nevertheless still quite small circle of decision-makers"

Obstacles to People's Participation

All the developmental agencies in the world now discuss about the participative rural development approaches, including non-governmental organizations, governmental and inter-governmental agencies. The apathetic situation occurs mainly due to the poor economic, political and social position of people. But some times the latter they do not always want to participate. A recent Overseas Development Administration funded study observes that people feel that development functions were primarily the government's responsibility. Rather they prefer to participate passively and / or through their community leaders.

Organization at village or even at district level is cither short or membership of poor people in such organizations is nonexistent. Hence local organizations easily become centers of formal power controlled by the few elites. 'The professional bureaucrats both at national and local level pose important barri-ers to efective local participation. Lack of community participation in projects can be the result of bureaucrats assuming the role of knowledgeable specialists who do not take user's views into account because users do not 'know enough' (according to them) to make decisions. However, some time the local people give their rights of decision to developmental professional thereby save confcts, time and energy. Moreover the desire of participation is likely depend on the 'product' ofered as much as on the development of channels and structures to make participation a practical possibility.

References

Adnan, S. et al. (1992) *People's Participation, NGO and the Flood Action Plan*, Dhaka Research and Advisory Services.

Arnstein, S. R. (1969) *Ladder of Citizen Participation Journal of the American Institute of Town Planning*, Vol. 35. pp. 216-224

Bergdall, D. Terry (1993) *Methods for Active Participation: Experiences in Rural Development from East and Central Africa* Nairobi: Oxford University Press

Cheema, G. S. and Rondinelli, D. A. (eds.) (1983) *Decentralization and Development: Policy Implementation in Developing Countries.* London: Sage

Conyers, Diana (1986) *Future Directions in Development Studies: The Case of Decentralization World Development*, Vol. 15, pp. 593-603

Guzman, R. P. (1988) 'Decentralization as a Strategy for Redemocratization in the Philippine Political System' *Philippine Journal of Public Administration* Vol. XXXII, No. 3&4, pp. 217-225.

Hoshino, C. (1994) *Land Development; Processes and Decentralization in Latin American Large Cities and Metropolitan Areas: Issue, Trends, and Prospects* Regional Development Dialogue, Vol. 15, No.2, pp. 29-60

8

Participation of Rural Women in Development

Rural women's participation in the development process has been the focus of intensive debates by most international forums in the past years. Among forums that have recognized the plight of Third World's women's participation in the development process are the 1995 Nairobi Forward Looking Strategies for the Advancement of Women held in Kenya, the 1995, The Beijing Declaration, and the United Nations Development Fund for Women. According to the philosophy of these forums, each member state should promote women's economic independence, which includes the creation of employment, access to resources and credit, the eradication of the persistent and increasing burden of poverty, malnutrition, poor health and illiteracy on women. Although such declarations have been able to increase an awareness and understanding of the problems facing women and their needs, as such they have not yet resulted in significant development priorities for rural women.

Rural women play a key role in supporting their households and communities in achieving food and nutrition security, generating income, and improving rural livelihoods and overall well-being. They contribute to agriculture and rural enterprises and fuel local and global economies. As such, they are active players in achieving the MDGs. Yet, every day, around the world, rural women and girls face persistent structural constraints that prevent them from fully enjoying their human rights and hamper their efforts to improve their lives as well as those of others around them. In this sense, they are also an important target group for the MDGs.

Rural Women's Poor Access to Infrastructure

Rural women spend more time than urban women and men in reproductive and household work, including time spent obtaining water and fuel, caring for children and the sick, and processing food. This is because of poor rural infrastructure and services as well as culturally assigned roles that severely limit women's participation in employment opportunities.

Faced with a lack of services and infrastructure, rural women carry a great part of the burden of providing water and fuel for their households. In rural areas of Guinea, for example, women spend more than twice as much time fetching wood and water per week than men, while in Malawi they spend over eight times more than men on the same tasks. Girls in rural Malawi also spend over three times more time than boys fetching wood and water . Collectively, women from Sub-Saharan Africa spend about 40 billion hours a year collecting water .

For these reasons and because rural women tend to underreport their employment as contributing family members, according to available data female employment in agriculture is consistently lower than it is for men across the total adult population in developing countries, although it varies greatly by region . The jobs of rural women who are employed tend to be shorter term, more precarious and less protected than those of rural men and urban people. The lack of flexible hours to accommodate family work combined with wage and job discrimination and limited representation of women in workers' organizations are partly responsible for this.

Despite women's lower overall employment rates, among employed women the proportion working in agriculture as opposed to other sectors is usually equal to or higher than the male equivalent. Almost 70 percent of employed women in South Asia and more than 60 percent of employed women in Sub-Saharan Africa work in agriculture . The substantial involvement of rural women in agriculture, primarily as unpaid or contributing family workers, highlights the importance of developing policies and programmes that address the needs, interests and constraints of women as well as men in the agriculture sector. This includes revamping and strengthening extension systems to be more responsive to and inclusive of women, addressing structural barriers to women's access to productive resources, and improving financial systems to respond to the needs of rural women producers and entrepreneurs, including to move out of the less productive segments of the rural economy .

Improving Rural Women's Access to Productive Resources

On average, women make up about 43 percent of the agricultural labour force in developing countries. Evidence indicates that if these women had the same access to productive resources as men, they could increase yields on their farms by 20 to 30 percent, raising total agricultural output in developing countries by 2.5 to 4 percent, in turn reducing the number of hungry people in the world by 12 to 17 percent . For rural women and men, land is perhaps the most important household asset to support production and provide for food, nutrition and income security. Yet an international comparison of agricultural census data shows that due to a range of legal and cultural constraints in land inheritance, ownership and use, less than 20 percent of landholders are women . Women represent fewer than 5 percent of all agricultural land holders in North Africa and West Asia, while across Sub-Saharan Africa, women average 15 percent of agricultural land holders .

Extensive evidence shows that rural female-headed households also have more limited access than male-headed households to a whole range of critical productive assets and services required for rural livelihoods, including fertilizer, livestock, mechanical equipment, improved seed varieties, extension services and agricultural education . Similarly, in seven out of nine countries across Africa, Asia and Latin America, female-headed households were less likely to use credit than male-headed households .

Rural Women's Economic Empowerment

A large body of research indicates that putting more income in the hands of women translates into improved child nutrition, health and education , yet data on child nutrition disaggregated by both rural/urban location and sex are sparse. In all developing regions of the world, rural children are more likely to be underweight than their urban counterparts. From 1990 to 2008, the proportion of children under five in developing regions who were underweight declined from 31 per cent to 26 per cent, yet in parts of Latin America and the Caribbean, and Asia, the disparity between rural and urban children increased . Figure 3 indicates that in South and Central America, rural children are about 1.8 times more likely to be underweight than their urban counterparts; other regions do not fare much better. Improvements in maternal nutrition, access to water and sanitation and health services, all of which are lacking in many rural areas in least developed countries (LDCs), would also contribute greatly to addressing this situation.

Inequality are Barriers to Universal Education

An extra year of primary school increases girls' eventual wages by 10-20 percent, encourages girls to marry later and have fewer children, and makes them less likely to experience violence , yet in many areas of the world, educating girls is perceived to be less important than educating boys. Furthermore, while significant progress has been made in reducing the gender gap in primary school enrolment, a large gap remains between rural and urban areas. Household data from 42 countries show that rural girls are more likely to be out of school than rural boys, and they are twice as likely to be out of school as urban girls .

In rural areas, there is often a greater prevalence of social and cultural barriers, labour requirements and distance "penalties," that keep girls out of school. In Pakistan, a half-kilometre increase in the distance to school decreases girls' enrolment by 20 percent . Decreasing the distance to school raises girls' enrolment and attendance; building local schools in rural communities increased girls' enrolment in Egypt, Indonesia and several African countries. The cost of education is another barrier, particularly for rural poor families.

Women make up over two-thirds of the world's 796 million people who are illiterate, and many of them live in rural areas . In some countries, far fewer rural women can read and write than rural men. For example, in Cambodia 48 percent of rural women are illiterate compared to 14 percent of rural men, while in Burkina Faso 78 percent of rural women and 63 percent of rural men cannot read and write . Yet literacy and education can be powerful tools for empowering rural women and fighting poverty and hunger. In fact, women who are educated are more likely to be healthy, generate higher incomes, and have greater decision-making power within their households .

Secondary school attendance has implications for future employment and economic opportunities as well as health outcomes. Evidence indicates that rural girls are less likely to attend secondary school than rural boys, and they are far less likely to attend than urban girls. According to Figure 5, 39 percent of rural girls attend secondary school compared to 45 percent of rural boys, 59 percent of urban girls, and 60 percent of urban boys.

Recent data from a number of countries from Africa, Asia and Latin America indicate that women are far less likely to participate in rural wage employment (both agricultural and non-agricultural) than men . Instead, they are most active in the informal rural economy, which operates outside of labour standards. When they do work for wages, rural women are more likely to be employed in part-time, seasonal, and/or low-paying work . Men's average wages are higher than women's in both rural and urban areas, and in some countries, the gap in wages between rural women and men is also wider in rural areas . Rural women are also more likely to be unpaid contributing family members than rural men .

Furthermore, rural women typically work longer hours than men, when one takes into account both paid productive and unpaid reproductive or domestic and care responsibilities. In Benin and Tanzania, for example, women work, respectively, 17.4 and 14 hours more than men per week, while rural Indian women work almost 11 hours more than urban women and 12 hours more than urban men .

In most regions, women are under-represented in politics and decision making Progress has been made in women's political representation since 1995, including in Africa and much of Asia, where there have been cases of notable increases in the presence of women parliamentarians. Strikingly, Rwanda made great gains, with women now making up 56 percent of the parliament, compared to 17 percent in 1995 . Globally, however, a gender gap in women's access to power, inclusion in decision making, and leadership remains at all levels, including in rural councils. Information available from Asia for 2010 indicates that women there represented between 0.2 percent (Bangladesh) and 7 percent (Cambodia) of chairs or heads of rural councils, while they represented between 1.6 percent (Sri Lanka) and 31 percent (Pakistan) of elected representatives in rural councils .

A key to ensuring rural women's empowerment and eradicating poverty is to address inequitable gender power relations and persistent norms and beliefs that maintain gender-based violence (GBV) and harmful traditional practices (e.g. female genital mutilation (FGM), early marriage, wife inheritance). According to a multi-country study conducted by WHO, rural women report more experiences of physical abuse than urban women . However, the data from the study show no clear pattern as to whether more rural or urban women are accessing services to assist them in dealing with the abuse. In general, women may doubt that services will offer the help they require. They may also fear for their children's or their own safety if they report abuse. Police, counseling and legal services may be more difficult for women to access in rural than urban areas due, for instance, to a lack of transport and distance to services.

Child Mortality in Rural Areas

Between 1990 and 2009, all the regions of the world saw a significant decrease in under-five mortality rates, with some developing regions reaching or approaching 2015 targets . Existing data, however, make it impossible to determine how child mortality varies between rural boys and girls. Although levels of child mortality vary widely between countries, rural rates are usually much higher than urban ones . Sub-Saharan Africa has the highest rates of rural and overall under-five mortality, but rural areas are often equally disadvantaged in countries with much lower rates of under-five mortality – for example, in Honduras, rural children under five are almost twice as likely to die as urban children. Of the developing regions, Latin America and the Caribbean and Eastern Asia have comparatively low levels of under-five mortality, but they also have the highest levels of inequality between rural and urban populations . Overall, rural children under 5 in developing regions are about 1.4 times more likely to die than their urban counterparts.

Women's Education is a Key Determinant in their Children's Survival

Available information from 68 countries with data on under-five mortality by mothers' education indicates that a woman's education is a key factor in determining whether her children will survive past the first five years of life. A child's chances of surviving increase even further when his or her mother has a secondary or higher education. Children of mothers with no education in the Latin America and Caribbean region are 3.1 times more likely to die than those with mothers who have secondary or tertiary education and 1.6 times more likely to die than those whose mothers have primary education . These facts suggest that rural women's deficits in education have broader and longer-term implications for family well-being and poverty reduction.

Women's Access to Health Services

Quality reproductive health services and well-timed interventions are fundamental for achieving good maternal health, yet hundreds of thousands of women die each year because of a lack of such services. In most developing regions, rural women have less access to skilled health personnel in delivery, even though the long-standing differences between rural and urban areas have declined in all regions and even been eliminated in a few.

Between 1990 and 2008, the proportion of rural women receiving antenatal care at least once during pregnancy grew from 55 to 66 percent, while corresponding rates for urban women increased from 84 to 89 percent over the same period. While this would indicate that antenatal coverage has improved at a faster pace in rural areas, a large gap still exists .

Available information from the mid-1990s to the mid- to late 2000s indicates that some predominantly rural countries (where at least 60 percent of the population lives in rural areas) have made substantial progress in antenatal care coverage (at least 4 visits) in rural areas . In Asia, Bangladesh made significant gains in antenatal care coverage, but still remained under 20 percent coverage in 2007, while India and Nepal also improved, but remained under 30 percent coverage in 2005 and 2006, respectively. In Sub-Saharan Africa, Namibia increased coverage by almost 20 percent between 1992 and 2006, but most other countries made little or no progress, and many actually saw coverage decrease.

Globally, women constituted half of the adults (15 years and older) living with HIV in 2010 . Young women are particularly vulnerable to HIV, and they account for 64 percent of HIV infections among young people worldwide . Yet only 33 percent of young men and 20 percent of young women in developing regions have comprehensive and correct knowledge of HIV . Youth in rural areas, and especially young women, are even less likely to know about prevention methods or to use condoms than their urban counterparts . WHO data from 25 countries indicate that rural women are almost always less likely than urban women to report knowing about means of sexual transmission of HIV, in some cases by margins as large as 20-50 percent. Interestingly, in several countries with high levels of HIV infection (Malawi, Namibia, Rwanda, Tanzania, Uganda, Zambia and Zimbabwe), the rural-urban gap is low, possibly reflecting the success of public interventions and awareness-raising campaigns in those countries.

The number of people accessing antiretroviral therapy in low- and middle-income countries reached an estimated 6.6 million (47 percent of those eligible for treatment) at the end of 2010. Antiretroviral therapy coverage generally appears to be higher among women than men. Across all low- and middle-income countries, an estimated 53 percent of women eligible for treatment were receiving it at the end of 2010, compared with 40 percent of men. Coverage was higher for women than men in East, South and South-East Asia, and in Sub-Saharan Africa. But in Latin America and the Caribbean, the reverse was true .

While research on utilization patterns is still in its early stages in terms of understanding differences in uptake by rural versus urban location, significant evidence from generalized epidemics indicates that rural populations have less access to treatment services than urban populations, although the situation is improving in some countries as services expand (e.g. Senegal, Uganda) .

Most of the care for people living with HIV is provided in the home, and women and girls account for 66 to 90 percent of all AIDS care givers (in addition to the many tasks they already perform). Conditions are most difficult for women and girls in rural areas. The disproportionate share of AIDS-related care giving by women and girls imposes a heavy toll on their own well-being, often leading to their increased vulnerability to HIV infection. HIV-associated stigma and discrimination, increases in the poverty of female- and child-headed households and a higher probability of dropping out of school at an early age could all add to the burden faced by female caregivers .

Women form the backbone of agricultural labour, especially in Sub-Saharan Africa – which is the epicenter of the HIV epidemic. The impact of HIV/AIDS on women, either in their own capacity or as care givers, reduces their time and energy and is associated with declines in agricultural productivity and, therefore, food insecurity . In the rural areas, households with one or more persons affected by HIV and AIDS are more likely to be food-insecure than non-affected households . HIV also exacerbates property insecurity and the disinheritance of women, especially widows whose husbands have died from AIDS-related causes .

Rural Women and Natural Resources

Environmental degradation has a great impact on natural resources, which rural women rely on for their livelihoods. For example, evidence suggests that women with fewer occupational options and less mobility rely on forests more than men do. Reduced quality and availability of land, game, forests, and genetic and aquatic resources increase rural women's time burden, reduce their capacities to cope with shocks and climate change, affect where they live and provoke conflict, which in turn undermine rural health, education and livelihoods. Furthermore, there is some evidence of causal linkages between gender inequality and environmental degradation. For example, gender inequality and deforestation were causally related in more than 100 countries between 1990 and 2010 .

Research suggests that women express more concern for the environment, support policies that are more beneficial to the environment and tend to vote for leaders who care about the environment. Evidence from 25 developed and 65 developing countries indicates that countries with higher female parliamentary representation are more likely to set aside protected land areas. A study of 130 countries shows that women are also more likely to ratify international environmental treaties .

While women's involvement has been associated with better local environmental management, their mere presence in institutions is not enough to overcome deep-rooted disparities. Institutional change and flexibility are needed to ensure that women can participate effectively in decision making. A recently published study of community forestry institutions in India and Nepal found that women's proportional strength in forest management committees has an impact on the effectiveness of their participation. The more women on the management committee, the greater the likelihood that they will attend committee meetings, speak up and become office holders .

In urban areas, levels of access to improved water and sanitation are generally high and above the MDG target. In contrast, poor rural populations still face great challenges accessing clean drinking water. Coverage in rural areas across all regions lags behind urban areas . In 2008, an estimated 141 million people living in urban areas and 743 million people living in rural areas relied on unimproved sources for drinking water. An urban dweller in Sub-Saharan Africa is 1.8 times more likely to use an improved drinking water source than a person living in a rural area .

Women's Partnership in Development

A recent study of 23 members of the OECD Development Assistance Committee indicates that in 2007-08, bilateral donors committed USD 4.6 billion to gender equality and women's empowerment in the economic and productive sectors (including agriculture) . This represents one-fifth of their total aid in these sectors . Forty-two percent of the aid for gender equality in the productive sectors was earmarked for agriculture and rural development .

While there is increasing donor recognition of rural women's important contributions to eradicating poverty and hunger and to overall well-being in rural households and communities, there remains a lack of data on the actual impact of aid on rural women's empowerment and gender equality. Progress towards such objectives is often translated into monitoring and evaluation indicators that assess 'progress' by numbers of rural women participating in particular interventions rather than the quality of those interventions and the broader impacts on rural women. There is an urgent need to invest in rural women and to develop more comprehensive and nuanced metrics and related measurement systems to assess the different impacts of agriculture and rural development policies and programmes, together with contributing aid allocations, on rural women and men.

To a great extent, the MDGs monitor general progress, providing the global community and individual countries with useful information for policy and planning purposes.

Although the MDG guidelines suggest that all indicators be disaggregated by sex and rural-urban location, this is only occasionally done owing to the nature of the indicators themselves, low capacity and poor data systems, or lack of interest. Some of the indicators – for example those under MDG 2 (Achieve universal primary education) and MDG 3 (Promote gender equality and women's empowerment) – are disaggregated by sex. MDG 5 (Improve maternal health) focuses specifically on women. Others – for example MDG 7 (Ensure environmental sustainability) – are difficult to disaggregate by sex. However, even when data are disaggregated by sex, they are rarely also disaggregated by urban and rural locations.

In addition, rural dynamics and women's roles sometimes require different types of indicators to characterize and monitor progress than those commonly used. For example, data to capture rural women's multiple job holding and seasonal work are particularly difficult to obtain with existing systems. Overall, with a few exceptions, the MDG indicators provide a rather limited base against which to measure progress for rural and urban women and men, and to identify and address specific disparities.

As we work toward meeting the MDGs and move toward developing new and better global targets, there are a number of areas that must be observed if we are to understand in greater depth the opportunities and constraints in rural women's lives, and to monitor progress towards rural women's empowerment and gender equality appropriately and effectively. Indicators and data collected must be disaggregated, at the very least, by sex and rural/urban location. These indicators could include, but are not limited to: MDG1: average annual dietary intake per capita; access to employment, including the informal sector and agricultural self-employment; access to productive assets and financial services (e.g. land, credit, extension services, agricultural technology); access to social security and safety nets; MDG2: ratio of orphans to non-orphans (10-14 years old) attending school; MDG3: prevalence of gender-based violence (GBV) and GBV knowledge/attitudes/perceptions; participation in institutions; MDG6: proportion of people living with HIV who receive anti-retroviral treatment compared to those who need treatment; access to other health services (e.g. malaria/tuberculosis treatment); and MDG8: the impact of aid to agriculture and rural development and of trade/debt on rural women's empowerment and gender equality.

Participation of Women in Rural Development: A Case Study

The impact of development on women in South Africa is quite different for both urban and rural women. In fact, there is substantial evidence that rural women are mostly neglected, and consistently have lost in this process. There is also overwhelming evidence of development policies and projects formulated bypassing the involvement of rural women in most African countries. The majority of the population in LDCs lives in rural areas, approximately 70% being women.

Development, according to Olopoenia and Pradip, is not an isolated activity, for it implies a progress from a lower state to a higher and preferred one. Development is a process by which people are awakened to opportunities within their reach. Development, therefore, starts with people and progresses through them. This is the reason, according to these authors, why rural women should be involved in on going development initiatives. They are the most marginalized group in terms of their needs, while being the people who produce almost 80% of the food consumed in most of Africa's rural areas.

These people have a certain consciousness about their position as rural women, although there are no strategies developed to affect change on them. Following the Lagos Plan of Action for Economic Development of Africa, it is advocated that the needs, rights and concerns of all women be fully integrated into individual country's development planning to benefit all sections of the population.

It is assumed that if these factors are not investigated and analyzed, they are likely to cause a continuous impediment on rural women's participation in on-going developments, as well as on the viability of development efforts in the country itself. This helps to increase our understanding and commitment toward upliftment and empowerment of rural women, by eliminating plans, policies and projects that constrain their increased participation in developments. The critical levels of poverty and unemployment currently experienced in South Africa mean that considerable pressure must be exerted on the economy to increase growth rates and to provide all people with access to economic opportunities.

(i) What could be the possible reasons for the low participation rate by women inrural areas in development?

(ii) Do rural women have capacities that are underestimated due to higher levels of illiteracy and/or traditional values and beliefs?

Review of Important Concepts

Given that rural women have an important role to play in development, it examines different contributions made by them to the improvement of their communities.

Background

To date, many scholars have written on the issue related to the participation of women in development in LDCs. The impression gained suggests that these on-going investigations seem to have not yet resulted in specific solutions to the problems facing rural women and development. Although each rural settlement in South Africa has its own particularities, there are still specific solutions or universally accepted development strategies to deal with development problems in these areas. Meer strongly expresses the opinion that unless more effort is put into organizing women in poor rural communities around their common interests, they are unlikely to benefit from favourable development policies. In the same way, Friedman stresses that unless development policies include guidelines for the process and practice of delivery, they are unlikely to challenge unequal power relations.

Women and Official Planning in LDCs

In the foreword to the alternative framework for structural adjustment programmes for socio-economic recovery and transformation, it is recognized that women play a crucial role as producers and agents of change in rural transformation, and that the negative effect on rural development is brought about by their marginalization. Ntomb'futhi Zondo advocates that very tradition regards women as inferior to men. The situation in rural areas is such that if you are female, you do not play any role in the societal debates. Even the 1994 African Common Position on Human and Social Development Forum describes women as part of the marginalized, vulnerable sections of the population and they are grouped with children, youth, elderly and the disabled. No matter which rural government option is chosen, it seems that women in rural areas will always remain where they are, and ultimately will end up in a worse position.

For this reason, to any change coming to their ways, they themselves need to stand up for it. A situation of past practices of relegating women to an inferior position in a society cannot be allowed to continue.To do otherwise will be a negation of commitment to social justice and equality. As part of development goals, there ought to be specific policies geared to the promotion of women's participation in local planning in most rural areas to contribute to overall welfare in society, so that whatever resource rationalization is undertaken, it is not executed to the detriment and disadvantage of rural women, because these women have attributes of which outsiders are unaware.

Women and Development Related Work

A study by Buvinic et al observed that women in most African rural areas women work an average of 12 to 18 hours per day compared to an average of 8 to 12 hours per day by men. Sneyder and Tadesse comment on rural women who worked almost 90% of roadwork under the "Food-for-work" programme in Lesotho. They expressed that the role of rural women is not only central to social, but also to economic progress in their respective countries. They also recommended work done by rural women in Gabon and Tanzania during the 200 days in a year, saying that men worked only

1,800 hours compared to 2,600 hours by women in agriculture, and that rural women worked harder than anyone else in these countries.

Women in South Africa's rural areas are the ones who run the families, while their husbands are working in the cities. Traditionally, women in rural areas have been regarded as people who belong at home, expected to minister to their husbands and children, but when it comes to making decisions on economic and political issues, men take the lead. In most African countries, rural women are the food farmers, and carry the burdens of life. Africa's 100 million rural women grow almost 80 % of Africa's food, including food for subsistence and food for markets. This amounts to food production of 3 metric tons each year per woman. Rural women do almost 80% of the work to provide the proper transport and storage of Africa's food. They do almost 90% of the work to process Africa's food, including the tasks such as threshing, drying, winnowing, peeling, grating, sieving, and pounding. They also do almost 60% of the work related to marketing Africa's food. Yet they face gender-specific barriers in accessing financial services, and can receive less than 1% of the total credit to small farmers and 10% of the total credit to agriculture.

Women and Economic Progress

While it does not directly address the role of women in agriculture, the African Charter for Popular Participation in Development held in Arusha in 1990, recognizes the critical contribution made by women to African societies and economies, and the extreme subordination, including discrimination, which they face. This forum posits that the attainment of equal rights by women in social, economic, and political spheres must become a central feature of a democratic and participatory pattern of development. The majority of women in rural South Africa believe that rural governments offer them no real hope for change or empowerment in terms of community power relations. Their experiences of these actions suggest that the more they are exposed, the more worried they become. This is mainly because whatever decision is reached, they are the ones who live with the implications.

Women make a major contribution to the economic production of their communities and assume primary responsibility for the health of their families. Their active support is crucial to the utilization of development objectives. There can be no societal transformation without their involvement, support, and leadership. Addressing the effects of gender discrimination and inequality is a necessary part of the socio-economic project of transformation. Despite the equality provisions in the South African constitution and land restitution process established since 1994, it has become highly unlikely that rural women will be in a position to make claims as individuals. Rural women are typically allocated small pieces of land, usually about 1000 to 5000 square metres, which are used to produce food crops such as vegetables, chickpeas and groundnuts for home consumption and, to a very limited extent, for sale. The family plot used to grow cash crops takes first priority, leaving the women only limited time to work on their plots, either very early in the morning or in the afternoon when they are not cooking, tending to the children, gathering firewood or otherwise engaged by their husbands. The restructuring of the South African agricultural economy requires affirmative measures to give effect to the principal of equality of opportunities. Women in Africa have a long tradition of participating in savings, production, marketing and mutual-aid organizations. Many rural women rely on cooperatives and market groups as a way to pool resources, reduce their workload, and optimize limited income. Micro-credit programme results have shown that women tend to be more prompt and reliable in their repayment of loans, and spend their increased earnings on children first, thereby improving nutrition, health and educational opportunities.

There has been insufficient political will and sustained commitment to meeting economic needs and interests of most rural women by the local authorities and governments. While many African countries have ratified the UN agreements on this issue, there seems to be no subsequent informed policy decisions. Most governments' macroeconomic policies do not incorporate gender perspectives in their design in order to

enforcing its application and implementation. As well, they often ignore the structure of households in Africa and the social relations that influence women's roles in production. To this effect, the United Nations Development Fund for Women acts as a catalyst within the UN system, to support efforts that link the needs and concerns of women to all critical issues on the national, regional and global agenda. It works to ensure the participation of women at all levels of development planning and practice. It plays a strong advocacy role, and concentrates on fostering a multilateral policy dialogue on women's empowerment.

Women and Education in Africa

The most fundamental reason for the existence of an educational system is that education plays a significant role in the economy of any society. In view of this, it is essential that the education provided meets the economic needs of that society, thus enhancing efficiency in the use of social and economic resources, ultimately leading to improved economic growth and social well-being. Ideally, education should contribute to economic development, equalize opportunities between social classes, reduce disparities in the distribution of income and prepare the labour force for a modern economy. International Organizations such as the United Nations, UNESCO, the World Bank and the Third World Countries are becoming increasingly aware of the importance of women in national development, and the fact that education can contribute to their playing a much more meaningful role in development.

There are many reasons as to why the education of women is important. Research has shown that there is a strong association between education and better life, nutrition, improved hygiene, low mortality and fertility rates, and economic development. Education for women in Sub-Saharan Africa has been noted to have a powerful developmental effect in light of their cardinal role of nurturing, upbringing, socialization and education of children. Women are well known for being active economically, as both producers and consumers of goods. Their capacity to serve actively in these areas can be enhanced if they are provided with adequate levels of education. A lack of education on the part of women deprives them of their productivity levels in the rural areas, because they will remain ignorant of ways and means of producing more on the farm. Cultural values, as well as economic realities of limited family resources and employment opportunities for women, which in the past have inhibited girls' entry into primary and secondary education, may now be prominent factors inhibiting Nigerian women from entering university.

Reasons for Investigating Rural Women

There are good reasons to focus on, and to emphasize rural women's participation in development. The most fundamental reason is that they play crucial roles in both subsistence and market food production in Africa. Not only because they are working harder than the average man, but also because they are reliable and committed to their tasks. Not only are women the majority in rural areas in Africa, but they are responsible for more than 50% of all productive activities, even in those households where men are present. In many rural areas of

LDCs, deforestation, loss of soil fertility, low productivity and poor living standards have been characterized as the features of these areas. All these have detrimental effects to the well-being of rural women. Therefore, overlooking the plight of rural women will have negative impacts on the development of rural areas and that of the nation. To this end, there is a need to reverse this negative approach to development by retrieving and revising the potential for participation by rural women. Equally important, those who are not in crisis are often the beneficiaries of development efforts, while those entrapped in poverty remain exactly where they are with no hope of release.

Population Survey and Sites

The sources of data for the purposes of the study were rural women drawn from three different rural settlements namely: Thintwa (in Natal Province), Tsheseng and Makhalaneng. These settlements were selected because of different particularities that allow for comparison. The purpose of such comparison was to determine if the same factors that contribute to the inactive participation of rural women in development were almost the same in these settlements. The study of these settlements included their respective land patterns and other relevant characteristics.

(i) Thintwa rural settlement is situated between Bergville and Harrismith towns. Following its landscape, it is dry, valley and hilly village. Its soil is poor and lacks agricultural potential. It has a minimal potential for livestock farming, as crop farming is almost non-existent. This village is scarcely populated without electricity and roads. Access to the accurate population statistic was not possible, as they were neither Councillors nor traditional Chiefs representing the people during the time of survey. Based on the researchers' observations, it appears that Thintwa has, on average, more old women than young.

(ii) Tsheseng rural settlement is in the former homeland of Qwaqwa, in the Free State Province. It has a low potential for crop production, but adequate for livestock farming. However, the potential for livestock farming is not well explored by many, and crop farming does not exist. This settlement is densely populated, and its soil is red, stony and hilly, symbolizing a rough landscape. This Village has also more old women, on average than young.

(iii) Makhalaneng settlement is another rural village in the former homeland of Qwaqwa. This village is also densely populated. Rocks and hills characterize its landscape, and it is dry. The land available is of low potential for agricultural crops farming, but suitable for livestock farming. The study selected these two settlements in Qwaqwa to investigate their similar, or different characteristics, even though the two are both located within the same district.

Population Sample and Data Collection

The final study sample comprised 152 respondents (rural women) compared to 240 respondents, as initially envisaged. The study interviewed 34% of respondents in Thintwa, 33% in Tsheseng and 33% in Makhalaneng respectively. The data was gathered using a non-probability sampling procedure. This method was used because of the lack of women's groups represented in these villages. Data collection basically involved traveling to the areas studied first, to familiarize with respondents for easy interactions as well as personal contact with them. Secondly, group discussions were organized by the researchers to facilitate an understanding of the whole study process. An easy designed questionnaire was used to collect data, and the filling in by respondents was carried out with the help of an interpreter, because most of the respondents could not read and write.

Interview Levels

Interviews for this study were conducted at three different levels. Firstly, among the different age groups of respondents (old, middle-aged and young women). This classification was necessary since at the different age groups, priorities and levels of participation in development process are also different, according to the needs, aspirations and expectations of individuals. The interviews dealt mostly with important issues of women's involvement in development initiatives, activities they are involved in, and why they believe they are left out of this process. The second level of the interviews was carried out with traditional healers, community leaders and chiefs. These interviews were centered on the issues affecting rural women's participation in development. They were attempting to discover various reasons for the disadvantaged position of rural women, and their contributions as the custodians of rural values. These were closed-ended interviews based on pre-made appointments with the respondents. The third level of interviews was carried out with the students and lecturers at the University of the North, Qwaqwa Campus, and Graduate School for Development Studies and Conflict Resolution. These interviews were aimed at seeking academic advice, knowledge, skills and their contributions in involving rural women around the University community into the on-going development processes and programmes on campus.

Results and Discussion

The study sampled 72 households representing a total of 152 female respondents. In terms of their age structure, they were classified into four groups, namely: under 40 years; middle-aged group; under 65 years and over 65 years. The highest percentage of 30.3% is attributed to the economically active group of women, comprising the 36 to 50 years age class. In terms of development strategies, great efforts should be made by planners to include this group of women in any development initiatives, because they are the majority. Women head of households represent the majority of South Africa's rural households. Women significantly outnumber men in most rural areas of South Africa, because they always remain behind, while men are away in search for jobs in urban areas. The number of poor rural women has increased dramatically in the past decades, notwithstanding the increasing female responsibility for agricultural production and income generating activities in the rural areas.

Its results suggest that all the three villages are characterized by single, married, divorced and widowed women, as well as those separated from their husbands because of the jobs. Following this table, 11.8% of women are single; 13.2% are married women; 23.0% are divorced; 18.4% are widowed and 33.6% are separated from husbands in search for jobs, and as a result they became the household heads. A study by Mazuri shows that in South Africa the migration of men to mines became more problematic when the government enforced regulations against families joining their husbands at the places of work. In return, this has exacerbated the high rate of women separated from their husbands.

Twelve and a half percent represents the number of children not stated either because of having none or death. The number of children less than four represents 25.7%. The number of children less than seven children represents 29.6%, while the respondents with more than nine children represent 32.2%. Tsheseng and Makhalaneng have 14% and 16% of more than nine children respectively compared to Thintwa with only 9.6%. The high birth rate is not only an attribute of the dense rural areas in South Africa, but also because rural urban villages share this problem in common.

Educational levels of respondents include both formal and informal education. Data on educational level of respondents suggest characteristics that discourage their active participation in development process, because most of them (respondents) are not educated. The number of respondents not educated represent 47.4%, with 23.0% of those having primary education, 9.2% of those with secondary education, 2.6% of those with college education and 17.8% of those with other types of informal education with skills such as sewing, candle making and to some extent small-scale business. It was also observed that among those respondents with primary and secondary education, many did not even complete the levels required. As a consequence, this has led to a higher illiteracy rate among inhabitants of the study area. This implies that they had no opportunities to attend formal education.

Educational level is an important tool, and is needed to stimulate, create, achieve and enhance active participation of rural women in development. The rate of women's participation in development initiatives is strongly influenced by their educational levels. The higher a woman is educated, the greater the likelihood she would be included in the labour force, and the lower the likelihood she would be unemployed. A lack of education is enhanced by inequalities and disparities in the labour markets, including absolute poverty in the rural areas.

All respondents were asked to provide the researchers with the kind of jobs, occupations, employment, or economic activities involved in as income generating ventures. This implies that only a few respondents were employed in formal or private sector with 9.2% having salaries, 13.8% engaged in trade, 11.8% involved in farming and 8.0% in other activities. Most respondents revealed that they are solely dependent on income from their husbands, and therefore they cannot survive independently.

Literacy is a mechanism that can transform and boost women's participation in development, because it can stimulate and enhance individual initiative. Innovation is, by and large, a major way to increase skills to participate in development initiatives, to eliminate dependency syndrome. A lack of initiative as a result of illiteracy has blurred rural women's mind-sets of believing in themselves that they would be the "initiators of their own developments".

Respondents were also asked to identify problem areas hindering their active participation in the development process of their respective communities. Many problem areas were identified and mentioned, from which six were the most outstanding, namely: a lack of information; lack of resources; lack of government assistance; lack of education and skills; consideration and belief in cultural values, and the influence of discrimination practices. This score describes that there are high expectations by the people in rural areas for the government to be doing things for them instead of shaping up their own destiny. Lack of education scored 20.4%, lack of resources with 16.4%, influence of discrimination with 13.8%, lack of information with 13.2% and belief in cultural value with 5.3%. Although in the presence of all these problems, Popkin found that rural women often contribute to family earnings in various ways. They assist family farms, produce handcrafts, brew beer for sale, or can work somewhere else in the farm to support themselves.

Willingness by respondents to participate in projects was identified by asking them the following question: "If new approaches to taking part in development initiatives are made available, would you be willing to participate?" This question was asked to all the respondents to assess their attitudes and readiness to participate in development. As a result of the above question, the "Yes" answers accounted for 77.6%, while the "No" answers accounted for 13.2%, with only 9.2% being "do not know". The "No" answers were mostly from women of 65 years and above, who claimed that they are no longer economically active to be involved in any development activities, while the percentage of "do not know" answers include the physically/mentally handicapped and other sick women. These women have the necessary know-how to initiate, plan, implement, participate and further the development process to high levels and so contribute meaningfully to its expansion. The local governments should address this issue by removing any barriers imposed on the development of rural women, presently preventing them from taking active part in these socio-economic development initiatives.

Lesson Learned

Rural women continue to remain obscure and invisible in the process of economic development, although they comprise the majority of the population in rural areas of South Africa. Virtually none are selected to participate in development initiatives at the individual level especially where they entail significant power and responsibility. Participation of rural women in economic activities at all levels is crucial for the development of South Africa and for economic advancement of women. The economic framework needs to be hypersensitive to the gender implications for rural women and to any economic policy in the future. Such policies need to be adjusted in terms of the impact on rural women's employment, economic advancement and empowerment. Investigating rural women's is crucial, because they are the backbone of rural economy, not withstanding being discriminated against.

Rural women's work is never done, farm work is part and parcel of their day's activities on top of household burdens of taking care of the children. Rural women in most African households carry out subsistence and near-subsistence agriculture, being over 80% of agricultural labour force. They are also responsible for many other tasks such as: planting, weeding, watering, harvesting, and storing of crops.

According to the case study that a lack of information, lack of resources and government assistance, lack of education, cultural values and discrimination against rural women were the most important factors contributing to the inactive participation of rural women in developments. Further inferences can be drawn in relation to the age structure of respondents, that it has impacted negatively on rural women participation, mostly for those in the category of 65 years and above.

References

Allen, T. & Thomas, A. (1992). *Poverty and development in the 1990s*. Oxford University Press, New York.

Hunger Project. (2000). *The African women food farmer initiative: Exclusion from development policy and programming equation,* New York.

Lightelm, A. A.& Wilsenach, A. (1993). "Development, poverty and the environment with particular reference to the Eastern Transvaal region". *Development Southern Africa*, 10 (1): 45-64.

Mwamwenda, T. S. (1994). "Women and education in Africa". *South African Journal of Sociology*, 25(4): 143-147.

United Nations Development Fund for Women (UNIFEM). (2000). *Women and economic empowerment*, New York.

9

Guidelines on Beneficiary Participation in Agricultural and Rural Development

The FAO Guidelines on Beneficiary Participation in Agricultural and Rural Development provide guidance for policy makers and practitioners how to incorporate group-based, participatory based approaches into large-scale investment projects. They include advice on a range of topics, including: strategies to promote participation, project formulation, group formation, financial arrangements, training, monitoring and evaluation, etc. They were based on experience gained in the design and implementation of FAO People's Participation Programme projects during the 1980s.

The Guidelines are meant as a tool for project planners and implementers, in particular for the experts involved in the identification and formulation of rural development projects.The latter can be large multi-component or smaller projects of any type: for example, those dealing with agricultural production, livestock, forestry, fishery, irrigation, land reform, inputs, extension, credit, marketing, research, training as well as those dealing with health, sanitation, nutrition, education and other social fields. This means firstly that the projects are to the largest possible extent oriented towards the rural poor, and secondly that they include provisions for the formation of self run beneficiary groups. As explained later, these two essential features do not substitute for but are expected to complement conventional development approaches and efforts.

In more concrete terms: the comprehensive Guidelines hereunder hopefully enable planners of any rural development project to select from the text those issues and elements which are necessary to incorporate in the overall project design specific objectives and workable components or mechanisms for active and lasting beneficiary participation.

This is not a luxury: the lack of feasible mechanisms to attain effective beneficiary participation is still a major deficiency in project designs among several other ones such as too tight schedule, under-estimated costs, production shortfalls, bad management and staff, poor engineering, procurement difficulties, wrong organization and structure, insufficient technical assistance, too many or unbalanced components, over-dimensioning, non-sustainability, inequitable benefit distribution, slow adaptation, insufficient government commitment, and recurrent budget shortage.

The Guidelines are based on a number of interesting consultations with experts in relevant FAO divisions and units who have experience with participatory projects and programmes. They are also based on scrutiny of relevant documents and reports on twelve FAO People's Participation Programme (PPP) and Small Farmer Development Programme (SFDP) projects as well as reports on other FAO participatory projects funded by UNDP, by FAO Government Cooperation Programme (GCP) extra-budgetary sources and/or under the FAO Technical Cooperation Programme (TCP).

In fact, these Guidelines evolved from a wealth of efforts and experiences gained in the field by UN (in particular FAO), government and voluntary (NGO) organizations. Since the mid-seventies and particularly the World Conference on Agrarian Reform and Rural Development (WCARRD), it was widely recognized that development efforts cannot be successful without the active participation of the people, particularly small and landless farmers, fishermen and other rural poor. Several of the above agencies launched therefore special programmes mostly on pilot basis. In order to test and develop participatory development approaches

In this perspective FAO promoted:

- the programme "People's Participation in Agricultural and Rural Development through the Promotion of Self-Help Organizations" (PPP);

- Community Action for Disadvantaged Rural Women (CADRW);
- Forestry for Local Community Development Programmes (FLCDP); and since 1987 "The Forests, Trees and People Programme (FTPP)";
- Programme for Small-Scale and Artisanal Fishermen;
- Support Programme for Farm Water Management;
- Freedom from Hunger Campaign/Action for Development (FFHC/AD: started already in 1959);

All of the above-indicated programmes promote group formation and action strategies designed to demonstrate to the disadvantaged people as well as to UN agencies and member governments the necessity and efficacy of adopting bottom-up or participatory rural development approaches as a complement to existing ones in order to reach the poor and guide them towards self-development efforts. And indeed the main outcome of these pilot programmes is that efforts of beneficiary participation in a project are most successful when the intended beneficiaries are systematically helped to organize themselves into small, self-run groups formed from scratch or within larger organizations. Through such groups they can better meet their economic and social needs, the project and/or delivery system can provide services and facilities more easily and on a wider scale, and the poor can engage much more in poverty alleviating efforts.

Popular participation and thus also beneficiary participation has become a fashionable, frequently used (and misused!) concept which is also often ambiguous, vague and abstract. It is presently applied in many projects in limited forms and manners. However, while considering also minor forms of participation as potentially valuable, it is tried in this guide to indicate how to design full beneficiary participation in larger projects which aim at reaching and involving mainly or exclusively the rural poor. This full participation can only be obtained by means of specific arrangements and/or mechanisms for grassroots institution-building in the form of group formation and action being the essence of participatory rural development.

The latter approach aims at improving conventional, area-based, all farmer or all rural people-oriented projects which lack specific participatory arrangements and consequently yield—as is well-known—mostly benefits to the better-off beneficiaries who have more assets, education and better access to the delivery system. Thus, participatory rural development does not replace other UN, government or NGO development policies, programmes and projects and should not be considered an alternative or exclusive development approach. It is instead a complementary approach which is indispensable for effective poverty alleviation.

It should here however be stressed that participatory rural development should not only be regarded as a set of techniques but also as a mental outlook or state of mind favouring a development approach which starts from the people concerned and treat them as subjects and not as objects of development.

The term participation is debatable because inadequate from the long term perspective. In the initial stages of development and for the time being, the poor must be encouraged just to participate in the economic system of the non-poor and thus raise their standard of living from abject poverty up to at least a reasonable survival level. However, later on the disadvantaged people should engage in self-development efforts and thus gradually also help to contribute to a more equitable socio-economic system of the non-poor which in its present form intrinsically and evidently leads to the exclusion of most have-nots from integral human development.

Another, often overlooked point is that a participatory development approach and project presupposes certain underlying basic values or value orientations such as sharing, cooperation, participation, coordination, mutual trust, delegation and concern, care for the disadvantaged people. For example, to be a valuable, active member of a small production group, of a supporting line agency or of a coordination committee, requires extra commitment and contributions of time, ideas, energy and other resources. A basic question is after all who and what could motivate the poor and also the supporting non-poor people to make these "sacrifices".

The right motivations needed can apparently only come from certain attitudes moulded by a religious and/or ideological belief system, or borne out of considering well one's own interest and/or out of fear for negative reactions of the grassroot people. The latter may increasingly exert pressure on officials and the better-off to provide (more) means of production, services and facilities, in other words to divide the cake of relative welfare more justly.

As several successful UN, government and NGO programmes show, have by now technically valid and well proven solutions to promote beneficiary participation but the main constraint to apply these solutions is indeed the political will in a country or project area to do so. Accordingly, the main problem is how to motivate in practice politicians, officials and elites to support or at least tolerate effect ive forms of participat ion of the rural disprivileged people in development.

In fact in order to plan and implement participation in projects, a number of strategies are required at various levels to sensitize and convince politicians and policy makers, the staff of UN, government, NGO and donor agencies, the field staff of development projects and the rural e lites.

As known, rural women have heavy, multiple and vital roles as wives, mothers, food producers and food providers. Particularly the poor women are nevertheless usually doubly discriminated, marginalized and exploited viz. as rural poor within their elite and male-dominated society and also as women in their own household.

They are in general also relatively disadvantaged in comparison with men in the development process. The main reasons are that they have more limited access to education, credit facilities and public life. Development efforts often target men—though not overtly but latently—as the recipients of projects. However, in general it would be inadequate and ineffective to treat women as a separate target group. Women cannot be separated from the family, just as children cannot. In most projects the disadvantaged nuclear or extended family should be taken as a target group.

This approach implies, however, that each participatory project must firstly focus specifically on the identification of the conditions, needs, resources and capabilities of the various categories of disadvantaged women and secondly on the provision of training, extension and other facilities for viable individual and/or group activities of women. The latter should regard not only the conventional but still indispensable topics such as health, nutrition, childcare, home economics as well as workload reduction and small-scale income generation, but also as soon as possible full participation in local development planning, decision-making and efforts. In this way the women will raise their economic and social status and thus their standard and quality of living, not in the least by developing their qualities of leadership and equal participation in local self-development.

Women's problems in the context of rural poverty are thus to be analysed and tackled carefully according to the different conditions of poor rural women in different regions, cultures and ecologies.

Project planners and experts have now-a-days at their disposal guidelines on various technical topics, some of which are prepared by FAO Divisions. They have however, notoriously time constraints to study and use these materials. It is therefore tried to formulate the present Guidelines as concise and operational as possible, although some basic issues are reiterated for clarity. Thus many items condensed in one or a few phrases, could not be elaborated more and also the necessary conceptual parts were kept at the bare minimum.

The Guidelines are inevitably presented in rather general terms in view of the wide variety of economic and social situations and needs in developing countries and thus of the types of agricultural and rural development projects and programmes. In fact, in successive phases more elaborate and concrete additional Guidelines are highly desirable for major types of projects like agricultural production, credit, irrigation (land and water), forestry, fishery and so on..

Beneficiary Participation in Rural Development Projects

Around the mid-seventies there was a growing awareness that various approaches for rural development like community development, integrated rural development and basic needs did not result in substantial rural poverty alleviation. Even subsequent efforts made in some countries such as rural works, concessional credit, rural employment programmes did not improve the plight of the poor on a sustained basis. Economic growth was insufficiently combined with equity or just distribution of benefits.

International, government and non-governmental agencies realized more and more that the main reason of many unsuccessful development projects was (and still is) the lack of active, effective and lasting participation of the intended beneficiaries. Consequently, several agencies started to promote the participation of people, in particular disadvantaged women and men, in development through various programmes, mostly on a pilot basis.

In these Guidelines the vast literature and considerable experience which by now exist regarding popular participation and participatory rural development in general cannot, of course be reviewed: only some key notes mainly on beneficiary participation in projects are given hereunder

To start with, there is a wide range of definitions and interpretations of participation. For example, it means (1) sensitizing people to make them more responsive to development programmes and to encourage local initiatives and self-help; (2) involving people as much as possible actively in the decision-making process which regards their development; (3) organizing group action to give to hitherto excluded disadvantaged people control over resources, access to services and/or bargaining power; (4) promoting the involvement of people in the planning and implementation of development efforts as well as in the sharing of their benefits; and (5) in more general, descriptive terms; "the involvement of a significant number of persons in situations or actions which enhance their well-being, e.g. their income, security or self-esteem"

There is furthermore a wide range of approaches in development projects to bring participation into practice. Some major types of participation found in projects are the following:

Type I: Induced involvement: the strategy, design and workplan of a project are predetermined and the intended beneficiaries are encouraged to participate in its activities and obtain certain benefits. In various projects people are invited to make contributions of labour and/or other resources which is also seen as a form of cost-sharing.

Type II: Transitory mobilization for community development: the people participate in certain specific temporary tasks mainly for the development of their community, but there is no institutional base or structure (groups or organizations) for more sustained participation.

Type III: Group formation: the project has a specific objective to help create new or strengthen existing self-formed and self-run groups and organizations through which the rural poor gain access to resources, inputs and services and participate actively in the project, also by means of self-proposed actions. This latter type of full participation leads also to empowering of the poor: through their groups and organizations they obtain not only access to resources, but also decision-making and bargaining power as well as a base for sustained self-development efforts.

Self development and self-reliance should in fact be an outcome of participation. The latter term is actually debatable when it is taken in the narrow sense that the poor should just only obtain a share of the "cake" or participate in the socio-economic system of the non-poor as mostly implied or expressed in a top-down project. A better, wider meaning is that through participation the poor not only gradually practise self-development, but may also contribute to modify the existing system of the non-poor which left them out of development to varying extents.

In accordance with the statement of the World Conference on Agrarian Reform and Rural Development (WCARRD) on this key issue and on the basis of the foregoing considerations, by participation in an agricultural or rural development project or programme is meant in these Guidelines that the intended beneficiaries, in particular the rural disadvantaged people, contribute to the planning of a project or programme, participate actively in its implementation and evaluation and share fully in its benefits. There is by now overwhelming evidence that such participation cannot effectively take place on an individual basis but needs a structure consisting of existing and/or new, self-created and self-managed groups or organizations. This implies of course the right of free association and also the full participation of women on an equal basis with men.

At present there is a widespread consensus chat effective beneficiary participation is practically indispensable to render a project successful. However, relatively few projects have an explicit design to attain effective participation. In fact, the existing development projects dealing with rural people can broadly be divided in two categories:

Conventional projects: these include objectives and components for productive and other (supporting) activities such as training, extension, credit, irrigation and try to involve the intended beneficiaries in these activities in order to achieve the project objectives.

The projects of this category have pre-designed project frameworks (objectives, action plans, inputs, outputs and time schedules) mainly based upon top-down planning. Many of them are large-scale, capital-intensive and heavily staffed. The projects are meant for all people in a certain area who are mostly not consulted beforehand on their needs and desires. As the projects focus moreover more on macro-economic than on social aspects and the poorer people's necessities, they yield mainly benefits to the better-off locals.

Participatory projects: these deliberately promote participation which consequently is explicitly incorporated in their objectives, approach and methodology.

The distinction between these two types of projects results mainly from the fact that in practice participation is basically conceived either as a means or as an end and in some cases in both ways.

Conventional projects which by and large still prevail are predominantly production-oriented and participation, when considered in the project design, is regarded as a means to achieve certain productive objectives which are pre-determined by an outside agency.

In a number of less conventional projects there are graduations of a partial participatory approach: the rural poor may have been consulted on their needs, aspirations, potentials and willingness, and may also be involved somehow in project implementation. Basically, they are expected to participate, however, to varying extents in project benefits. These partial participatory approaches are certainly very useful and may help to avoid project failure; it may also lead to increased participation in the future.

In truly participatory projects, participation is seen also as an end and thus taken up clearly in the objectives which however mostly include also productive goals. In fact, these projects have two legs: participation and production and practice shows that in the long term they "run" or "walk" better.

Given the importance more and more placed on beneficiary participation, no wonder firstly that the number of participatory projects are increasing; they are supported by FAO, ILO, IFAD and other UN agencies, various progressive governments and furthermore to a great extent by NGOs. Secondly, that conventional projects, though easier to design and to manage, are regarded increasingly as out-dated and after all less feasible, cost-effective and prone to be successful.

Finally, it should be stressed that the positive aspects of both conventional and participatory projects should be more and more merged. For example, the economic (feasibility, marketing, etc.) and technical (research, technology transfer, etc.) requirements for the development of certain (sub-) sectors (e.g. irrigation, crop production, livestock, extension, credit) must be fully taken into account also in participatory projects. Top-planning (e.g. by a national body or a district development committee) and grassroot (bottom-up) planning (e.g. by groups or federations which come out with small-scale production plans) must be matched, for example by a workable coordination committee. Indeed feasible forms of vertical integration of development efforts are indispensable.

How is participation as an end in concrete expressed in the objectives of participatory projects? The common essential elements in the overall objectives are the following: to raise the family income and standards of living of low income rural people; to Identify and apply for this purpose a sub-village development approach for and with the intended beneficiaries by actively involving them in development through the promotion of economic and social need-fulfilling group activities.

The common essential elements in the specific objectives are:

1) to help identify, plan and implement employment – and income-generating and other group activities for small farmers, tenants, fishermen and/or labourers;
2) to assist the beneficiaries to organize themselves into self-run groups and organizations (or to use existing ones) in such ways that firstly they have (increased) access to programmes of training, credit, inputs, marketing and processing as well as education, health and sanitation and, secondly, they can more and more satisfy their economic and social needs and become eventually self-reliant;
3) to assist line departments and other agencies including banks and NGOs to increase their effectiveness to better serve the rural weak, to develop innovative farm and also off-farm income-raising activities, and to encourage self-development efforts;
4) to develop a strategy for expanding the successful features of the project in the country.

The important elements found in the practice of participatory development projects are the following:

1) Process instead of project approach: Conventional projects are usually planned too much in detail ("pre-cooked") over a too short time span to obtain tangible results and spread effects. A participatory project can substantially contribute to solve these problems by replacing or at least complementing the standard project approach by the process approach and to conceive a project as the first phase of a longer process enacted and sustained by a rolling programme. The project design must accordingly be more flexible and such that It can be expanded and replicated in similar areas with minimal outside assistance and recurrent costs.

2) The target group is predominantly or exclusively formed by the rural disadvantaged people. However, also non-poor or better-off rural people (local leaders, influentials, etc.) as well as government and NGO officials are to be actively involved in various project actions, in particular to improve the delivery of services and facilities to the target group and to learn from each other.

3) Education for participation which is given in addition to the classic (teacher-student) types of training provided in conventional projects to transfer technical know-how. A major objective of the educational process is awareness creation or conscientization: the poor will gradually become critically aware of their economic and social conditions, the causes of their deprivation and dependency syndrome as well as their potentials to change their plight through joint efforts by clustering into small action groups. Participatory education attempts to develop capabilities among the beneficiaries to strive for full participation as well as self-development particularly when the project is over. This education is non-directive, dialogical (two-way) and built upon indigenous knowledge.

4) The structuring of the target group by means of group formation and group action. This entails strengthening of existing groups or organizations and/or the promotion of new, self-created and self-managed ones. The existing groups may be traditional groupings, farmer associations, cooperatives, women's, youth and village groups and/or trade unions. The groups and organizations which may later on somehow federate, form the basis for sustained participation and can be regarded also as a "receiving system" through which the poorer people can mobilize their own resources and be "reached" effectively by any development agency.

5) Resource mobilization by group members which includes pooling of know-how, ideas, assets, savings and/or labour as well as obtaining services and facilities like training and credit. This is done in a gradual learning process.

6) Economic and social activities. Starting with small, low-risk, well-known income-raising and socio-cultural group activities of any feasible type, the groups will undertake gradually larger, more complex ones, also on an inter-group basis.

7) The inclusion of group promoters in or attached to the project staff with the following two main roles: a) to help develop the economic and other activities of project groups and facilitate their access to resources and services; b) to help develop adequate participatory education and training activities for, with and between beneficiaries in order to increase critical awareness and stimulate meaningful and increasingly independent group actions (self-reliance). The above roles could best be performed by specific change agents (group promoters or the like) who work exclusively and directly with the beneficiaries and their groups to enhance participation. In projects which unfortunately have no arrangements and/or funds to recruit group promoters, the roles of the latter could be performed in part by ad-hoc trained technical project staff.

Promotion of self-reliance and self-development. The relationships between supporting government, NGO and project staff and the intended beneficiaries is deliberately shaped in such ways that self-reliance and self-development are encouraged amongst the target group and dependence on project inputs is gradually reduced. Project staff members encourage the beneficiary groups to identify themselves problems and seek adequate solutions and actions. Self-reliant groups are the main indicator for a successful participatory project.

9) The development of coordination and cooperation mechanisms which enable the beneficiaries to participate actively in as many project actions as possible. The latter include identification of needs and potentials, setting of project objectives, planning and carrying out of activities as well as monitoring and evaluation. The project avoids thus by all means to become just only a delivery vehicle.

The above are all important elements in any project design to attain full participation; they are, however, not all indispensable for certain forms of "minor" or partial participation.

Why Participation and what are the Obstacles?

Group and Individual Development Approach

As explained earlier, participatory projects include one or more components or elements of group formation and action but not exclusively: many development activities will continue to emerge from individual initiatives and incentives, in the areas of such projects. Group formation/action is thus not the exclusive solution or panacea for achieving certain development objectives. Groups can be instruments to (better) meet certain but not all needs and/or to (better) perform certain functions. Group formation should of course never be compulsory or a sine-qua-non condition, but spontaneous and voluntary. Freely formed, well-performing groups are "contagious" and have a beneficial spread effect.

In sum, "individualistic" types of involvement in project formulation and implementation can work satisfactorily in various instances. However, it is by now well realized, that only through group approaches the large numbers of marginalized rural people can be "reached" effectively by government and other organizations. There is also overwhelming evidence that the predominantly "individualistic" approaches largely applied by conventional development agencies, bring benefits mostly to the better-off-people. For the types of projects supported by FAO, ILO, WHO and (pre-) investment agencies, group approaches are normally also more cost-effective.

A problem occasionally raised is how "individualistic" people and societies can be motivated for group-wise development efforts. It is erroneously observed that the propensity for group action amongst disadvantaged rural people is significant for social but not for economic development purposes, unless there is a strong and evident incentive (e.g. group credit, irrigation or marketing). However, firstly the economic and social actions of the rural poor are mostly still very much interwoven and less compartmentalized as in modern societies. Secondly, the participatory approach builds wherever possible, upon numerous traditional and other forms of cooperation and groupings found amongst the rural poor including those living in so-called "individualistic" societies. For example, individual profit making makes less sense in traditional societies where profits are to be shared by larger kinship groups. Finally, the activities of group members can take the form of group or individual production or a combination of these: individual operation but sharing of common facilities, joint input-purchasing and/or marketing.

Although the participatory approach has certainly not a narrow focus, it is specifically meant for the economic and social development of the rural poor and thus does not cover in a strict sense wider forms of people's participation such as community participation. The latter refer to the involvement of the entire population of a village or community in the planning and implementation of a project and is thus not target-group specific. Such "holistic" forms of people's participation are certainly required for area-based operations which affect all inhabitants like environmental protection, soil and water conservation, provision of physical, economic and social infrastructures (civil works) and irrigation, sanitation and health schemes. It is also clear that the groups formed under the participatory project approach can considerably facilitate and widen community participation.

Arguments for Beneficiary Participation

Various foregoing points highlight that the participatory approach gives advantages to the rural poor as well as to the agencies which implement or support a project. The main reasons are the following:

1) Coverage: to reach and involve on a wider scale the disadvantaged rural people through institution building, that is the creation of adequate "receiving" systems at grassroot level as well as of corresponding "delivery" systems;
2) Efficiency: to obtain a cost-efficient design and implementation of a project. The beneficiaries will contribute more in project planning and implementation by providing ideas, manpower, labour and/or other resources (cost-sharing). Consequently project resources are used more efficiently;
3) Effectiveness: the people involved obtain a say in the determination of objectives and actions, and assist in various operations like project administration, monitoring and evaluation. They obtain also more opportunities to contribute their indigenous knowledge of the local conditions to the project and thus facilitate the diagnosis of environmental, social and institutional constraints as well as the search for viable solutions;
4) Adoption of innovations; the beneficiaries can develop greater responsiveness to new methods of production, technologies as well as services offered;
5) Production: higher production levels can be achieved while ensuring more equitable distribution of benefits;
6) Successful results: more and better outputs and impact are obtained in a project and thus longer-term viability and more solid sustainability.

By stressing decentralization, democratic processes of decision-making and self-help, various key problems can be better solved, including recurrent costs, cost-sharing with beneficiaries as well as operation and maintenance; Self-reliance: this broad, ultimate objective embraces all the positive effects of genuine participation by rural people. Self-reliance demolishes their over-dependency attitudes, enhances awareness, confidence and self-initiative. It also increases people's control over resources and development efforts, enables them to plan and implement and also to participate in development efforts at levels beyond their community;

8) Supporting institutions like UN agencies and NGOs can fulfil better their mandates: e.g. for FAO the WCARRD mandate.

Constraints of Participation

These are mainly the following:

1) The political conditions/power structures of the country and project area. These may vary in different forms and degrees from a decentralized, laissez-faire and/or free enterprise system to a fully centralized, strongly planned and/or controlled one. They may vary furthermore in regard to their degree of stability. Accordingly, widely differing situations can be found ranging from full support of the central and/or local government to participation of the poor to indifference and hostility versus this approach.

   In fact, in a number of countries the urban and rural elites, particularly the latifundists and landlords, influence the political and administrative structures to such an extent that any policy to encourage genuine participation of rural people is either inexistent, or strongly opposed, and/or by various means neutralized or strained. For example, by prohibitive legislation, exasperating government control, alleged unavailability of funds and/or personnel and so on.

2) Legislative obstacles. In various countries freedom of association either does not exist or only formally; in other ones where the right of association, including of small farmers, labourers, etc., is recognized in the laws, the labour legislation is inadequate and/or scarcely applied in practice. Under the influence of vested interest groups the laws might further be interpreted and/or applied in such ways that (part of) the rural poor are prevented from organizing themselves.

3) Administrative obstacles. Centralized public administrative systems that control decision-making, resource allocation and information, may ostracize participation. The staff in such structures frequently disdain people's involvement. Also complex, bureaucratic procedures impede genuine participation as well as one-way, top-down planning performed solely by professionals; the same can be said of rural development planning done in urban centres and hardly based on need assessments in the field.

4) Socio-cultural impediments. A serious obstacle is the widespread mentality of dependence, sense of frustration as well as distrust in officials among low income rural people. The latter are frequently dominated by local elites to whom they have to leave key decision-making. All this forms part of the "culture of poverty" of the silent, excluded majority for whom survival is the sole aspiration. Furthermore, the poor form a heterogeneous "group": there are various categories with class, caste, tribal and religious differences and also with different interests, needs, access to resources as well as potentials. Accordingly, also participation must be planned and promoted according to different local contexts and factions.

Other impediments are: the isolation and scattered habitat of the poor, their low levels of living and heavy workloads especially of the women. Furthermore, their weak health conditions, low level of education and of exposure to non-local information, ignorance of their rights to self-organize groups and lack of leaders and know-how to move in this direction in order to promote their interests.

Some constraints of implementing and supporting agencies are the following:

1) There is often pressure from the side of implementing institutions and/or of supporting government or donor agencies to produce visible results quickly: quantity of funding and results prevails over quality. Unlike tangible physical infrastructure works and production outputs, most of the arduous participation efforts remain less visible and measurable as they have to focus—prior to concrete productive actions—principally on training, changes of attitudes and fostering of awareness of local needs and potentials.

2) Many implementing agencies are designed for centralized planning, decision-making and implementation; such set-ups do not favour participation.
3) There is usually lack of skilled staff to promote participation. It is indeed often problematical to find well-motivated and capable animators for group formation and action. And yet the latter are the key women and men to make a project successful as they live and work directly with the intended beneficiaries. Most participatory projects obtained, however, eventually well-performing group promoters (in various instances from the extension field staff), also through effective training.

Most of the above listed possible obstacles can gradually be overcome as evidenced by practice in many areas. However, the list indicates that for determining the form and degree of beneficiary participation the environmental, economic and social context of a project must be fully taken into account: participation is a site-and project-specific process.

Strategies to Promote Participation

Constraints

The main constraint of genuine participation is the political will to promote this in a country or project area. This basic problem can be overcome by means of various strategies at international, national and lower levels. The strategies should all aim at informing, sensitizing and motivating various categories of key persons in one way or another involved with rural development efforts such as: (a) politicians and governmental policy-and decision-makers; (b) the top and other staff of government, UN and donor agencies as well as of NGOs; (c) the (field) staff of development projects; and (d) the elites and better-off people in rural areas.

The practical outcome of the strategies must be that politicians, officials, experts and elites become motivated to accept, support or at least tolerate effective forms of participation of the disadvantaged rural people in development. For this purpose it will be of course very useful to demonstrate the experience and successful results of (pilot) participatory projects like the FAO/PPP and their great benefits for the rural poor.

Sensitizing Governments

Politicians, top decision-makers and planners, etc. need to be convinced of the necessity to incorporate participation in rural development policies, plans and programmes. This can be and is done in many ways e.g. by:

1) organizing ad-hoc conferences, seminars and missions. These are so far occasionally arranged by UN bodies, donors and NGOs. An example of an interesting huge effort with wide impact is the FAO WCARRD Conference and its on-going follow-up Plan of Action under which so far several missions and other activities were carried out;
2) inviting key government officials in field trips and workshops of participatory projects and also in inter-country workshops dealing with participation issues;
3) using mass-media and audio-visuals: distributing and showing of concise promotional materials: pamphlets, slide shows, films, etc.

A number of actions indicated in the following strategies will also have direct or indirect sensitizing effects on top government officials.

Promoting Policy Dialogues

Promoting dialogue between key officials, planners and decision-makers of national and international development agencies at country level is important. The latter may include one or more UN bodies, international and regional development banks, donors, aid consortia and voluntary organizations such as international NGOs. They could encourage, organize and/or participate in policy dialogues with selected governmental agencies in order to obtain rural poor-oriented economic and social policies and institutional arrangements that are required for participatory projects. The dialogues may indicate the need for a differential strategy as no government is monolithic: certain government agencies may be participatory development-oriented while others may be still rather cop-down, centralized, bureaucratic and/or technocratic.

The most important policies required for participatory development regard appropriate legislation for rural people's organizations including full freedom of association or group formation as well as reorientation of the delivery system, in particular the extension services, towards the needs of the rural weak.

Other special policies required include full integration of women in development, decentralization of decision-making, planning and resource allocation, rural poor-oriented input supply, extension, credit and marketing, enhancing non-agricultural income-generating activities as well as just fiscal and pricing systems.

In sum, projects and programmes cannot be implemented with effective (full) beneficiary participation before a minimum of certain favourable national policies have been (or are likely to be) adopted in a country.

In order to obtain strength in policy dialogues, the participation and concerted action is needed of all national and international development organizations which strive to combat rural poverty. In fact, international agencies as well as NGOs can influence a country's policy and institutional framework for effective poverty-alleviation.

Finally, the strategy of promoting dialogues between government agencies and NGOs appears to be particularly useful. FAO, UNDP and other UN agencies are now becoming quite active in this direction; they have also created special units for dealing with NGOs.

Promoting the Planning and Implementation of Participation in Larger-Scale Projects

In a project cycle various institutions are involved such as one or more government agencies, international development, funding and/or donor organizations, NGOs, etc. The lack of understanding, sympathy and/or experience regarding participatory projects of one or more of these cooperating institutions often makes it particularly difficult to render a project or at least some of its components participatory. The institutions involved may have different, e.g. predominantly macro economic and/or technocratic views and approaches regarding rural development efforts. Furthermore, experience on how to attain effective beneficiary participation may be lacking as the country's projects are either not participatory or do not properly monitor and evaluate beneficiary participation.

There is thus a wide scope for strategies to motivate officials, project planners and implementers through, among others, the following methods:

– meetings and field workshops at various levels
– periodic informal exchanges of views
– briefing sessions and documents on participatory development

- the inclusion of participatory experts in mission teams
- incorporation of participatory issues in the terms of reference of identification, preparation, appraisal and evaluation missions – provision of background materials on on-going participatory projects and/or visits to the latter, if any, in a country.

A direct result of the above actions will be that project planners become convinced that participation must be included from the very beginning in all stages of the project cycle. This implies in practice, that they urgent necessity and importance to start with the intended beneficiaries on their needs and desires by means of pre-project identification or reconnaissance missions.

Systematic Sensitization

The sensitization of the traditional, administrative and other influential leaders at project area and higher levels.

Practice shows that the support of village leaders is crucial for a participatory project. Many villages, especially in Africa, still form very traditional communities which have a closely knit social system of clans, lineages and extended families. The indigenous chiefs are powerful and "their" poor people over-dependent upon them. Will such chiefs give their consent and support for a project specifically designed for the poorer people? The required support, advice and assistance from the elites is indeed often important. In many cases, local chiefs and elders are prepared to support project actions for rural poor groups as well as for the delivery of the required services and facilities to these groups.

In order to obtain their support, the local traditional, administrative and other influential leaders in the project's entire action area have to be systematically sensitized and motivated beforehand on the participatory project approach through meetings, initiation workshops and other actions. The local leaders have to become convinced that it is in their own short- and long-term interest to support the project: the latter yields viz. economic and social benefits also to the better-off inhabitants. The sensitization campaign(s) must be project area-wide so that it becomes more difficult for non-favourable village and other leaders to oppose the project's special attention to disadvantaged villagers.

Finally, the sensitization of administrative and local leaders involved in a project is also realized through on-going participatory training.

Increasing Support

The increasing support of donors and development agencies and banks for participatory projects. Efforts to obtain this support aim mainly at the following:

- to convince donors and agencies which support participatory projects, to continue this assistance until they yield sufficient successful results for demonstration to governments;
- to insist that donors, development banks and agencies will only support a project if a participatory approach is incorporated in it;
- to attain more assistance to developing countries for participatory projects on a large scale up to the point of creating a critical mass.

For these wide scopes donors as well as international development agencies and banks should participate in, initiate and/or organize various of the earlier proposed promotional actions such as policy dialogues, seminars, field workshops and visits to participatory projects. It will be crucial to show the actions and results of participatory projects also by means of good monitoring and evaluation systems. Moreover, case studies on the benefits and cost-effectiveness of participatory projects (ection 14) as well as promotional materials will be quite helpful.

Other actions include: studies on the policies and commitments of donors and development banks as well as identification of opportunities for assistance.

Actions to be taken by FAO and other UN Agencies

Apart from the active involvement in most of the aforementioned strategies, other very much required actions are that FAO and other UN agencies:

1) sensitize on participatory development methods their top officials, the staff of technical divisions as well as mission and project teams;
2) strengthen, help, expand and multiply existing participatory projects and promote new ones including on a pilot basis;
3) build up a strong support unit for participatory projects and promotional actions, also to assist technical divisions and to increase the interest of donors to support such projects;

4) increase the limited manpower as well as technical and financial resources for participatory development in the technical and operational divisions of aid agencies;
5) ask each technical division to review its projects in the light of participatory principles and also to refine the participatory methods in its subject matter areas;
6) promote networking amongst UN and other agencies, banks and NGOs which are involved in participatory development projects as well as those which could be involved in such efforts in order to exchange experience, expertise and audio-visuals. Furthermore to organize workshops and field visits and share promotional literature. Periodic meetings of cooperating agencies, donors and project field staff are particularly useful.

Point (4) above needs special attention and action as illustrated in the following:

"There is a limited staff in FAO of specialists who have a wide experience not only of the PPP but of many other participatory forms of development including cooperatives, small farmer organizations and agricultural trade unions. They also increasingly maintain contact and dialogue with a wide range of NGOs. These are supported directly by a core group of specialist consultants with a wide knowledge of participatory development and of FAO's programmes and procedures. A second source of human resources may be found in the cadre of PPP project field staff who have been trained during the implementation of the PPP programme. Many of these trained people are actively working with PPP projects and can be called upon to share their knowledge with others. The third important human resource is resident amongst FAO's staff in various Technical Divisions, and which has not yet been fully mobilized. These are specialists in all the different sectors and disciplines that are normally involved in the large-scale projects and some experts are also involved in participatory project.

Financial resources are in short supply and will have to be increased if FAO is to make use of the accumulated rich experience of the last ten years of PPP. Without sufficient support for a new strategy to further promote participation in agricultural and rural development, FAO will fall behind other UN agencies that are actively involved and will have difficulty in meeting requests from governments and donors for technical assistance involving a participatory approach".

Identification of Project Areas, Beneficiaries and Their Needs

Identification of Project Areas

For an efficient development strategy poor and "better-off" rural areas need to be demarcated in a country. An area is poor when it presents (part of) the following conditions: poor physical resources, lack of physical infrastructure, of trained manpower and of basic services and facilities, inequitable land tenure conditions, production levels below potentials, administrative backwardness, shortage of on- and especially off-farm opportunities, institutionalized forms of oppression and exploitation of the poor, and/or lack of people's participat ion in local decisio n-making.

For the identification of poor areas, data regarding some of the above key criteria may be obtained by means of rapid rural appraisal methods, while information on other ones is mostly hard to collect in a relatively short time span. Other reasonably precise criteria could be applied more quickly in most countries. For example: areas affected by floods, salinity, erosion, desertification, un- and under-employment, relative inaccessibility, areas with sizeable numbers of poor tribal people and/or refugees, zones with strong out-migration, etc.

Additional preferential criteria for starting participatory projects are e.g. areas: a) with above average concentration of one or more categories of poor rural people; b) with a sufficient number of actual and/or potential viable economic activities and also market outlets; c) areas in which the essential services and facilities are present and can be delivered to the low-income people; (This is to ensure that the beneficiary groups once formed, will have a fair chance to have their production and other requirements met in time.); d) areas where these groups can have an influence and multiplication effort on existing projects; and e) which are not too a-typical. i.e. have such specific hard geographic, economic, social and/or political (unrest) conditions that a participatory project is likely to become unsuccessful, at least for the time being.

For the identification of initial action areas consisting of one or more village clusters where project field actions for beneficiary participation are to be started, exploratory socio-economic surveys are needed. Such surveys are to be carried out by well-selected action-research experts on participatory lines. It is very desirable to involve these agents as early as possible in this operation, in particular in the search for suitable village-clusters and within these core villages where the field actions will start.

The village-cluster approach to be adopted in most cases implies that the project's participation activities will start in one or two selected core villages and gradually be spread to the surrounding villages. The advantages of the village-cluster approach include:

1) Better handling of the guidance, coordination and supervision of the project activities;
2) Rapid spread effect of the project's impact from the pioneer villages to the adjacent ones;
3) When the rural poor production groups are located close to each other, they can form a suitable type of federation which will give them more bargaining power;
4) A cluster enhances economies of scale: it facilitates the provision of input supply, processing and marketing points and facilities, as well as other (health, education, etc.) services.

A final point: the misconception that in poor areas all people are poor is based on insufficient distinction between area and family level poverty. Area-wide or all farmers development approaches are to be applied for certain area-based project components like the provision of physical, economic and/or social infrastructures and water and soil conservation. For other components specifically meant for benefiting the poor people, such as (special) delivery of inputs, credit, training, etc., the identification of the "target group" and the application of a feasible participatory approach remains a must.

Identification and Classification of Poor Rural People

Definition of poor rural people: all people who a) live in a rural area at or below subsistence level; b) are dedicated full- or part-time to agriculture, forestry, fisheries, handicrafts and/or related occupations; and c) are over-dependent for work and livelihood on others with more power and means of production.

The main categories of rural poor people are: small and marginal owner-farmers, tenants, sharecroppers, landless labourers, small fishermen, forestry workers, and part of the rural artisans, of tribal people as well as of nomads and refugees. The poor women can belong to any of these categories. Various combinations of the above categories are frequently found.

Given the operational importance of the topic, two other, rather similar ways to classify the rural people are given below:

The rural population consists broadly of five categories: 1) the rich having an abundance of means of production; 2) the middle class having secure and sufficient access to income and assets; 3) subsistence producers having some access to income and assets; 4) the very poor having very little access (labourers, hawkers, etc.); and 5) the destitutes including the handicapped: those who are not able for whatever reason to help themselves.

The disadvantaged people are also classified as follows: 1) the marginally poor (small farmers), 2) the poor (small farmers-part-time labourers), 3) the very poor (labourers and part-time micro farmer-labourers) and 4) the destitutes.

The first two categories can be more easily encouraged to self-organization as they have some assets, and can thus profit better from gainful group activities also by means of credit. Instead, the very poor being mainly labourers often migrate for work, have no economic activities of their own, are more indebted and more dependent on their better-off employers.

Most participatory projects have a specific target group and attempt to benefit only or mainly the rural poor. However, given the various types of poor people and the gradations of their poverty, a project may benefit the subsistence poor and only part of the very poor and the destitutes. In fact. in some projects the subsistence poor form initially a reference group for the "lowest-level" ones who cannot take any risk and certainly not before they concrete local examples. A project though meant for all categories of the poor, need thus not necessarily start with the most needy people (the very poor and destitutes) who may be attracted and stimulated to engage in development actions by the subsistence poor only in successive phases.

How to Identify Poor People

For the identification of the intended beneficiaries firstly available data on the rural population of the country and project area(s) are to be gathered. This could include data on population, land tenure, economic activities, income, (un- and under-) employment, housing, etc. Many of these data are required anyhow for a development project. With this information an overall direct assessment can be obtained of the numbers, proportions, etc., of the various categories of poor and non-poor farmers, fishermen, artisans et alias when taking into account the following:

1) all landless farmers belong to the poor; some exceptions are however, e.g. larger scale tenants or above poverty line regular wage earners;
2) the identification of landowning poor is more problematic. Statistical criteria, like area of land owned (all who own less than, say, two or three acres are poor) are notoriously relative and arbitrary as farm productivity on such plots varies greatly. Moreover, land tenure data are frequently lacking or deficient.

For the sorting out of the poor, specific criteria need to be developed as poverty is an area-specific variable and refers to specific economic and social realities. Possible criteria are:

1) availability or less of production assets of a family such as types and amounts of arable land, land tenure conditions, labour, animals, equipments, tools, etc.;
2) available skills in the family;
3) on- and off-farm family income (including of emigrants);
4) degree of indebtedness of a family;
5) housing conditions; building materials, available facilities, room occupation rates, etc.;
6) nutrition: calories intake, nutritional status of children below 5 years, consumption of certain types of food, etc.;
7) level of education for women and men: literacy, school enrolment rates, etc.;
8) health conditions in a family; presence of handicapped dependents, incidence of diseases, etc.;
9) economic dependency rates within the households;
10) lack of participation of the poor in formal and informal rural people's organizations and in local decision-making.

Most of the above data are usually available at national, and less at lower levels (no breakdowns).

Examples of identification criteria used in various participatory projects are:

1) (near) landless labourers;
2) small farmers, tenants and sharecroppers operating plots of land below the project area average, e.g. 3 or 5 acres;
3) small, traditional fishermen and artisans;
4) the people as under (2) and (3) who largely lack access to water, inputs, credit, markets, education, training, extension and other services (the "rural excluded");
5) the total annual family income is below the average in the area concerned; the families' main source of income is agriculture, fishing and allied activities and the family members are the principal source of labour.

The above criteria need to be specified and operationalized for each project area. Local informants and particularly the poor can be involved in participatory identification when needed, that is they may assist in applying the selection criteria and reach agreement among themselves to solve doubtful cases as to who belongs to the poor. In many areas entire categories of people such as the landless, sharecroppers, small artisans, traditional fishermen, tribal and low class/caste families belong to the poor, whereas the non-poor like big and middle level farmers and fishermen, merchants, money lenders, etc. form a well-known minority that easily can be identified.

The participation of the non-poor in a project. When considering the basic question how the rural poor can be "sorted out" in "communal" or tribal societies, it should be reminded that the identification of low-income families in participatory projects concerns only their eligibility for rural poor group membership and for certain services and facilities provided by a project. Consequently the non-poor inhabitants of a project area are to be systematically informed on the objectives and actions of a project and are furthermore to be invited very much—also by the groups—to participate in a project for the provision of advice and moral and other support to the disadvantaged people. For example, in local implementation or coordination committees as well as in various activities such as crop and livestock production, training, extension, research and/or evaluation.

Furthermore, as various projects show, most better-off locals find it below their status to participate directly as members in rural poor groups.

Identification of Development Needs and Aspirations of the Intended Beneficiaries

Area and Beneficiary Needs

On-going need-assessment is essential to obtain the active participation of the people in project preparation and implementation. For this purpose area and beneficiary needs are to be distinguished. Area needs are related to area poverty encompassing the needs of an entire territory and of all its inhabitants. For example: more and/or better physical resources, trained manpower, economic and social infrastructure, services and facilities. For meeting such needs an area-wide or "all rural people" development approach is required.

Beneficiary needs are directly related to group and family level poverty. They can be divided into physiological (food, clothing, housing, health), psychological (e.g. safety, self-realization), economic (employment, income), and socio-cultural needs (e.g. group belonging, education, recreation and social recognition). Needs have a certain hierarchy: some are for bare survival, some for sustained and other for dignified human survival. Beneficiary needs are interrelated with one another and also with certain area needs.

Apart from needs, people also have aspirations and expectations: their aspirations may, however, not coincide with their needs as perceived by outsiders. The rural poor are in general quite able to bring up the nature and priority order of their felt needs and desires.

How to Identify Beneficiary Needs

Organize project cycle surveys and missions in a participatory way, that is, consult on the needs and desires of as many future project participants as possible, in particular the intended beneficiaries and other village level informants.

The best way is to establish or send to the area prior to project identification missions, or reconnaissance work teams for say 2-3 months.

The need-assessment should focus on the identification of priority needs as perceived by the low-income people concerned. This is particularly necessary for the promotion of rural poor groups which are best formed around felt priority needs.

The information collected, though sufficient to plan a flexible project framework, will still be provisional and usually in part suspect: more reliable and in-depth data can only be gathered by field workers who work with the people for longer periods during project implementation and gain their confidence.

Needs identification, or the search for ways to satisfy intended beneficiary needs, form part of an on-going participatory process and can be done more systematically and effectively when groups and organizations involved in a project bring up their felt needs, among other to perform gainful activities, whereas the delivery staff hopefully endeavours to meet these necessities. Group Promoters are to be trained to help the disadvantaged people to understand their own situations, to win their confidence by closely working with them and getting the poor to articulate their needs. The Group Promoters will also learn to stimulate the delivery staff to help meet these necessities.

The Formation of Rural Poor Groups and Organizations

Need for a Receiving-cum-Delivery System

The existing groups in a certain project area may be farmer associations, cooperatives, women's, youth and village groups, trade unions and other formal and informal groups. In many cases traditional tribal, nomadic, clan or community groupings can be effective vehicles for participatory development. In other cases, these may be so strongly dominated by land-owners, money lenders and other influential people and elites that new participatory groupings initiated and run by the under-privileged people themselves, are required for adequately involving one or more categories of the poor in self-development efforts.

The existing or newly formed groups involved in a project are to be firstly starting bases for economic and social self-help activities, secondly receiving mechanisms for services, facilit ies and inputs at the local level, and thirdly instruments for participat ion in local decision-making and for increasing the bargaining power of the under-previleged through their "pressure groups."

Through such a receiving system the rural population can mobilize their own resources and be "reached" effectively by any development agency for the delivery of services and facilities to support economic and socio-cultural activities. The economic activities which aim at income and employment generation, could include crops, livestock, fishery, public works, irrigation, agro-processing, transport, marketing, handicrafts, and so on. The socio-cultural activities may regard the fields of health, sanitation, nutrition, education, training, recreation, etc.

The term "Receiving System" is, however, not fully adequate. Firstly, it could give the wrong connotation that the groups and organizations are mainly conceived as passive recipients of services and facilities (likewise also the term beneficiary has a quite passive connotation). Instead, they are to be regarded in the first place as starting bases for self-development efforts to be rendered more fruitful by the effective utilization of the services received, and moreover as instruments for participation in local decision-making.

Secondly, the rural poor are, also through their groups, not only receivers but also deliverers among others, of new ideas, methods and practices for self-development based on their previous experience. They are also deliverers of labour and other means of production as well as of many types of agricultural and other products.

The delivery system consists of government agencies and other (NGO) organizations that provide services and facilities to the intended beneficiaries.

Most conventional projects give attention only to the building of a delivery system from the centre and down to the village and not or scarcely to the creation of an adequate receiving system. A delivery system may be transformed so that it becomes geared to the real needs and aspirations of the rural poor people. A participatory receiving system should become an effective instrument in this transformation of the delivery system. Through mutual adaptation both systems will form jointly an appropriate local receiving-cum-delivery system.

Inventarization of Existing Groups and Organizations

For the planning of beneficiary participation, it is indispensable to identify existing forms of local people's organizations. As indicated earlier, some of the existing groups and organizations may be traditional and some others are "imported" and more modern such as farmer associations, cooperatives, rural workers' organizations or trade unions. The question is whether they do represent the target group. This is only the case when an organization supports in its mandate and activities specifically (part of) the rural poor.

Larger farmers' associations and cooperatives have often elite-dominated structures and the involvement of such well established organizations in participatory projects must be considered with great caution.

For the inventory of existing groups and organizations a distinction has to be made between standard and participatory organizations. The former, usually formal organizations (among others, most cooperatives and farmer associations), are set up, managed or controlled by outside agencies, hierarchical leadership, employed managers and/or other elites. Participatory groups and organizations are started and run by low-income people themselves and have consequently a more active membership and better performance.

Self-Formation of Small Homogeneous Groups

In project areas where the above stocktaking indicates that participatory groups are lacking, it will be indispensable to promote their formation. This can be done either from scratch or from or within existing groups or organizations. The latter may be either traditional or formal ones like cooperatives. Informal smaller action groups could be formed within or from the large organizations for certain enterprises. Traditional African situations with customary or communal land agriculture may require location-specific approaches for small group formation.

In any case the basic prerequisites for the creation of groups from or within existing groups or larger organizations are, however, that the latter have objectives compatible with those of the participatory groups to be formed, are furthermore not dominated by the better-off, can promote the interests of the poor and lastly give sufficient autonomy to the groups for self-management.

Small homogeneous groups are to be formed by poor people themselves around certain starter income-raising activities. Essential group formation guidelines are:

a) Viable income-raising group activities are to be identified before the formation of groups.

b) The beneficiaries must themselves select the members, leaders, activities and rules of their groups. In other words, the groups should be really participatory. Each group selects its own members as they like on one or more of the following bases: adjacent farm lots and/or home plots, family ties, common (community) interests, friendships, religious affiliation, etc.; furthermore, willingness to accept mutual responsibility for group activities. This willingness may regard joining a nucleus enterprise, sharing production aids, possession of special skills or a pool of implements (among labourers) and so on.

c) *Composition:* the groups should be homogeneous, that is, consist of members who 1) live under similar economic and social disadvantaged conditions and have close social affinity; 2) accept mutual responsibility and joint liability for self-help activities; and 3) trust each other to such an extent that none of them would dominate or exploit the group. The homogeneity of a group is to be based on these three factors and other ones like gender, age, neighbourhood, and occupational affinity may be helpful but are not essential.

In certain projects a relative flexibility regarding the participation in groups may be allowed. As an exception and for good reasons based on the local social structure and culture, a project may allow that a group of rural poor includes also a better-off member (as done e.g. in the PPP Thailand). The latter should, however, identify with the poor and share their interests, her/his presence should enhance the attainment of the group objectives and also be acceptable to all other members. The non-poor member should, however, not hold a leadership position in the group.

The promotion of homogeneous rural poor groups is an indispensable core feature of a participatory project. This is because: (a) homogeneous groups facilitate effective communication which develops mutual trust, interest and concern and thus group cohesion and the bond to meet common needs, and (b) experience shows that in heterogeneous groups conflicts of interests are more likely to arise and one or more better-off members may capture the benefits, resulting in group failure.

Members of a group should thus belong to one or more categories of the rural poor who are willing to cooperate with each other on equal terms. A preliminary household survey should indicate customary patterns of cooperation, preferred co-operators and group activities. The homogeneity of groups does of course not refer to all economic and social issues that concern the potential group members. Moreover, it does certainly not mean strengthening existing class, caste or clan biases. For example, a group of landless labourers may agree on land reform but disagree on irrigation, land use or marketing and the members may belong to different (rival) classes, clans, or political parties. A group of water users may agree on the distribution of water from an irrigation channel in order to make more efficient use of it, but the members may have divergent views on land reform or housing.

d) *Size:* the group should be compact, cohesive and flexible, and thus small. The size of the groups to be formed depends largely upon the numbers of farmers/fishermen who will engage in a joint activity and will accordingly benefit from a common source of production or from common facilities. For example, those who could be served by a common tubewell, or who could jointly bring milk to a common milk collection centre, or who could operate a joint processing unit or act as a joint labour team for rural works, etc. (Huizer: 1982). However, the groups should be compact and also flexible to allow free informal discussions and to perform economic activities on a shared basis. Experience shows that the optimal size is 8-15 members, otherwise sub-groups and/or tensions may arise more easily. Other reasons to start with small cohesive groups are that these facilitate communication and dialogue between the members, form optimal learning laboratories and are the necessary "bricks" to build later on well-functioning, larger groupings such as (pre-)cooperatives, associations or federations.

Steps in the Process of Group Formation

These are the following:

a) collection of relevant information on eligible households by means of household surveys;

b) organization of informal meetings with prospective group members to discuss, among others, the purpose, methods of operation and benefits of the groups as well as possible group enterprises, joint means of production, etc.;

c) the self-selection of possible group members: this includes decision-making on whether to form groups only with small-holders, tenants or landless, furthermore only with women or men, or to create mixed groups of women and men and/or small-holders and tenants, etc.;

d) listing by the group promoters of potential group members and leaders, of possible group activities and required inputs; furthermore, distribution of membership cards or other symbols to the members of each group formed;

e) group discussions regarding group liabilities, resources and needs as well as recording of the production activities and income of the group members;

f) group members assign among themselves responsibilities and duties by consensus or formal voting. This includes the election of a chairperson, secretary and treasurer. The rotation of leadership positions is very recommendable as this offers opportunities to members for leadership training and minimizes domination of a group by a few members holding office for too long periods. It promotes also shared leadership;

g) establishment of group rules including, among others, rules on compatibility of membership of other organizations, how to rotate group leadership functions, how to organize group credit and repayment, how to establish and use a group credit to ensure its repayment, how to establish and use a group savings fund and how to tackle possible land (tenancy) problems. Planning of the required meetings: where, when and with what agenda.

It is clear from the above steps that the formation of viable and stable groups requires patience and sufficient time: for this important process a period of two to six months is usually needed, depending upon the local circumstances. Both too quick formation (e.g. to obtain credit) as well as too much delay (which may kill the interest of the potential group members) should be avoided. When is a group really formed? When it is stable, that is, retains the majority of its members, holds regular meetings attended by most members, carries out beneficial activities and has accrued a reasonable amount of group savings.

Incentives and Disincentives for Group Formation

Why should the rural poor form or join groups? For most outside development agencies the advantages of the group approach are by now evident. The incentives for the poor themselves to plan and carry out group-wise development actions are of course situation and location-specific but derive in general from the following three main rural poor group functions.

a) Groups are attractive starting bases for undertaking gainful economic and social self-help development activities. The members can pool together to varying extents their capabilities, experience, information, assets, labour and other resources and perform successfully certain profitable self-planned actions which cannot be carried out on an individual basis or with much more effort and risk and/or less profit.

The low-income people may also be attracted to groups as these provide new training opportunities, where they can learn from the group promoters and one another to articulate, discuss and solve their problems, to plan, carry out and record joint enterprises, to keep accounts, etc. Furthermore, they may soon become aware of the advantages of economies of scale by sharing group-wise inputs and production aids. The rural people actually have long traditions of informal group actions and they need no special incentive once they that they can cooperate in face-to-face groups which are more efficient, fruitful and conducive to their (self-)development. The basic stimulus for the poor to form or join groups is that these can meet certain clearly identified priority needs and aspirations. Groups are best formed around priority needs as perceived by the intended beneficiaries, like better use of scarce land and water resources, and (thus) more and better crops and livestock, cheaper inputs, credit and saving, agro-processing, transport, marketing, etc., but also more training and know-how, better technology, education, sanitation, primary health care, housing and recreation.

b) The groups are useful, if not indispensable receiving mechanisms for inputs, services and facilities provided by the delivery system to meet the needs of the poor. This is increasingly realized not only by the deliverers in the development agencies who want to reach and serve the poor in an efficient and cost-saving way, but also by the intended receivers and utilizers themselves who feel that individually they will remain out of reach and marginalized.

c) For the rural poor groups are also attractive as instruments for participation in local decision-making, as indispensable means to gradually obtain bargaining power and to exert pressure to improve their lot. Through their self-run groups the poor become increasingly self-confident and recognized by their wider community and – as experience shows – may even be elected as representatives in local councils or other formal organizations.

The disincentives for group-action to be identified and tackled may be: (a) opposition of local power holders to rural poor organizations; (b) lack of support of village leaders and influentials who feel that age-old patron-client relationships may become endangered; and/or (c) obstruction even by slightly less poor farmers/fishermen who do not accept that their labourers or servants build up group power.

Overcoming the opposition of local power holders to Rural Poor Organizations

In various countries and/or project areas, local and national level elites or power holders (political and religious leaders/authorities, landlords, traders, moneylenders, etc.), as well as slightly better-off groups of farmers or fishermen with different vested interests, may overtly or latently oppose any more stable grouping or organization of low-income rural workers. This opposition stems usually from the strong drive of local and other elites to maintain their position and/or to continue their domination and/or exploitation of the poor rural workers, who frequently live in a state of semi serfdom. Most peasants live and work in extreme economic dependence upon bigger landowners, traders and middlemen and may fear intimidation, manipulation, victimization, or expulsion from their land, etc., when involving in peasant organizations.

Group and Inter-Group Activities

Group Activities

The project staff and in particular the participation agents, together with potential group members, line staff and ad-hoc experts including knowledgeable local farmers or fishermen, identify a range of possible common productive and other activities in the action area for which groups of disadvantaged people will be formed.

The types of group activities in a certain area depend of course upon the local economic, social and institutional potentials, furthermore upon the needs, desires and capabilities of each group formed as well as upon the design, objectives, staff and resources of a project. The many viable group activities carried out by beneficiary groups range widely but four broad types can be distinguished as follows:

a) Direct income-raising activities: These may consist of improved and increased production in existing or of new enterprises in any economic (sub-)sector like agriculture, livestock, fishery, forestry, handicrafts, processing, transport, trading, marketing and so on. Practice shows hundreds of different group undertakings which yielded economic but also social benefits. The latter include more skills, risk-taking, group cohesion and eventually self-management. Some examples for illustration are:

- intensification or improvement of various food and cash crops such as rice, plantains, pineapples, coco, yams, maize, pepper, oil seeds, cotton, vegetables, fruits and so on;
- development of small-scale animal husbandry activities such as poultry, rabbit, duck, turkey, goat and sheep raising, bee-keeping and so on;
- development of small-scale aquaculture (fish ponds), riverine fishing, etc.;
- introduction or improvement of low-cost facilities for processing of produce such as rice, fruits, etc., and also for dairy and fish products;
- introduction or improvement of low-cost, small-scale irrigation, drainage and/or anti-erosion systems;
- development of low-cost storage, transport and marketing facilities
- creation of supply points for inputs such as fertilizers, etc.;
- establishment of utility stores for farming essentials, household articles, etc., as well as petty trading;
- development of production and marketing of local handicrafts (handlooms, etc.). cottage industries, trades such as carpentry and blacksmithing, charcoal making, household utensils, production of local building materials and so on.

b) Income enhancing activities: these include:

- cost reduction and income maximizing activities which aim at reducing production costs and/or obtaining better prices, e.g. bulk purchasing of inputs, group transport and/or marketing or products;
- consumer savings: e.g. obtaining consumer goods at lower prices by joint purchasing;

- social savings: reaching agreement through group pressure to cut expenditure on costly customs like ceremonies (weddings, funerals) but also on bad habits like unreasonable spending, drinking, gambling, etc.;
- social insurance: group-wise protection against emergencies or calamities by means of group (welfare) funds or collective insurance arrangements so that group members do not become over-indebted.

c) Production facilitating actions which create proper conditions for group production, e.g. action for enforcement of land reform laws, for consolidation of holdings for joint production, etc.

d) Socio-cultural group activities. Many groups feel the need for social and cultural activities. For example, in the field of health and sanitation (mother and child care, latrines, piped water, etc.), education (functional literacy courses, activities for school-going children and so on), family planning, folk-culture, theatre; village beautification (tree planting) and so on. In many areas there is an acute need for group actions aiming at better nutrition: adequate diet and food preparation, better food storage, proper distribution of food in the family, clean water supply, improved personal and environmental hygiene, utilization of biological waste (biogas), etc.

Most projects emphasize, at least initially, direct production activities which strengthen the group's cohesion, management skills, and economic base. It is however important that each group identifies, chooses, plans, executes and evaluates as much as possible on its own a feasible activity and reaches self-reliance; the participation agent and other field staff should give guidance mainly in the initial stages and withdraw as soon as possible. Practice shows that the most preferred types of group activities are those that yield clear economic benefits and are based on the felt needs of the group members.

The identification of viable group (production) actions forms part of the on-going action-research e.g. from the household survey data collected a number of ideas/proposals may emerge.

The income-earning activities in particular for new or "young" groups should be low risk, based on local experience and low-cost, intermediate technology. They must furthermore yield quick, tangible returns and thus be of short duration: in most cases less than one year, so that groups become more motivated and encouraged for further action.

The activities can take the form of group or individual production or a combination of these such as individual operation but sharing of common facilities or joint input-purchasing and/or bulk marketing. Thus certain phases of productive activities may be done better jointly and other ones better individually. It is in the interest of the group members to act jointly when the (sub-) activities are more cost-effective and offer economies of scale.

Each group prepares a simple group production plan which includes: a) the socio-economic conditions, resources and problems of the participating households; b) the plan for the group undertaking including a schedule of operations; and c) possibly the plans for subsidiary on- or off-farm income-raising activities of individual members which may require some group help.

Some major constraints to carry out successfully income-raising activities are: insufficient, inadequate or too late delivery of inputs, lack of training of local field staff and group members in group dynamics and group enterprise management, lack of mobility (means of transport) to help groups in planning adequately their activities and insufficient consideration of the feasibility, cost-benefit and credit-worthiness of a group enterprise.

Once a group has performed successfully its initial undertaking, it will undertake additional, more complex profitable activities. All necessary guidance and support for the groups is to be obtained from or through the group promoters who liaise the groups with the local delivery system.

An overall point is that there are two levels of management of group activities. One is strategic management whereby groups must anticipate the impact of occurrences external to them (e.g. new price policies or environmental damage like over-cropping or over-fishing). The other is operational management where groups deal with issues arising from their day to day operations. However, in particular for the latter type there is a great need for instructional manuals on group dynamics, group business management, monitoring and evaluation, savings/credit, etc.

When is a group mature? The indicators of group maturity and self-reliance are: (1) regular meetings with active participation of all group members; (2) savings accumulated and less dependence on credit; (3) self-sustenance through food production; (4) joint preparation of group production plans; (5) ability to handle inputs and supplies; (6) ability to market the produce profitably; (7) adequate profits and just distribution of these among the group members; (8) effective record keeping; (9) effective links with line agencies and NGOs; (10) involvement in social activities e.g. literacy classes, home management, contributions to community development works, etc.; (11) number of activities successfully undertaken; (12) more women and youth participation; and (13) rotation of leadership.

Towards Federations of Groups

After one to two years well-performing groups may be encouraged to engage in inter-group activities, e.g. for joint input purchase, storage, marketing, processing, training, appropriate technology, etc., not only to obtain economies of scale, but also as a move towards inter-group associations or federations of say 20-25 groups at secondary level. The emphasis will be on functional associations for the economic and social emancipation of the rural weak. In the federations accountability to the primary groups should be maintained as a basic principle. A federation represents thus groups and is not an executive body.

Inter-group associations should have an educational orientation towards their member groups and become a source of technical assistance, economies of scale, managerial guidance and coordination. They can offer training to new groups and even help finance their activities from accumulated savings. Moreover they can serve as reference points and examples for new inter-group associations and eventually perform (part of) the functions of group promoters.

In most cases it is more advantageous and preferable to create multi-activity inter-group associations instead of single-activity ones (e.g. for one crop) in order to meet better certain common needs of the groups: e.g. training, information exchange, and more massive pressure on the delivery system.

The federations may be legalized as (pre-)cooperatives or associations in order to obtain more recognition, legal status and services and facilities.

The groups may also link themselves to participatory, rural poor-oriented cooperatives or other people's organizations, if any, while maintaining their necessary autonomy. It should be stressed here that the groups do not replace cooperatives and other village institutions: they will remain interest groups taking part in production programmes.

The federations of groups and/or linkages to existing organizations will not only facilitate the delivery of services and facilities, but also the consolidation of group plans into multi-group or federational plans to be matched with area and regional development plans through local coordination committees. In this way a two-way (bottom-up and top-bottom) planning process will be developed.

Through inter-group activities and federations of groups, the poor become increasingly self-confident and recognized by their wider community; they obtain organizational power and will eventually also be represented in local government bodies.

When groups become more self-propelling, the participation agents will gradually withdraw and become eventually redundant for these groups, which is a main indication for a successful participatory process. They can then give more attention to new groups and may also perform specific functions for associations of groups.

Institutional Arrangements for Beneficiary Participation

Institutions to be Involved

For the active participation of the intended beneficiaries the project needs to involve relevant government institutions such as line departments, banks, training and research centres and/or women and youth councils. Furthermore also NGOs such as rural people's organizations, church-related development agencies, national federations of NGOs and/or small rural development-oriented NGOs. The inclusion of selected NGOs is of course important as they have usually more the confidence of the people, are less hierarchic and bureaucratic and provide services more expediently and timely.

Either NGOs or Governments or both can thus be project implementers. But whatever the case, emphasis on overall support by the government is to be guaranteed from the commencement of a project. The continued support of FAO and/or other aid agency is also needed.

Where the political climate is good, governments that are willing should implement a project. In other cases, NGOs with experience at the grassroots level should be allowed to implement it solely or in cooperation with one or more government agencies.

The selection of government bodies and/or NGOs depends naturally also upon the type of project and upon the capabilities and willingness of these agencies to provide the beneficiary groups with the required services and facilities. It should also be considered whether one or more of these organizations are able and prepared to second to the project some of their capable field workers (e.g. extensionists, social workers) as participation agents.

For the selection of training and/or socio-economic research centres (in or outside a university), it should be considered whether these institutions have genuine concern for disadvantaged people and can provide on an institutional or personal basis the necessary expertise for participatory training, action research and evaluation.

Coordination

In order to obtain the required project support for the beneficiaries workable linking and coordination mechanisms are needed for obtaining effective policies, allocation of resources and delivery of services to meet the various needs of the groups. The main coordination mechanisms are explained hereunder.

Project Coordination or Participation Committee. At project area level this Committee is formed with representatives of: a) all relevant local agencies which deal with and (are to) serve the intended beneficiaries; b) the project staff, in particular the group promoters; c) the beneficiaries or their groups where these have been formed; and d) where opportune, selected local leaders. The Committee aims at promoting beneficiary participation and at solving related implementation problems, in particular the timely delivery of services and facilities to the rural poor groups.

The main functions of a participation (or coordinating) committee include: 1) to provide to the project staff the main orientations and guidelines for the planning, implementation and evaluation of beneficiary participation according to the basic project documents; 2) to help recruit and train the required project staff such as the participation agents (group promoters); 3) to promote effective two-way communication channels between low income groups in the project areas and supporting government and NGO officials at various levels; 4) to obtain the necessary training and support for the beneficiary groups from government and/or NGO bodies; 5) to help administer and control the project funds for group formation and action; 6) to promote the consolidation of the project's participatory actions and their multiplication In other areas of the country; and 7) to perform any other function that will enhance the success of the project.

Where a larger project has a coordinating committee, task force or the like for all project operations, the participation committee could be constituted as a sub-committee or even "coincide" with the larger coordinating committee.

Within the participation committee small technical committees could be created for e.g. the training, approval of group loans, and monitoring and evaluation.

A larger project may also have a special National Coordinating Committee or Task Force, or be supported by an existing National Committee for similar projects or efforts. It would be very desirable that also such a National Committee has a sub-committee or special task force to deal with participatory issues such as general policies, personnel, finance and other matters of national importance.

In the project itself there is a need to designate a preferably local staff member as the participation coordinator who is specifically encharged to support, coordinate and supervise all agents and operations concerned with beneficiary participation. He/she should be a member or possibly the chairperson of the specific participation (sub-) committee(s) at project area and national levels, brief periodically the members of these (sub-)committees and assist in the selection, training and guidance of the participation agents.

The required qualifications of the participation coordinator are: 1) acquaintance with grassroots realities and motivated to assist the poor; 2) experience in working with field agents such as extensionists and social workers; 3) experience with the operators of government and international bodies at various levels; 4) experience with organizing training activities; 5) academic degree or the equivalent in economics, social or agricultural science; and 6) good knowledge of the local language.

Need for flexible organizational set-ups: Though the above set-up is desirable, the coordination mechanisms may vary according to the conditions, possibilities and already existing coordination bodies of a country and project area as well as to the type of participatory project, e.g. one participation committee may sometimes replace the committees at national and/or lower levels. Moreover, for a project mainly involving government agencies a different coordination set-up may be required than for a project implemented mainly by one or more NGOs. For the latter type of project one or more small Task Forces (at national and/or at lower levels). including representatives of the NGOs concerned and possibly of the supporting government bodies, may (initially) be appropriate for project implementation.

Coordination of project support activities is to be foremost undertaken at the local level. Encouragement and support from national level is however, quite necessary to enhance the local level coordination.

Finally, delegation of responsibility to lower levels should be a disengagement process whereby most higher level functions are gradually delegated to lower levels, e.g. FAO to the implementing agency, which in turn delegates to the group promoters and/or the inter-group associations, and these to the groups.

Financial Arrangements

Project's Financial Arrangements

The promotion of economic and financial self-reliance on the part of the rural poor (groups) and the re-direction of financial institutions towards the disadvantaged people requires that the project's financial arrangements of relevance to the beneficiaries contain the following major elements:

1) involvement of the rural poor groups for administering savings and credit.
2) Equal priority to credit activities and mobilization of savings to ensure both economic and financial self-reliance and increased production by the beneficiaries.
3) Social instead of physical collateral for group loans; this group guarantee is a major factor in loan security.
4) Placement of a Credit Guarantee Fund (CGF) with the participating banks as an additional security for its loans to the poor and as an incentive for its active collaboration.
5) Establishment of realistic interest rates on deposits and loans which are normal in the recipient country, in order to foster group financial self-reliance and ensure that the relatively high costs of the financial services (loan delivery and supervision, etc.) provided by participating institutions are adequately covered. Normal rates would also cushion the withdrawal shock when project support terminates. However, in

situations where interest rates are too high for small farmers, it would be necessary to negotiate for lower rates.

6) Provision of financial (including savings) training for groups.
7) Establishment of group emergency funds and food banks as a group insurance system.
8) Planning with flexibility to suit the specific financial and institutional situation in each project area.

Group Savings and Loans

Formal or informal group savings are to be encouraged from the outset because they: (a) strengthen the economic base of the groups and their capacity to increase production; (b) discipline the minds of the group members and indicate their commitment to groups; (c) facilitate access to credit; (d) relieve dependency on moneylenders and avoid the danger of over-indebtedness; and (e) foster cooperative spirit and self-reliance.

Group activities should begin with the help of savings rather then credit. Savings may start as a group welfare fund created and controlled by the group itself. Certain rules for managing a group savings fund are necessary, e.g. the ceiling, interest rates and time periods of loans to persons in or outside the group. When a fund becomes sizeable, the group may act against new members. In such cases new members may be allowed access to the fund in proportion to their contribution to the group fund.

It is in most instances beneficial to encourage groups to open a savings account in a nearby bank so that they become familiar with the banking system and can obtain loans in proportion to their savings. In this way savings are linked to loans; they may even be a prerequisite to become eligible for (project) loans. The application of contractual savings—always after consultation with the beneficiaries—is another possibility. In this system a certain percentage (say 10-15%) of a group loan is credited to the group savings account.

A Credit Guarantee Fund (CGF) may be established in a local credit institution (or a suitable substitute like a cooperative, credit union or an NGO) in order to encourage this institution to provide group loans from all its available credit funds. The CGF should ideally thus not function as a revolving fund or form the basis of such a fund created as a special line of credit for low-income people. The credit institution provides loans to groups to finance the inputs for their income-raising activities according to their group plans. An adequate procedure is that the loans are examined and approved by a local Loan Appraisal Committee. The loans will be provided against group liability: each member is responsible for the repayment of the total group loan. In other words loans are given with social instead of physical collateral, and as indicated earlier, at locally prevailing and not preferential, lower interest rates.

A Guarantee Fund should be used in accordance with the project document. After the project terminates it needs to be used to finance the same or similar rural poor-oriented participatory projects.

One of the main problems of groups in obtaining a bank loan is the usually considerable time spent to reach a bank and its usually complex credit procedures. On the other hand, some of the main problems of the banks is scarce familiarity with group liability, insufficient savings of the groups, the bank's bad experience with repayment rates in past conventional credit schemes and high transaction costs for a sizeable number of small loans (which are however reduced by giving "package" or group loans).

Practice shows that repayment rates on loans given to the disadvantaged people with group liability are generally higher than those on normal loans to "bankable," non-poor locals. In cases where defaulting occurs, the groups should exert social pressure on defaulting members and not the participation agents who should never perform the roles of loan collectors and controllers.

In various countries, selected banks have convenient small farmer credit schemes which could be tailored to meet the required credit demands for the group activities.

Finally, it should be stressed that the small groups are promoted for self-reliant development and not merely for credit delivery. Loans can only be provided when the groups are cohesive and active and show sufficient self-initiative and capability to prepare production plans.

Selection of a Suitable Bank

The main criteria for the selection of a suitable bank are that the bank:

1) has a widespread network of branches in rural areas, in particular in or near the project areas;
2) is willing to provide group loans to the so-called unbankable low-income people with social instead of physical liability;

3) accepts to incur initially higher transaction costs to attract new clients;
4) is agreeable that part of its top and field staff receives training in key participatory development issues;
5) is able to provide services through mobile loan officers; and
6) has preferably experience in working with low-income rural people.

The establishment of linkages with suitable financial institutions in a project area is difficult and time-consuming as they have no or scarce experience with credit for the rural poor and usually a low level of financial consolidation. Evidence in various countries shows that rural poor groups can administer finance provided training is given to them according to well-defined area-specific guidelines. This role is particularly important where the beneficiary groups carry out jointly an income-raising activity, which requires more elaborate financial management.

In some countries the group savings approach is followed, while in others individual savings are emphasized and individual deposits accepted by the collaborating banking institution.

The initial credit recovery rates vary considerably between participatory projects, but are usually far beyond normal loan recovery rates. This is because loan security is provided partly or totally through social collateral as a replacement of physical collateral which the rural poor usually cannot provide.

The general tendency in participatory projects is to apply statutory or normal interest rates for group savings and credit. In some countries where the project itself operates the credit activities, a special interest structure has been developed ranging from interest free loans for tools to 25 percent interest (including transport and marketing costs) for repayments made in kind.

There are so far only a few instances of the formation of special group emergency funds and/or food banks for insurance and food security purposes. However, certain groups have retained a large proportion of the surplus generated from group production activities as collective savings or investments. These resources, which cannot be drawn upon for individual purposes, could be used as emergency funds in case of accident, illness, death or crop failure of one or more group members. With current, unfavourable climatic conditions in many countries, the question of insurance coverage acquires added importance.

Variety in the Design and Operation of the Financial Component

The differences in the design and operation of the financial component in various participatory projects reflects the necessary adjustment and flexibility in relation to local socio-economic conditions, as illustrated by the following examples.

Particularly at the beginning of the implementation of a participatory project in Ghana, the country suffered from extreme inflation and the shortage of foreign exchange. To facilitate project operations, the guarantee fund was increased and transferred into an Input-Import Fund held in convertible currency outside the country, while the Ghanaian Government allocated funds sufficient to cover most local currency costs. The collaborating bank receives the inputs, which are then distributed to the beneficiaries on credit. The price of the inputs in local currency is determined by an agreement between the government, the project and the bank.

In Sierra Leone, where a participatory project itself provides the required credit, a detailed system has been developed for provision of loans and their recovery in cash or kind. In Kenya credit has also been administered by a participatory project, while in Zambia this is done by cooperative organizations.

Other local level project-specific arrangements include group marketing of surplus in Ghana to bypass middlemen who previously provided usurious loans; the formulation of by-laws to regulate financial and other group operations in Sierra Leone; and preparations for forming local credit unions in Ghana and Lesotho.

The Nimba County Rural Development Project in Liberia has been able to base its local financial activities on a modified form of traditional savings and credit groups ("susu"), thus exemplifying an imaginative adjustment to the socio-economic environment.

In Zimbabwe the Savings Development Movement constitutes a genuine grassroot action, where local people—mainly women—organize themselves in savings clubs for financial self-reliance and self-help production purposes. This movement was found to have an impressively decentralized structure and self-propelling capacity rooted in the local social system and culture, making it an interesting example of local arrangements for the financial component of a participatory project. It is now planned to establish a Savings Development Bank to provide the clubs with safe access to savings deposit facilities and to utilize the savings mobilization of the clubs more effectively for rural development purposes of value to the clubs. The proposed bank structure appears to have an interesting and viable set-up that could provide an example to participatory projects, particularly in their expansion phase, of a large and growing number of groups with expanding savings and credit activities, and which show a considerable degree of financial self-reliance. The participation of savings club members in the design and operations should be structured in such a way that the benefits go primarily to members of the savings clubs, with less emphasis on creating bank surpluses for general rural development purposes. Moreover, club members' savings deposited in such a bank should not be required to cover all credit issued.

Specific Seminars

Selected rural banking institutions are to be sensitized, for example through specific seminars on participatory principles in general, and the feasibility of group-based rural finance operations for participatory projects in particular. The banks should be included to enter into collaboration with participatory projects also by the following means:

1) Full briefing about financial guidelines for participatory projects, including the benefits of the group approach.
2) Detailed information about the financial arrangements and achievements of relevant ongoing participatory projects.
3) Channelling group savings to the prospective bank partner.
4) Encouraging credit repayment in cash to facilitate an increase in bank deposits.
5) In case a revolving fund should initially be necessary, the establishment of a revolving fund account with the bank should be given preference, with a view to transforming it as soon as possible into a fund in support of regular credit for rural poor groups from the bank. If no initial credit relationship with a bank is possible, the operation of the credit guarantee fund as a project revolving fund could be undertaken to show banks the feasibility of group credit.
6) Exposing bank officials to participatory project operations by inviting them to participate in field workshops and coordination committees.

Project Operations

Project operations for credit delivery at local level should not begin until the financial arrangements are organized satisfactorily. Clear criteria for credit eligibility, size and duration are to be worked out together with adequate procedures for assessing credit applications based on group production plans. Training should be given to project and bank staff as well as beneficiaries on the project-specific financial procedures.

A small Loan Approval or Credit Committee could be established in the Project Coordination or Participation Committee in order to give technical guidance to prepare group production plans and approve the required loans. The Credit Committee should include the concerned participation agent, extension worker, local bank branch manager and any other technical officer, as and when required.

Credit

Finally, credit from whatever source is essential for participatory development, but should not breed over-dependency on credit or constitute the main incentive for group formation. In order to avoid these risks in various projects groups become only eligible for credit after a certain period during which they show their capacity to form a cohesive group, to work with their own very small resources and to create a group fund from their (tiny) savings.

Participation Agents/Group Promoters

Participatory change agents may be designated as animators, facilitators, development activists, field action promoters, group organizers or motivators, etc.

Roles

The group promoters are the key persons to render a participatory project successful. They assist the disadvantaged people in their action area:

a) to identify viable economic and social group activities;

b) to form small groups for these self-selected activities;

c) to obtain—as liaison persons—from the delivery system the required training and support (credit, inputs, etc.) for the group activities; and

d) to perform the necessary action-research and self-evaluation.

Group promoters are animators, enablers and catalysts of the groups (to be) formed and thus the pivotal grassroot workers for promoting a local receiving system. They work with and not only for the people and avoid leadership roles so that after their departure people are not left "orphanized".

The tasks of group promoters are different from those of normal extension workers, for the following reasons: 1) government extension workers are responsible for all the people of a village or area, including the non-poor, whereas the group promoters are dedicated only or at least mainly to the disadvantaged people; 2) the group promoters have to live and work with the village people for two, three years whereafter they withdraw, whereas extension workers usually do not live with their target population and enjoy also a more permanent assignment; and 3) the group promoters are (or at least should be) mainly accountable to the rural poor groups, whereas extensionists respond to and are supervised by their government agency.

A group promoter is thus not a typical government official, teacher, welfare worker or leader

Selection

Group promoters should be chosen carefully: the principal qualifications required are:

1) experience in working with people and local organizations in rural areas and well-acquainted with the problems of the poor;

2) capable, motivated and committed to live, work at least two years with the poor in the field;

willing to leave any decision-making and leadership to the people, promoting among them attitudes of self-help and self-reliance;

4) familiar with the local language and culture; they should thus come preferably from similar rural areas in the same district or from the same ethnic or linguistic group, but not from the project area, in order to be able to better introduce new ideas for action to the people. However, in some cases group promoters can be and are recruited from and posted in their own village or zone of origin. Apart from cost savings, the advantage is that their experience and know-how could be utilized more easily also after withdrawal of a project;

5) desirable qualifications are: rural background, a minimum of secondary level education and experience in community or rural development as well as in such fields as social work, elementary economy or sociology, agriculture or extension.

There should be flexibility on the gender. Preference for men or women should be determined by the context. There should not be rigidity on the number of males and of females to be employed as group promoters in a project.

From the above roles and required qualifications of group promoters, it follows that their many-sided tasks require in practice a full-time availability and secondly that beneficiary participation can be promoted much more efficiently and with less cost by locally recruited staff.

In projects which unfortunately have no arrangements and sufficient funds to recruit full-time group promoters, the roles of the latter could be performed in part and, of course, with less impact, by ad-hoc trained project staff who have other technical duties. However, such staff should preferably also be local and their other tasks such that they are to be performed in the field in direct contact with the intended beneficiaries. It is moreover to be stressed that anyhow all project and local staff needs to be briefed and trained on-goingly on the participatory issues and operations of the project.

The search, selection, recruitment, training and guidance of group promoters are important operations in a participatory project. In order to find capable group promoters, which is often problematical, candidates must be recruited from wherever they are available in a country: government agencies, NGOs and/or otherwise. Each source of recruitment has advantages and disadvantages. Several participatory projects obtained well performing field workers from the government extension field staff. This increases project sustainability as the recurrent costs are lower, and may moreover enhance project expansion and multiplication.

In some countries, it is desirable to give preference to candidates with secondment prospects as they will expectedly continue to propagate the participatory approach after they return to their seconding agency. In this way the latter agencies will be sensitized and enabled to better serve the rural poor. Group promoters on secondment from government should be given their annual income increases and seniority promotions. Participation agents need, of course, very much specific initial and follow-up training especially in group dynamics, group enterprise management, savings/credit and other key topics.

Posting and Payment

In the project area(s) a number of village clusters are to be identified during project preparation. At least two group promoters (one female and one male) are to be assigned to each village cluster; the female group promoters will of course give special attention to women. Teams of husband-wife couples would be the most desirable field staff.

Ideally the male and female field workers should live in the action villages with the people for constant availability and guidance. Depending upon the local culture, unmarried female field workers may however, have to reside in a nearby centre. Each couple of group promoters starts to work in the core community of a village cluster.

Important is the image of group promoters amongst the locals in their action area. Their role should repeatedly be explained to all villagers and also shown in practice. Through their helpful spirit, kind attitudes, wise considerate manners and patient actions, they will gradually be regarded as animators and guides and not as typical top-down officials or aliens interfering with the local culture and living habits. It will be of primordial importance to build up gradually confidential friendship relationships in their action communities starting with the poor and thereafter with the less poor villagers: otherwise they could be regarded by the poor as being mainly on the side of the better-off.

It would also be strategic to ask the influential and other villagers prior to any action whether they really accept in their community the proposed outsiders as participation agents.

As group promoters have hard pioneer tasks and work often in the evenings and on non-working days when the poor are available for meetings, they should receive just payment: in various projects they receive e.g. a hardship allowance or the like on top of their usually low field worker salary. They should also obtain means of transport (motorbikes or bikes). The latter are best given "on purchase/lease", that is the (motor) bikes become the property of the group promoters after they have paid them back to the project in say 24 monthly instalments. This guarantees better proper operation and maintenance.

Expected Performance in Group Formation

For the planning of a beneficiary participation component, it can be assumed that in not too unfavourable circumstances, each of the group promoters can help the beneficiaries to organize themselves into a total of at least 11 groups (on the average 15 groups) over three years. The third year is in particular also needed for consolidation of all groups formed. Each group promoter will thus reach directly over three years some 150 households (taking a rather low average group size of 10 members) which means an involvement of at least 900 rural people (assuming an average household size of 6 persons).

Disengagement of group promoters. While a group promoter is promoting self-reliance of her/his groups, she/he is working towards self-redundancy in her/his action area, so that she/he can be useful elsewhere. Self-reliance can be promoted by: involving the group members in all activities so as to build their capabilities, developing leadership skills through training and rotation of leadership functions, encouraging group-to-group learning, teaching record keeping, helping to establish linkages and to build up savings, reducing visits to groups and ensuring the presence of one or more group members whenever she/he contacts the line agencies, banks, etc. Self-reliance may not always mean total disengagement of group promoters: the latter could be maintained by inter-group associations to perform certain specific functions.

Career Prospects

Many non-seconded, well-motivated group promoters feel the temporary character of their employment and the lack of career prospects as a serious problem. The participatory approach implies a long term process and effort in any developing country. Consequently, well-performing group promoters will most likely find opportunities and/or demand to continue working with the poor after their assignment with a project as exemplified below. Employment of group promoters on secondment is of course often preferable to ensure their career prospects.

1) The participatory project itself, once sufficiently successful, usually will be expanded. The implementing agency (line department and/or NGO) will then require a number of experienced senior group promoters or coordinators, in particular for the training of new group promoters to work in extended or new project areas.

2) Graduated or anyhow gifted group promoters may desire to follow an academic career, particularly in such fields as applied development sociology and economy, agricultural extension; etc. They conceive the experience gained with the poor as an enlargement of practical knowledge regarding the promotion of self-development of the rural poor. Experience shows that research and training institutions are increasingly eager to employ group promoters, in particular those who gave special attention to action research. Moreover, some projects provide fellowships to selected group promoters for professional advancement.

3) As the magnitude of rural poverty is growing, various governments tend to encharge one or more agencies with the planning and/or implementation of specific rural poor oriented programmes and projects. Accordingly also the demand for capable participation agents will increase. This is still more the case with UN supported programmes for poverty alleviation.

4) Although the rural poor groups will federate themselves and become eventually self-propelling, they may still need help in or outside the normal government delivery structure for solving production, marketing, processing, etc. problems. Experienced group promoters could perform valuable functions on payment for inter-group associations, primary or secondary level cooperatives or the like.

Participatory Training

Objectives and Characteristics

The main training objectives are; a) to improve the economic and social conditions of the poor; b) to assist the beneficiaries to become active and productive group members and leaders; c) to encourage group promoters and other supporting staff to adjust their standard training to meet the needs of the rural poor; and d) to stimulate all project participants to develop adequate training contents, methods and also materials.

The essential training characteristics are: 1) participatory; every trainer is a trainee and vice-versa; 2) on-going: the training is conceived as a continuous process and is designed and carried out within the context of any project action to improve the production. income and social conditions of the beneficiaries; 3) pragmatic and problem solving: the training is based on solving immediate and recognized problems; 4) in-service, on-the-job, on-site training, learning by doing; 5) self-learning: individually but also group-or team-wise; 6) reality-exposure: both trainers and trainees are to be exposed to the realities of the rural people and their living areas; and 7) dialogue and cooperation on equal terms; no we-they dichotomy between staff and beneficiaries.

Conventional training has a top-down approach, is entirely pre-planned and uses mainly the classroom (teacher-pupils) method. Instead participatory training is based on the felt needs of the trainees, recognizes that the poor can also be resource persons, stresses learning from each other, facilitates building of team work and links knowledge much more directly with action and problem-solving.

The innovative training approaches include: 1) stimulation of farmer-to-fanner and group-to-group training to attain self-reliance; 2) the trainees are not passive recipients and objects, but subjects of training; 3) training in specific technical fields is not exclusively given to group leaders (whose workload often hinders proper dissemination of the know-how obtained) but also and preferably to group members selected by one or more groups. This will enhance shared leadership, inter-group cooperation, self-reliance and farmers becoming informal grassroot extensionists.

Moreover, an accounting system of payment for services rendered could be developed by the beneficiaries themselves in order to decrease over-dependence on outside aid, while the delivery system could gradually obtain adequate cost recovery.

Training Target Groups, Personnel and Committees

The main "target groups" are: a) the intended beneficiaries; b) the project staff, including the participation agents; and c) supporting government and NGO staff such as line agency and other (field) officers, but also local leaders and influent ials.

The trainers must have practical experience. They include: the group promoters and other project staff, technical officers of the delivery system, experienced farmers/fishermen and also successful groups which enlighten, train and motivate other ones.

A small training committee which would include interested technical officers, group promoters and beneficiaries, could be very useful to assist in the planning, implementation and evaluation of feasible training programmes.

Beneficiary Training

The types of topics are the following:

a) Certain general subject matters which aim at enhancing beneficiary participation through efficient group formation and action and should be given to all intended beneficiaries. These matters include group dynamics, shared leadership, planning of group activities, savings and credit, accounting, cooperative management, monitoring and evaluation as well as negotiating and bargaining. In some projects certain basic issues like fostering thrift habits and overcoming bad customs such as irrational spending, drinking, gambling, etc. are also very much stressed.

   Specialized training is to be given according to the type of project as well as to the specific, felt group needs. For example, in crop production, small livestock development, soil and water conservation, small-scale fishery, aquaculture, forestry, group marketing, etc., but also in non-farm activities such as (agro-) processing, weaving, tailoring, pottery, production of house-building materials or of artisanal items in wood, bamboo, metal, leather, etc., as well as maintenance and transport.

c) Training could furthermore be given in: home life and community development, in particular for women: health, sanitation, first aid, nutrition, child care, etc., but also management, leadership, village development, etc.

d) Other very useful training subject matters include: legal and procedural matters, e.g. land reform, tenancy rights, mortgaging, wages, employment (rural works programme, etc.), the use of banks, and of local administration etc. Pragmatic information on these topics is frequently not or badly communicated to the poor

e) Functional literacy for adult women and men, which help them to analyse their problems, plan actions and also to reduce their dependency upon literate villagers or group members.

The training opportunities include: 1) short courses, preferably given at field (village) level; 2) advice and consultation between group members, group promoters and technical officers; 3) information given by knowledgeable successful farmers or fishermen; 4) exposure media: audio-visual aids, radio (rural broadcasting programmes), films, slideshows, public meetings, etc.; 5) demonstrations organized jointly with group members for improved crop cultivations, livestock rearing, aquaculture, handicrafts, etc.; 6) written extension materials; 7) simple newsletters prepared together with the beneficiaries; 8) initial and successive field action workshops; 9) inter-group exchange visits; 10) (inter-)group evaluation exercises; and 11) where appropriate, role playing and socio-drama.

Training equipment and materials. Each group needs at least extension materials, a blackboard and elementary stationery. Each cluster of groups needs a flannel or black board, a camera, folding exhibition boards, transistor radios and possibly a slide-projector and a videotape recorder. The local production by the groups of simple training materials is to be encouraged.

Training of Participation Agents (Group Promoters), the Project Coordinator and Other Project Staff

This training, a central project operation, aims at: a) introducing the field workers into the approaches and procedures of participatory development; b) fostering adequate attitudes, motivations and team-spirit; c) experimenting innovative ways of poverty eradication; d) teaching basic technical topics which are needed for group guidance and are also taught to all group members; in particular: philosophy and methods of participatory development, group dynamics, savings and credit, accounting and monitoring and evaluation); and e) stimulating group self-learning and self-development of training contents, methods and materials.

Also the project coordinator needs of course, to be trained as early as possible by the implementing agency and FAO (or another agency) in all the aforementioned topics.

The initial orientation training of group promoters should be well structured and sufficiently long. It should mainly consist of familiarization with the objectives and operational aspects of the project.

An inception training workshop for group promoters and other project staff is to be given for at least three weeks in or near the project area with not more than 30 participants including the candidate group promoters (half of whom female), the project staff and selected key officials of the delivery system. It is recommendable to invite twice as many candidate participation agents as needed initially in the project in order to obtain a reserve pool of these field workers. The curriculum should be pragmatic and include work experience presentations by the participants and course evaluation exercises. "Sandwich" type training (classroom and field experience combined) is very recommendable.

The group promoters need thereafter initial field training of 2-3 months which is at the same time the starting period for their field action in the project area. They will learn team-wise, among others, to prepare and carry out village and household surveys, to solve work and living problems met in the field, to cooperate with the delivery system and to plan the project initiation workshop.

The follow-up training of participation agents includes: a) periodic (preferably monthly) review and evaluation meetings for group promoters and other staff to evaluate team performance, to identify and solve work problems and to prepare workplans; b) field action workshops; c) refresher courses in such subjects as new rural development policies and programmes, innovative income-raising activities and credit schemes; d) issue of a periodic (project) newsletter; and e) exchange visits of group members. group promoters and officials between different areas of their own and similar participatory projects.

Training of Government and NGO Staff as well as Local Leaders

This training aims at familiarizing those involved in the project with the approach and procedures of the project and its participation efforts, the handicaps of the poor to have access to the delivery agencies and the roles of the latter to help solve the problems of the rural poor. In many instances, the above mentioned officials and leaders need to be to a certain extent "de-trained" and then re-trained to perform well their participatory roles. On-going exchange of experiences and views particularly in field workshops, is crucial in this learning process.

The training opportunities for the government and other staff consists mainly of their participation in: 1) training courses for group promoters and other project staff; 2) field workshops; 3) briefing sessions with the use of promotional materials; 4) project coordination committees; 5) the programming, provision, and evaluation of beneficiary training; 6) intra-or inter-country seminars related to the objectives and issues of the project; and 7) inter-group and/or inter-project exchange visits.

Participatory Action Research

Conventional and Participatory Action Research

The essential differences between conventional and participatory action research is that in the latter research the poor are actively involved in all stages: both researcher and respondent are active including in the design of research instruments, interviewing, data analysis as well as in the reporting, evaluation and discussion of the results.

The research results are to be shared with all project participants. Participatory research is to be included in any participatory project as it is indispensable firstly for the collection and analysis of the necessary information on the action areas and the disadvantaged people and secondly for project expansion and replication. It is to be carried out during the entire project period by the participation agents and other project staff together with the local people, in particular the actual and potential group members. Guidance in the design, methods of collection, tabulation, analysis, interpretation and reporting is to be provided by rural poor-oriented economic and social research institutions. The latter obtain in this way also opportunities to learn the participatory development and research concepts and methods. In cases where the services of a research institution prove too costly, it is preferable to obtain the help of well-motivated experts on an individual basis who in many countries appeared to be available.

Objectives

The main research objectives are:

1) to select the project area(s) and within these the village-clusters where the group formation actions will start;
2) to identify and classify the rural poor and non-poor in the action areas and to obtain pragmatic information on their living conditions, needs and aspirations by means of area, village and household surveys;
3) to determine whether, how and to what extent the locals are so far involved in development efforts, in particular through rural people's and other local organizations. Where needed, it should also be clarified on one side why most low income people do not actively participate in these efforts, and, on the other side, why most of the local people's organizations, if any, in their present form do not attract them;

4) the potentials, efforts and problems of the formation of rural poor groups from scratch and/or within or from existing groups and organizations;

5) to plan and implement together with the beneficiaries, group promoters, project and line department staff as well as, where opportune, with ad-hoc experts—viable income-generating and other group activities. In various instances small feasibility studies may be needed before engaging in such activities;

   to plan and conduct appropriate training programmes for the beneficiaries as well as the concerned line department and other staff. Furthermore, to provide grassroot data to the field workshops of the project;

7) to develop and sustain a workable participatory monitoring and evaluation system;

8) the research may also include case studies of successful and deficient rural poor groups;

9) identification and/or development of appropriate technologies for the small farmers or fishermen with the support of the concerned line departments and other technical bodies

Surveys

To attain the above objectives, simplified action area, village and household surveys are needed periodically. This research may be based on the interesting methods and procedures developed in various countries. The surveys will help to establish economic and social benchmarks, which highlight the status of the beneficiaries in the initial phase of the project so that any progress can be evaluated successively by the project participants.

A baseline survey, to be conducted before the field action starts, is useful but only if the grassroot people are really involved. This type of survey may be part of project preparation and serve among other, for target group identification. Sampling of households is to be avoided as this may lead to resentment of those not included in the sample. Only those data are to be collected which are really relevant for project operations. The outcome should be used for discussion by the group promoters and the groups.

Some constraints to conduct a baseline survey early in the project cycle are: a) scarcity of suitable research staff in the initial phase; b) the information obtained on the intended beneficiaries may be insufficiently reliable as their confidence has to be gained first through the project's field actions; and c) lack of funds for this project preparation action. In fact the survey is to be kept low-cost including by being quite selective in data collecting. Moreover in areas where projects with grassroot people were or are being implemented, many useful data may already be available.

Participatory Monitoring and On-Going Evaluation (PMOE)

PMOE should be a management tool above all for the beneficiaries, but also for the project staff, government agencies, NGOs and donors. It is indispensable for securing active participation of all project participants in the assessment of the progress of a project.

Participatory Monitoring

In order to obtain useful information on project progress, successes and failures and to develop a methodology for its expansion and replication, the beneficiaries, participation agents and other project participants should all be involved in developing and applying a locally workable monitoring and evaluation system.

Participatory monitoring is a process of measuring, data collecting, processing and communicating to assist the beneficiaries and project staff in decision-making. The purpose is to provide all concerned with information as to whether project objectives are being achieved and whether the operations, performance and impact of a project is "on course". The information should also indicate inadequate operations, shortfalls in performance and discrepancies between planned objectives or predicted impact and those achieved in order to modify inadequate objectives and rectify project deficiencies.

In order to set up a workable participatory monitoring system the beneficiaries are to be motivated in particular and this implies that:

a) their felt needs, desires and problems are taken into account;

b) simple, understandable and attractive methods are introduced and repeatedly explained; and

c) the results are presented to them on a continuous basis and by adequate means including regular group discussions and audio-visual aids.

Participatory monitoring is to be conceived from the beginning as part of the group formation and action process. Therefore, not only the baseline and benchmark data need to be recorded, discussed and kept to be used later, but also effective recording is to be undertaken of inputs, outputs, workplans and progress made in strengthening the cohesiveness of the groups and/or organizations of the beneficiaries.

Records are to be kept of the (bi-)weekly group meetings on major problems discussed, decisions made, actions undertaken. This is to be done by each group with elementary (standard) forms designed with the groups, and contained in some kind of simple log-book. The items of such forms are to be reviewed periodically in order to verify their usefulness. Each group has to learn also a minimum of bookkeeping in order to keep track of inputs and outputs related to credit and savings. This bookkeeping goes parallel with the recording of group loans and repayment by the agency (bank) concerned. A systematic accumulation of data on loans and repayment as well as simple cost-benefit analyses give essential insights into the quality of groups to manage their affairs and improve their conditions.

The group members would also benefit greatly when each of their households would record cash in-and outflows on simple schemes.

Monitoring is usually hard to introduce to (illiterate) peasants. It can be made simple for them by using e.g. symbols, pictures and graphics. Even literate children of group members may be engaged as "secretaries*' in groups in which none of the members is literate. Training of group members in functional literacy remains of course, of utmost importance.

Monitoring could give much satisfaction to the beneficiaries and also considerably facilitate benchmark and/or other studies including on the "thorny" issues of income and expenditure of households.

In sum, the main tools of participatory monitoring are: 1) recording of group meetings, workplans, progress made, problems met, etc. in group log-books; 2) group bookkeeping for inputs, outputs, credits, savings, etc.; and 3) action-research.

Participatory Evaluation

On-going evaluation is the systematic analysis by beneficiaries and project staff concerned of the monitored information with a view to enabling them where necessary, to adjust or redefine the project's objectives, policies, institutional arrangements, resources and activities.

Participatory evaluation should also take into account the needs and desires of the beneficiaries and include self-evaluation on an individual and group basis by all project participants in order to strengthen local capabilities for self-learning and joint problem-solving. In particular the rural people themselves are to discuss what progress they are making and how to overcome what problems. The rural poor groups should also evaluate the activities of the delivery system in order to improve its performance. This helps groups to "talk back", to pick up issues which have not been dealt with by the delivery system and to identify its bottlenecks. The results may be brought up in field workshops.

If evaluation is done in the above ways, it will stimulate critical awareness and motivation for better group self-management. The self-evaluation results need to be presented systematically to other project participants at local and higher levels.

The evaluation should include not only the tangible and measurable results of group activities but as much as possible also their spill-over benefits that improve the group members' economic, social and integral human development. For example, acquiring skills in speech, writing, presenting ideas logically and clearly, overcoming shyness in dealing with officials and conducting meetings; furthermore, learning to solve problems including household conflicts through dialogue, inculcating thrift habits. record keeping and money management techniques as well as gradually reducing vices like gambling, alcoholism and gossiping, and also group-wise helping persons in acute necessities like house building or land preparation.

The main evaluation tools based on those for participatory monitoring, are:

1) group promoter log-books containing an overall picture of the group recordings;
2) group promoter diaries for the "private" observations and reflections on the process and results of beneficiary participation. In these diaries attention is to be given to possible difficulties, conflicts and setbacks. Logbooks and diaries help the group promoters to learn from each other's experience;
3) periodically (preferably monthly) review and evaluation meetings of group promoters;

4) periodic (e.g. quarterly) group and inter-group evaluation sessions;
5) newsletters in the local language based on information provided by the groups;
6) evaluation studies and surveys; and
7) periodic field workshops, a total reflection upon the whole field action process by project staff, beneficiaries and concerned outsiders.

The above listed cools should all be used to promote a constant two-way flow of information between groups and the project staff.

Estimated Costs to Promote Beneficiary Participation

Cost-Effectiveness

The cost-effectiveness of the participatory approach is for the time being difficult to determine as economic and social parameters are only in part adequate to measure costs and benefits. The assessment of the latter is however, important as it indicates economic and financial viability and facilitates communication with officials and experts in government, aid and donor agencies who development predominantly from an economic point of view.

Benefits

The main direct benefits of rural poor groups include the following:

1) income generation,
2) employment generation,
3) capital formation, also by means of savings,
4) accumulation of other (tangible) assets,
5) access to credit,
6) development of community assets,
7) upgrading of skills.

The indirect benefits include:

1) on-going exchanges of information, experiences and views,
2) better management of group enterprises,
3) ability to articulate and solve problems,
4) development of grassroot organizations (institution-building),

5) more social security through group-belonging,
6) prevention or resolution of conflicts at household, group and village levels through dialogues,
7) spirit of participation, cooperation, sharing, self-confidence and self-reliance, other indirect "spill-over" benefits may include:
8) skills in speech and writing of the poor, and presenting ideas coherently and clearly.
9) overcoming shyness in dealing with officials and conducting meetings,
10) inculcating thrift habits,
11) acquiring ability in record keeping, money management and responsible spending, e.g. by reducing the expenditure of costly customary ceremonies,
12) reduction of vices like gambling, alcoholism and gossiping, and group-wise helping persons in acute necessities like house building and land preparations.

The direct benefits can be measured mostly quantitatively to a sufficiently reliable extent, whereas the indirect ones can mostly only be described qualitatively.

A participatory project may very well be cost-effective when also its indirect benefits are assessed adequately and added to the direct, quantifiable outputs. There is however a great need for studies to develop a methodology to determine the cost-effectiveness of participatory projects.

Since the groups in participatory projects select usually low-risk activities, it may safely be assumed that the benefits outweigh considerably the costs both for beneficiaries and implementing government agencies and/or NGOs. Moreover, most governments in developing countries are charged with the responsibility of social uplift of the disadvantaged classes of people. Participatory projects assist in organizing the needy and thus enable the governments to provide services to these people and thus to discharge effectively in part their mandate. The projects offer to beneficiaries, among other advantages, economies of scale and social benefits by building organizational capabilities; they offer above all effective receiving/utilization systems.

Costs

A participatory process is usually supported in its initial stages by external staff and funds from local, national and/or other sources. However, the costs of the specific participatory elements or operations in a larger project are relatively minimal in relation to those of technical and other project components and are also temporary. The very essence of the participatory approach is its strong orientation towards self-reliance which implies, among other things, low and decreasing recurrent costs and cost-recovery by the beneficiaries. Although usually a participatory process thus needs some "start-up" external aid from a development or donor agency (never to be a major actor!), the basic objective is that the process becomes self-propelling as soon as possible and also expandable to larger numbers of poor people with no or minimal outside personnel and funds and thus with no or very low recurrent costs.

Extra Costs

The extra costs to make a project participatory consist of the following:

a) Financing in total or in part a relatively small number of locally recruited field workers who act for a limited project period (say three years) as participation agents. The latter could be and in several instances are selected from a country's extension staff and in these cases the field workers need only special training in group formation and action and preferably also some additional "hardship" allowances for their pioneer work. Also means of transport are to be provided to the field workers.

(b) Extra funds are required also for one or more inception and follow-up training field workshops on the participatory approach and procedures to be held in or near the project area(s), and some periodic (yearly) follow-up evaluation workshops including at national level.

c) Some extra funds are moreover needed for training in (beneficiary) participation, particularly in group dynamics and other topics directly related to group formation and action.

d) Finally, some limited funds are to be made available for participatory socio-economic research as well as for grassroot monitoring and evaluation, both regarding the formation, action, performance and constraints of the groups.

Field Experience

Various elements which have been taken from field experience and illustrate the above points follow hereunder.

FAO launched under its People's Participation Programme since 1982 twelve self-sustained pilot projects in Africa. Asia and Latin America. Eight of these projects have a three year period of field actions completed and show the following results and costs.

Over a period of on the average three years in total 864 groups were formed and guided with the help of 77 GPs (of whom 49 or 64% were female); each GP assisted thus in the formation of on the average 11 groups.

The 864 groups had in total 10.557 members: on the average 12 members per group. The eight projects served accordingly in total about 10.557 families and reached at least 63.342 beneficiaries when assuming an average family size of 6 persons.

In conclusion, on the average each project covered in its first three years of field action two project areas with in total ten GPs (of whom six were female). The latter promoted in total 108 small groups with 1.320 members. This means that each project reached in-depth on the average at least 1,320 families and covered thus not less than 7,920 beneficiaries.

1) Contractual services: (about 21% of the donor contribution) to finance: a) the basic salaries, hardship allowances ("topping up") and travel costs of the project staff (usually one coordinator and the group promoters (when seconded or recruited from the field action villages themselves, these costs are of course, lower); b) action-research on the groups (including small feasibility studies); c) local expertise and skilled, non-voluntary labour as and when required for possible physical works needed for certain selected group activities; d) project evaluation including by an independent institution; e) preparation of reports.
2) General operating expenses (about 8% of the donor budget) including part of rental and maintenance of equipment, communications and miscellaneous expenditures.
3) Supplies, equipment and materials, first for a Credit Guarantee Fund (about 16% of the budget) as a security for the lending institution to provide from its funds collateral-free group loans for inputs. Secondly, this budget item includes also various types of equipment including means of transport (13% of the budget), usually one vehicle for the participation coordinator and motorcycles for the group promoters.
4) Training on participation and other issues (about 17% of the budget) of beneficiaries as well as project and other supporting staff. This

includes: courses, training materials, field workshops in the project areas and fellowships for well-performing group promoters.

5) Personnel services and official travel (about 13% of the budget): the salaries, travel and daily subsistence allowance of short-term local and/ or expatriate consultants for technical backstopping (in total for three to six person/months).

6) Project servicing costs (about 7% of the budget) and special factor for inflation (5% of the budget).

The proportional sizes of the various donor budget items vary per project of course, and in practice are also in part interchangeable as participatory projects or components need a flexible design and budget.

With the foregoing global indications the order of size of the cost of group formation and guidance can be roughly estimated for any participatory project according to its number of intended beneficiaries and/or of small groups' to be formed as well as to its number and size of action areas.

The amount of $175,000 includes all budget items of the earlier indicated self-sustained participatory projects except the credit guarantee fund which forms on the average 16% of the donor budget. The credit fund has been excluded from the cost estimates because many larger projects dealing with the rural poor. include already a credit fund or provisions to obtain such fund for income-raising activities of the beneficiaries.

On the basis of the above given costs per project and beneficiary (which refer to small, self-sustaining pilot projects and are thus relatively higher than for other, larger projects). It can be assessed that the cost of effective beneficiary participation viz. by means of group formation and action, is in the initial three years about $220,000 for 10.000 beneficiaries or about $162,000 for every 100 groups formed and guided. In subsequent years these costs are far lower as many groups become more self-sufficient and need thus much less GP assistance. Moreover, well-performing groups have considerable spread effects: they facilitate the formation of new groups.

It should also be reminded that the average cost per beneficiary for larger (multi-million dollar) projects with sizeable technical components and target groups may, however, well be lower due to economies of scale.

The above figures are of course to be taken only as very global and rough estimates as firstly the participatory projects or components considered vary in size and design and secondly in each country various factors may considerably affect the specific costs of beneficiary participation as well as the total project costs. For example, the local salary levels of the group promoters, the availability and cost of transport, the experience of the poor with group action and the accessibility of the beneficiaries. The latter factor is related among others, to the remoteness, geography and physical infrastructure (roads, etc.) of the action areas and the type of local settlement patterns ranging from scattered to concentrated.

In conclusion, to render a conventional project fully participatory some elements like employment of group organizers, working through small groups, training, field workshops, action research and evaluation need to be added. These elements mean however, a far better design and chance of success of a project. The long-term economic and social benefits of such a project will outweigh considerably the relatively low additional costs.

In some instances extra budgetary allocations may not even be needed, but rather a reallocation of existing funds and staff. It is thus in certain cases preferable to reallocate existing funds and personnel to participatory projects or programmes rather than to increase public budgets and employment. Furthermore, as explained, participatory elements will cost comparatively less than self-sustained (pilot) participatory projects in isolation (like FAO's PPP) as there will be economy in administration, coordination, supervision, technical guidance and evaluation.

Project Continuation, Expansion and Multiplication

Continuation: Need for Process Approach

Projects with adequate beneficiary participation provide the means to self-organized rural people, group promoters and other staff to make full use of their skills and resources for basic rural development. The major building blocks come from the communities themselves unlike many conventional development projects which often require sizeable funds, technical expertise and extensive administrative support including for "reaching" the beneficiaries.

A participatory project aims at institution-building at grassroot level by promoting beneficiary groups and at higher levels by adapting and/or creating delivery agencies which serve effectively the rural weak. For this wide scope a project must overcome various constraints and bottlenecks of such a nature that it simply cannot become self-sustaining and illustrative for expansion and widespread multiplication in a few years.

Consequently the conventional project duration of three to five years is too short for a participatory project and can only be considered as the first stage in a complex participatory process sustained by a rolling programme to attain tangible results and spread effects.

Another basic point is that the investment in manpower and other resources would be underutilized, if not actually wasted, if a project is discontinued because of lack of outside support. For all these reasons a participatory project usually requires some additional years of limited outside assistance for a successful continuation and expansion.

At this point the question arises: when is a participatory project as a whole mature to the extent that external assistance to it can be terminated? Although field research on this topic is lacking, some of the characteristics or indicators of project maturity could be the following:

1) degree of economic viability and profitability at group and family levels, shown e.g. by mobilization of savings, types and numbers of profit-making activities, continuing access of the poor to the delivery system and economic self-reliance of the groups;
2) the types, levels and spread of technical, entrepreneurial, leadership and other skills acquired by the group members; furthermore ability to tap and use technological know-how;
3) degree of social development and political recognition, shown e.g. by the maturity of the groups, decision-making capabilities, level of participation and leadership roles of women and youth, efficient links with agencies which deliver services and facilities, level of literacy, and participation of group members in local institutions like cooperatives and government bodies.

Other factors to be considered before terminating external assistance include: (1) The self-sustainability of the groups which do not any more enjoy the guidance of the group promoters; the time taken by a group to become self-propelling is of course, location-specific and varies between 3 and 7 years. (2) The capability and willingness of the implementing agency to manage the project and to handle its expansion; and (3) the political will and efforts of a government to incorporate the participatory approach of the project in its policies, plans and/or programmes.

While outside support is normally indispensable in the initial project phases, strong and systematic efforts must also be made to sensitize policy and decision-makers of relevant government bodies and NGOs to provide more and more local support so that a project can continue and expand in a self-supporting way. It is essential to convince decision-makers that participatory projects are basic to enact sustained rural development. In this perspective each country concerned needs one or more strategies to expand participatory rural development.

Expansion and Multiplication

The wealth of experience accumulated in participatory projects indicates that beneficiary participation can be successfully planned and implemented under a variety of socio-economic conditions and with different types of beneficiaries. However, project planners at national and international levels may still be reserved and this is mainly due to the lack of information on participatory projects and their achievements. Insufficient efforts were made to diffuse participatory experience and encouraging results among key policy and decision-makers. Another reason is that participatory projects have usually a low visibility because they stress—in addition to productive activities—education for participation, and they are furthermore implemented mainly at grassroot level and on a limited scale, except in some countries like e.g. Nepal, Sri Lanka and Thailand.

By expansion of a project is meant hereunder an extension of its operations in new areas which are adjacent to the project's initial ones and by multiplication a propagation of (part of) its operations in other, non-adjacent areas of a country. By the way, multiplication is a better term than replication which has a connotation of "mechanical" or rubber stamp repetition.

Expansion and multiplication of a participatory project may refer to two different types of cases:

a) a project as a whole is launched—with an improved design—in one or more adjacent (expansion) or other areas (multiplication) in a country;

b) only the project's beneficiary participation component (or its successful elements and/or methods) is propagated in the same project area or adjacent ones (expansion) or in other areas (multiplication).

The type of propagation under b) may proceed in two ways viz. either applying the beneficiary participation approach and methods of a project in other projects or programmes, or applying it autonomously under the normal delivery system. The types of propagation under b) are naturally more difficult but still possible, in particular in adjacent zones affected by the spread effects of the field actions of a participatory project.

In this perspective there is a great need for ongoing exchange of information and also cooperation (e.g. pooling of staff, training materials, and other resources) between the participatory projects in a country and outside. This would stimulate the multiplication of genuine beneficiary or rural people's participation which should become an essential part of the overall development strategy of each country (M. Perera, op. cit., 1988).

The Planning of Project Expansion and Multiplication

Given the need of a process approach a participatory project is to be conceived as a first phase of a longer process. Therefore it turns out usually necessary to prepare—as early as possible before a project terminates—a flexible plan for the next phase. The data required for this exercise are to be obtained mainly from the project's monitoring and evaluation system as well as from an evaluation study carried out by independent experts. A well-devised monitoring and evaluation system is the only way for a project to ensure firstly proper management, and secondly that its participatory trial-and-error efforts can be shared and provide sufficient evidence to outsiders that the project deserves support for its continuation, expansion and/or multiplication in other areas of a country.

With the information obtained it will be possible to improve the design of a successive project phase, that is e.g. to redefine objectives and to plan and coordinate better certain operations, in particular those required for wider and more active beneficiary participation.

For the preparation of an expansion or multiplication plan the following points appear important.

1) A first necessity is to engage in dialogues with governmental policy-, programme- and decision-makers at national and lower levels.
2) The plan should stress consolidation of the project's ongoing institution-building process that is of the existing beneficiary groups and organizations (federations) as well as of the service delivery agencies. Without these consolidation efforts the project may lose its quality during its expansion phase. By quality is primarily meant

effective management, solid self-run groups engaging in viable economic and social activities, well-tailored training programmes, qualified and motivated participation agents and other staff, fruitful cooperation with the delivery system, and meaningful research as well as monitoring and evaluation. The risks of expansion are indeed dilution and distortion of the key features of a participatory project.

3) The new areas to be covered by a project during its expansion phase should preferably be adjacent to its existing earlier ones. Such concentration facilitates project management and supervision, mutual information and cooperation between actual and potential (intended) beneficiaries as well as service agencies. In other words concentration leads to better spread effects and has eventually a wider and larger, because aggregated impact. The advantages are in part comparable to those of the village cluster approach. For the identification of new areas extensive action-oriented field research is needed.

4) Expansion and multiplication implies more field staff, in particular participation agents. In order to maintain project quality the latter should be carefully selected and thoroughly trained. For this training it is very recommendable to engage selected qualified senior group promoters who performed well during the project's first phase, and, where needed, also similar fieldworkers from other participatory projects.

   The expansion and more so the multiplication of a project's participatory efforts may require a sizeable number of participation agents. As usually only a relatively small number of exceptionally qualified and motivated group promoters are available in a country, it is a question of realistic planning to anticipate that mostly only average level grassroot workers can be recruited. Such staff can perform reasonably well if provided with solid training, attractive incentives and where possible with study and/or career prospects.

   It is a sound policy—also to keep the (recurrent) costs of an expanded project as low as possible—to recruit as many group promoters as possible on secondment from public and private organizations such as extension agencies and NGOs including religious bodies, and preferably from those operating near the new project areas. This policy implies of course, the redeployment, relocation and re-training of part of the field staff of line agencies and/or other organizations concerned.

In certain instances expansion or multiplication may grow out to such magnitude that a project must arrange timely internal cadres which are recruited from the action areas. For example, in some ongoing participation projects well-performing groups are encouraged to select each a few members for in-depth training not only to impart the know-how acquired to their peers, but also to help establish and guide new beneficiary groups. In other cases internal cadres are gradually formed by recruiting suitable locals on a (part-time) voluntary or semi-voluntary basis. These multiplying agents perform (part of) the functions of group promoters. The major advantages of such policies of forming internal cadres are that they reduce dependency on outside aid, are cost-effective and imply low recurrent costs.

5) Inter-group associations can play an important role in project expansion: they can assist in recruiting internal cadres, in the process of the formation and training of new groups and associations, in the dissemination of improved technology and in meeting other needs.

6) For the establishment of fruitful linkages in the expansion phase it will be indispensable to obtain pragmatic information on existing groups and organizations of the intended beneficiaries in the new project areas and furthermore on the public and private agencies as well as relevant ongoing projects and programmes with which the expanded project could cooperate or coordinate efforts.

7) As transpires from the foregoing points, for the planning of an expanded project and particularly of its beneficiary participation component, various operations of the project identification and preparation stages indicated are to be carried out again. This needs, of course, to be done in modified ways: e.g. data collection can be more selective as considerable information is already available; furthermore socio-economic reconnaissance work, in particular field surveys, can be better organized as the experience at grassroot level gained by the project to be expanded, can be fully taken into account.

How to Ensure Beneficiary Participation in the Project Cycle

The project cycle consists usually of seven main stages: Reconnaissance or Pre-identification, Identification, Preparation, Appraisal, Approval by the supporting agency and Government, implementation and Evaluation. For participatory projects this cycle is (to be) conceived as a flexible and fluid process; for example in some instances one or more phases could be merged or even suppressed.

It deals mainly with the operations required for the reconnaissance, identification and preparation or formulation of a participatory component in a project. The main ones are:

a) collecting relevant information, as explained below;
b) sensitizing the staff of appropriate Government and Voluntary or Private Organizations (NGOs), furthermore local leaders and representatives of the intended beneficiaries on the nature and need of a project as well as of its participatory approach;
c) reaching agreements with potential project participants and the authorities concerned on the type of project needed and the best ways to plan and implement it.

Although it deals mainly with projects initiated and supported by an external development agency, many points are mutatis mutandis also relevant and applicable for projects and programmes initiated in a country without external aid.

Need for Flexible Project Designs

Practice shows that effective beneficiary participation can be incorporated in the design of a project of any type: agricultural production, livestock, forestry, fishery, credit, irrigation, input-delivery, research, training, extension and so on. For this purpose, a participatory project (or at least its participatory component) is, however, to be prepared with considerable flexibility. This should be reflected in the project documents which should have flexible frameworks. The beneficiaries must be offered sufficient scope and space to help define and implement economic and other activities and to organize themselves around these according to their own needs and possibilities. Thus e.g. participatory preparation of detailed work plans is part of the project implementation and such plans can and should therefore not be elaborated in detail beforehand in project documents. Otherwise the essence of the participatory approach, viz. self-initiative, self-reliance and self-development together with group democracy and shared leadership could be seriously compromised.

Reconnaissance Stage

In this stage, also called pre-identification phase, a project idea or proposal will undergo a first examination and elaboration. For this purpose relevant operational qualitative and quantitative data need to be collected. This requires firstly a desk review for the analysis of all available reference materials. Secondly, the data collection requires socio-economic field surveys in the potential project areas of the country concerned. This type of data collection can usually not be carried out satisfactorily during relatively short identification missions. It will therefore be indispensable to establish in or to send to a country before an identification mission, a small team to perform reconnaissance work during a period of two to three months. The team should collect—in particular at the local level—the data required for building in a project efficient beneficiary participation.

In the reconnaissance stage as much as possible identification work should be done as any amount of data collected prior to the identification mission will contribute not only to less longer and costly as well as more fruitful identification and formulation missions and work but also to far better project designs and thus—what after all really counts—to more successful project implementation and results. It is moreover a relatively cheap but rather fruitful investment to send out a small reconnaissance team and even more so when such team can consist wholly or in part of local experts.

The members of a reconnaissance team or mission should consist of: a) an applied female and/or male sociologist/anthropologist-cum-social planner, and b) one or more experts in agronomy or other fields depending upon the type of project and its prospective action area(s). Wherever possible the team members should be local, at least in part.

The team will carry out pragmatic social and economic studies in the potential project area(s). For the surveys a representative sample is to be taken including spokesmen and—women of the local people, in particular the poor; furthermore, key members of local people's organizations as well as traditional and other leaders and influentials.

Identification Stage

In the identification phase it should be thoroughly examined whether and how a project can be designed in a truly participatory way, in other words whether, to what extent and how beneficiary participation can be built into a project design. For this purpose it is firstly necessary to obtain a socio-economic country profile and secondly on the basis of this, relevant information on the overall feasibility and. thirdly, the social feasibility of a participatory project.

It is of course understood that part of the above information such as a country profile is necessary for any project and furthermore that the data required for drafting a beneficiary participation component or mechanism depend upon and are to be consistent and compatible with the many economic, technical and other data collected in the identification phase for the overall project design. Just to mention one key point in respect: the social feasibility of a project is to be correlated with its economic, technical and ecological feasibility.

Country Profile. This profile should be concise and operational and contain a number of relevant economic and social data. The latter are usually either already available or can be easily obtained. The information required on the potential project area(s) is to be collected mainly by means of reconnaissance work and concerns only the minimum necessary data for a participatory project.

Firstly, overall geographic, demographic and economic information is of course to be obtained which is usually readily available. The economic data may regard land tenure, agrarian reform and production structures, numbers/proportions of the various categories of farmers, farming systems and income, small-scale coastal and inland fisheries and other relevant economic activities. Secondly, various socio-economic and socio-cultural data need to be collected as explained hereunder.

Overall feasibility of participatory approaches and projects in a country.

In order to determine this feasibility, information is to be gathered on relevant policy and institutional issues which may imply the following key topics.

1) The political environment: Is the government de facto in favour of assisting rural poor people and in particular of the participatory development approach? This implies: do relevant government agencies fully, partly or not endeavour to: a) identify and classify poor people and poverty areas, and b) give them preferential attention by means of specific policies, institutions and programmes? Furthermore, in what forms and to what extent are people's participation, self-development and self-help part of the government's policies?

2) Has the country the required supporting legislation regarding rural people's organizations? This includes: freedom of association and group formation, adequate interpretation and application of the rights

of association, possible restrictive provisions (e.g. in some countries registered cooperatives are the only rural people's organizations allowed) and appropriate labour laws.

3) The forms and degrees of decentralization of public administration, planning as well as resource allocation and control. Among others: do government agencies at local levels have sufficient space and delegation of power to help implement a participatory project? What about the stability of the government system?

4) Policies to strengthen women's roles in rural development particularly in agricultural and other productive activities.

5) Policies concerning rural poor-oriented training, extension, credit, input-supply and marketing.

6) Policies to increase non-agricultural income- and employment generation opportunities for the rural low income women, men and youth.

7) Are fiscal, pricing and other key national policies consistent with poverty-oriented projects?

8) Foreseeable political, financial and other support to participatory projects at national and lower levels: to what extent is the government prepared to support the creation of an adequate receiving system in addition to the strengthening of the existing delivery system and gearing it to the needs of the rural weak?.

Social Feasibility Studies

The overall feasibility information and the country profile form the main basis on which one or more participatory projects as well as possible project areas can be identified. In this exercise, the emphasis should be on seizing opportunities to build on ongoing local development efforts and promising local initiatives. For participatory projects not only economic/technical but also social feasibility studies are indispensable. In the latter studies priority attention is to be given to the following:

1) identification and classification of the rural poor people: how defined and identified by government and other bodies, average incomes, poverty line(s), changes over time, etc.; the main categories of the low-income people and their numbers and proportions, also per region/zone; furthermore summaries of studies, if any, on the poor in the country including on their needs and aspirations;

2) identification of potential project areas on the basis of data under 1);

3) the local traditional and modern (usually dual) power structure; among others; types and influence of local power holders and groups as well as the forms and degrees of (over-) dependence of the poor upon them;

4) other relevant aspects of the local social structure and culture such as: ethnic and/or tribal groups and their mutual relationships, traditional social units (extended families, lineages, clans, etc.), prevailing values, norms, customs and taboos which could affect a participatory project;

5) the delivery system at local and district (provincial) levels: the structure, functions, policies, programmes, staff, resources, activities, performance, external relationships and constraints of Government agencies and NGOs which could be involved in a participatory project;

the relevant formal and informal, standard and participatory rural people's organizations: their genesis, history, objectives, membership, leadership, activities, results, and constraints. Furthermore, their external relationships to: national and district level units of the same organization, other local people's organizations, government and/or NGO bodies and local power and vested interest groups;

7) the numbers and percentages of rural people, particularly poor and disadvantaged groups, who are not organized in formal and/or informal organizations conducive to their economic and social development, and why;

8) existing forms and levels of locally available technical knowledge regarding project-relevant fields such as farming, fishing, handicrafts, self-organization, group-management, etc.

Project Preparation or Formulation Stage

The information needed for the preparation of a beneficiary participatory component in a project is to be obtained among others, through Project Preparation Missions but also, when needed, follow-up feasibility studies. The information regards mainly the following:

1) identification and description of the government agencies and NGOs which could effectively be involved in the implementation of beneficiary participation in a project;

2) selection and detailed operational profile of the institution(s) to be responsible for the above implementation; moreover, its/their position

in the local administrative and organizational network as well as its/ their image and prestige among the poorer locals;

3) pragmatic proposals to establish the minimum required (or to make use of the existing) coordination mechanisms at national and lower levels for project implementation;

4) workable proposals for the financial arrangements required for a participatory project such as agreements with one or more cooperating credit institutions, establishment of credit funds for (group) loans, and (group) loan conditions including social liability and interest rates;

5) manpower resources for locally recruited project staff. In particular to recruit the required participation coordinator and group promoters;

6) identification—by means of exploratory surveys—of initial action areas (village clusters) within the project areas where the group promoters will start their field actions ;

7) potentials and strategy of group formation: a key issue is whether to promote the self-creation of small groups of rural poor people within existing rural organizations, and/or on the basis of existing informal groups, and/or from scratch;

8) group activities: potentials in the project area for viable income-raising enterprises in agriculture, fisheries, forestry, processing, handicrafts, marketing, etc. Furthermore, as and when required, preliminary planning of small-scale feasibility studies on certain potential group activities;

9) participatory training; identification of training needs and preparation of a programme for (a) the intended beneficiaries, (b) project personnel, and (c) supporting government and NGO staff; furthermore search for suitable training institutions, personnel, methods, opportunities and materials,

participatory action research: types of pragmatic socio-economic research needed, search for institutions and/or expertise to assist in research design and execution;

11) participatory monitoring and evaluation; outline for workable local systems;

12) organization of project initiation, training and other field workshops in or near the project area(s) to discuss with all potential project

participants, especially the intended beneficiaries and supporting staff, the participatory development approach and project Once the earlier indicated overall and social feasibility data as well as the above information is obtained, the beneficiary participation component(s) and/or elements can be formulated taking of course, into account the other economic, technical and ecological components or features of a project.

PARTICIPATORY DEVELOPMENT PROGRAMMES SUPPORTED BY FAO

People's participation has become an increasingly important component of FAO's programmes and projects for agricultural, fisheries, forestry and human resources development. In this Appendix, the main participatory efforts promoted by FAO up until the early 1990s are briefly described.

People's Participation in Agricultural and Rural Development through the Promotion of Self-Help Organizations (PPP)

The People's Participation Programme (PPP) is a concrete follow-up of the Declaration of Principles and Programme of Action of the World Conference on Agrarian Reform and Rural Development (WCARRD) held in 1979. The Programme which started in 1980, was in part based on the ongoing FAO Small Farmer Development Programme (SFDP) carried out in various Asian countries, as well as on the FAO Rural Organizations Action Programme (ROAP) implemented in various countries worldwide.

The main *objective* of PPP is to develop and test through pilot field projects an operational method of people's participation through the promotion of self-help organizations which method would hopefully be used in larger rural development programmes and projects. The main *specific objectives*are firstly to help identify, plan and implement income-generating and other group activities for small farmers, tenants, fishermen and/or labourers. Secondly to assist the beneficiaries to organize themselves into self-run groups and organizations or to use existing ones in order to engage in income-raising activities and to have access to services and facilities so that they can satisfy their economic and social needs and become eventually self-reliant. Thirdly, to assist line departments and other agencies including banks and NGOs, to better serve the rural weak. Fourthly, to develop a strategy for expanding the successful features of the project.

The basic elements of the PPP approach are:

— focus on the rural poor

— the formation of small, homogeneous groups around common income-raising activities

— the stimulation of self-organization and self-reliance by eliminating undue dependencies and encouraging group savings

— the use of local group promoters as catalysts for group formation and guidance

— the involvement of NGOs

— participatory training, action-oriented research and monitoring and evaluation

— orientation towards expansion and multiplication by developing linking mechanisms

— seeking preferential policies for the poor

— obtaining sustainability by combining low cost with effectiveness.

PPP projects are funded from various government and other sources; the main donors were so far Sweden and the Netherlands. FAO provides administrative and technical support from its own staff and budget; ESHA is PPP's major supporting unit. The projects are small-scale and have an average donor contribution of about US $200,000 over three years.

The PPP has thus far been implemented in 12 countries viz. 8 in Africa, 3 in Asia and 1 in Latin America. It involved in early 1989 over 10,600 small farmers as direct beneficiaries and when including their family members, over 60,000 rural people of whom 44% are women. The farmers organized themselves with the help of 85 group promoters in over 850 PPP groups and 112 inter-group associations. Three PPP projects (Sri Lanka, Ghana and Zambia) are presently in a second three year phase. Various successful national and international workshops on the PPP have been held.

Community Action for Disadvantaged Rural Women (CADRW)

This Programme was initiated in 1981 in the ESH Division in response to the mandates of the WCARRD as well as the World Conference on the UN Decade for Women to give direct attention to the needs and priorities of disadvantaged rural women - the landless, dispossessed, abandoned and malnourished - as determined by rural women themselves.

The basic innovative aspects of the Programme were: 1) to take into account women's multiple roles as food producers, providers, parents, and partners in family and community life; 2) to promote support activities that address the women's multiple needs in an integrated way; 3) to promote village based rural centres for demonstrations and other activities of the community's choice; 4) to involve the community, men and women, in identifying their needs and improving their conditions; 5) to develop women's groups for income-raising activities; 6) to assist governments to adopt policies and strategies to provide women with access to resources and services.

The rural centres were to become focal points for attracting women leaders and for promoting women groups engaging in income-raising and other activities like new farming practices, nutrition, leadership, literacy, legal right courses, group child care and appropriate technology.

The Programme which ended in 1984 has been implemented in Egypt, Indonesia, Jordan, Kenya, Mexico, Sri Lanka and Zambia with original funding from SIDA (Sweden) and later on from other sources. The projects succeeded to varying extents in reaching their targets by promoting women's groups and activities; they were also useful in drawing attention of Governments to the needs of the poorest women and in promoting solutions by the beneficiaries themselves. The projects were, however, less successful in generating long-term economic benefits also because the viability of certain activities were insufficiently considered.

A basic difference between the CADRW and PPP is that the former applies a village wide approach to reach the poor women. However, in such approach most actions and benefits are usually taken by the not so poor or better-off women.

Community Forestry Programmes

The FAO Special Action Programme entitled "Forestry for Local Community Development (FLCD)" was started in the Policy and Planning Service, Forestry Department and carried out from 1979 to 1986. The SIDA-supported Programme was conceived as a means to stimulate awareness of and establish the basis for community forestry.

Under the Programme forestry managers from 62 countries participated in three Regional Seminars in Mexico, Thailand and Senegal. Some 51 countries took part in study tours to visit community forestry projects in Africa, Asia and Latin America. In-depth evaluations of the programme were carried out in Korea, India and the Philippines. Publications were prepared including on assessing people's needs, monitoring and evaluation, legislation and extension.

FLCD supported furthermore 44 field projects in 37 countries. Initially help was provided mainly to assist countries to define what to do, establish pilot projects, and train core groups of people in community forestry approaches. The emphasis was mainly on fuelwood, and on meeting other household and farm needs from self-help tree planting and management programmes. Later on income-generating activities became increasingly a major objective. Various countries were assisted in solving particular problems in on-going programmes. For example: the evaluation of the performance in the Social Forestry Programme in Gujarat (India), development of strategies to help people introduce trees into small farm systems in Malawi and into grazing systems in Sudan, and the development of a monitoring and evaluation system for use on all state social forestry projects in India.

With the successful outcome of the FLCD Programme, there was a need for wide-spread replication and adoption of community level forestry. Accordingly a catalyst follow-up programme called Forest, Trees and People (FTP) was started in 1987. The FTP Programme aims at enabling people - through their own efforts - to benefit more from forests and trees.

The Programme's specific objectives are: 1) to assemble, analyse and disseminate information needed for planning and implementing sound participatory forestry projects and programmes; 2) to contribute to rural development based on trees and forests for food, fodder and other products and for environmental stabilization; 3) to develop strategies, systems and methods by which people's participation is promoted in tree growing; and 4) to encourage donors to support participatory forestry activities in developing countries.

A solid information base is being built up by gathering data from literature, in-depth studies and field activities. Of the eight FTP field projects, four are SIDA-funded, FAO Trust Fund projects (Burkina Faso, Nepal, Thailand and Zambia). Two projects (Tanzania and Vietnam) are bilateral and coordinated by the Swedish University of Agricultural Services (SUAS), and two projects (Ethiopia and Kenya) are run by Swedish NGOs. Both FAO and SUAS provide technical support to and learn form the 8 projects.

The FTP field projects are located in countries where the chances of participatory tree growing on a larger scale are high. Baseline studies focus on factors such as people's need for trees and how trees can be integrated into local production systems, furthermore on nutrition, fuelwood availability, employment and social conditions. The projects stress participatory monitoring and evaluation and also effective two-way communication between villagers and field agents. Public awareness is raised by using media such as radio, and utilizing school and informal educational facilities. Forest-based small-scale forest enterprises are very much encouraged.

Programme for Small-Scale and Artisanal Fishermen

In the seventies it was increasingly realized in FAO and outside that the conventional economic or business approaches were not effective for the development of the world's artisanal fisheries. Consequently various attempts were made to focus on the poorer fishermen rather than on profits. In some cases the efforts were combined with concerns for the environment, food security, employment and intermediate technologies. In the FAO South China Sea and Bay of Bengal Regional Programmes, FAO started to explore alternative artisanal fisheries development policies. The 1984 World Conference on Fisheries Management and Development formulated on the basis of this new thinking a strategy with principles and guidelines for small-scale fisheries development. This strategy reflected the recognition of the need of the latter sector, of its value (production of over 20 million tons of protein food per year), and of its provision of employment (10 million full-time and 10 million part-time jobs). The Programme for the Development of Small-Scale Fisheries, based on WCARRD and the above-indicated conferences, concentrates on assistance for the integrated development of fishing communities. The Programme is based upon: 1) an integrated approach taking into account both technical aspects of development and the socio-economic needs of fishing communities; 2) active participation in development planning actions by small-scale fishing communities; 3) mobilization of local and national resources, skills, finance and markets for the development efforts, so that outside support remains supplementary and catalytic; 4) long-term technical support and in-service training; 5) a continuing and assured share as well as management of the fishery resources for small-scale producers; and 6) explicit attention to enhancing the economic and social role of women in fish production and marketing and in family maintenance.

The Programme activities are being carried out through regional and sub-regional small-scale development teams. The latter provide assistance and advisory services to national teams working on integrated small-scale fisheries development. They establish - where possible together with NGOs - also demonstration projects for in-service training, assist governments to identify the needs of the small-scale fishery sector and to formulate projects. The teams also liaise with bilateral projects, promote technical cooperation and training, encourage the adoption of appropriate technology, evaluate social and other factors affecting small-scale community development and improve village level capability in project planning and implementation. In all this due attention is given to the participation of women. For this purpose the Fishery Department published in 1988 Guidelines for Women in Fishing Communities. The Programme includes the location of Small-Scale Fishery Development Groups in 9 different zones. The Programme approach is furthermore applied in the FAO Regional Programmes Bay of Bengal and Integrated Development of Artisanal Fisheries in West-Africa (IDAF). Under these Programmes also small. informal fishermen groups are being promoted.

International Support Programme for Farm Water Management

This Programme which started in 1980 in FAO's Land and Water Development Division, as a follow-up of WCARRD and other international meetings, had the following objectives: 1) to identify the specific needs of individual countries in water management improvement; 2) to promote and formulate national action plans; 3) to coordinate support to and collaborate with the national action plans and projects; and 4) to monitor, evaluate and provide means for the dissemination and exchange of experience.

The plan of action comprised *at the farm and village level* the implementation of pilot improvement projects cum training programmes. The activities included: diagnosis of deficiencies and constraints, creating awareness of improvement potential, preparation of frameworks for implementation, operation and maintenance of irrigation systems, backstopping and follow-up services, and training of field extension assistants.

At the national level the activities focussed at build-up of research capacities to handle technical and socio-economic field problems, the promotion of institutional arrangements for the development of water management improvement policies and the implementation of these through the creation of irrigation extension services and the introduction or strengthening of teaching programmes in water management. For broad support an Advisory Panel was established in 1981 which included administrators and specialists from donor and developing countries.

Key components and results of the Programme which ended in 1986 were:

1) *Field projects* implemented in several countries. These were characterised by farmers' participation, simple technology, use of local manpower and resources, and low-cost implementation.
2) *Training*: Education and training programmes carried out for farmers as well as irrigation operators, advisors and technicians; furthermore study tours for farmer leaders and the preparation of several information materials. Also various international and national workshops and seminars were conducted, among others, in Pakistan, the Philippines, Surinam, Kenya, Indonesia and Sierra Leone.
3) *Institution building*: The capacity to plan and carry out water management improvements were strengthened in a number of countries, specifically through setting up irrigation Services at national level.

The Programme has actively dealt with a number of technical, socio-economic and institutional issues and problems at grassroot and higher levels. In particular with those of farmers1 participation: e.g. with water users associations, farmers' involvement In irrigation development and water management and technical constraints of farmers' participation in water management at the tertiary level. In fact, at the request of several countries, the Programme contributed considerably to the study and promotion of irrigation farmers' participation in a number of different irrigation zones. In the latter case studies were conducted of potentials, successful efforts and constraints of participation. Moreover several recommendations to increase farmer participation were made to government agencies and donors, including in workshops and publications. Some of the latter deal in-depth with participation problems in water management and provide suggestions for pragmatic solutions.

Freedom from Hunger Campaign/Action for Development (FFHC/AD)

This unique Programme was created, already in 1959, to support the participatory development activities of NGOs with special focus on the rural poor, as well as to promote public debate and exchange on development issues. Over the past three decades the FFHC/AD Unit in FAO has built up a network of relations with NGOs operating at grassroot level in Africa, Asia and Latin America. At the request of its NGO partners, FFHC/AD carries out several activities which are complementary to those of the NGOs as well as of governments and include the following:

— *Training*: FFHC/AD organizes training courses for NGO staff and field workers on various aspects of participatory development, from skills training to project formulation and management, to communications and cultural forms of expression.

— *Exchange programmes*: FFHC/AD helps national NGOs and local people's organizations to visit and learn from each others' experiences, within and between countries.

— *Networking*: FFHC/AD supports NGO partners' efforts to build up networks of communication and collaboration at country and regional levels. It provides funds to enable them to meet, discuss and plan together, and to study problems and issues of common concern.

— *Project support*: Over US $8 million in NGO donor assistance is currently being channelled to projects which FFHC/AD has helped partner organizations in 35 countries to formulate. At the same time, FFHC/AD works with NGOs in the South to improve the quality of their project work by assisting them to evaluate their programmes, training their staff, helping national NGOs to build more continuous links with community-based groups and giving NGOs access to FAO's technical expertise.

— *NGO/Government relations*: Because it is part of an inter-governmental organization and because it has won the confidence of NGOs in the South, FFHC/AD is in a good position to facilitate dialogue between governmental organizations on the one hand, and NGOs and their field workers on the other. FFHC/AD also helps to provide support and legitimacy to local groups vis-à-vis the governments of their countries.

— *North/South solidarity*: FFHC/AD provides a forum for dialogue and discussion among NGOs in the North and in the South about how to improve the quality and the effectiveness of their relationships. FFHC/AD also helps Northern NGOs to identify valid partners in Third World countries, and vice versa.

— *NGOs and inter-governmental organizations*: FFHC/AD constitutes a channel whereby the inter-governmental community can learn from the experiences and insights of NGOs in the field of participatory development.

— *Information and documentation*: FFHC/AD publishes two regular bulletins "Ideas and Action" (recently discontinued due to financial restrictions) and "Development Education Exchange Papers". It maintains a documentation centre with materials of particular interest to NGOs, and provides Southern NGOs with advice on improving their own documentation work. Collection and dissemination of documents of interest to NGO field workers is also carried out by FFHC/AD staff in the regions.

The small FAO FFHC/AD team consists of seven professionals of whom four are based in the field (Accra, Addis Ababa, New Delhi and Rio de Janeiro). The Unit has full access to FAO's wealth of technical expertise and its network of representatives in 74 countries. FFHC/AD does not receive funds from FAO for field projects; It helps Southern partners to formulate projects but they are funded by Northern NGOs.

References

Huizer, Gerrit: (October 1982). *Guiding Principles for People's Participation Projects: Design, Operation, Monitoring and On-going Evaluation*, FAO, Rome.

Van Heck, Bernard: (1977). *The involvement of the Poor in Development through Rural Organizations, Framework for Research-cum-Action*, FAO. Rome.

Oakley, Peter and Dillon, B.: (April 1985). *Strengthening People's Participation in Rural Development*, University of Reading.

Mckone, C.E.: (1989). *FAO People's Participation Programme: The First Ten Years - Lessons Learnt and Future Directions*, FAO, Rome.

Uphoff, N. Cohen, J.M. and Goldsmith, A.A.: (1987). *Feasibility and Application of Rural Development Participation*, A State-of-the-Art Paper, Cornell University, Rural Development Committee, Ithaca, New York.

Samuel, Paul: (1987). *Community Participation in Development Projects. The World Bank Experience*, World Bank Discussion Papers, The World Bank, Washington, D.C.

Bibliography

Adnan, S. et al. (1992) *People's Participation, NGO and the Flood Action Plan*, Dhaka Research and Advisory Services.

Agrawal, A. and K. Gupta (2005) 'Decentralization and Participation: The Governance of Common Pool Resources in Nepal's Terai'. *World Development,* Vol. 33, No. 7, pp. 1101–1114.

Aldaba, Rafaelita M. and Caesar B. Cororaton. (November 2002). "Trade Liberalization and Pollution: Evidence from the Philippines". EEPSEA publications.

Alkire, S. (2002). Dimensions of human development. *World Development* Vol. 30 (2): 181 – 205.

Allen, T. & Thomas, A. (1992). *Poverty and development in the 1990s*. Oxford University Press, New York.

Amin, A. (1993) The regional development potential of inward investment in the less favoured regions of the European Community. *Paper presented at the Conference on Cohesion and Conflict in the Single Market, Newcastle upon Tyne.*

Annan, K., (1999). *Facing the humanitarian challenge: Towards a culture of prevention*. Paper read at the 54th session of the United Nations General Assembly, New York.

Arnstein, S. R. (1969) *Ladder of Citizen Participation Journal of the American Institute of Town Planning*, Vol. 35. pp. 216-224

Asian Development Bank ADB RETA (2002). Regional Technical Assistance for the coastal and marine resources management and poverty reduction in South Asia – 5974. Situation analysis report - Sri Lanka component. Asian Development Bank and IUCN Sri Lanka

Bandyopadhay, D., (2007). "On poverty, food adequacy and hunger in West Bengal"', Delhi, *Mainstream*, 19 June, Tuesday.

Bastian, S. and N. Bastian (eds) (1996) *Assessing Participation: A Debate from South Asia.* Delhi: Konark.

Bergdall, D. Terry (1993) *Methods for Active Participation: Experiences in Rural Development from East and Central Africa* Nairobi: Oxford University Press

Bhatta, S. D. and Sharma, S. K., (2006). The Determinants and Consequences of Chronic and Transient Poverty in Nepal, CPRC Working Paper No. 66, Manchester, Chronic Poverty Research Centre.

Blakely, E.J. (1989) *Planning Local Economic Development*. Newbury Park CA, Sage.

Buhl, S., Wei, Q. and Xuixeong, W. (2004). *Report Card – Satisfaction Survey, An initial observation from China*, Technical Report 2, Beijing, GTZ, July.

Carney, D. (editor). (1998). *Sustainable Rural Livelihoods.* Department for International Development, UK.

CBMS Survey, (2008). "Community Based Monitoring System". Tabaco City Government.

Chambers, R. (1994) 'Participatory Rural Appraisal (PRA) Analysis of Experience'. *World Development,* Vol. 22, No. 9, pp. 1253-1268.

Chambers, R., (1993). *Challenging the Professions Frontiers for Rural Development,* London, Intermediate Technology Publications, 1993

Cheema, G. S. and Rondinelli, D. A. (eds.) (1983) *Decentralization and Development: Policy Implementation in Developing Countries.* London: Sage

Cloke, P.T. (ed) (1988) *Policies and Plans for Rural People: An International Perspective.* London, Unwin Hyman.

Conyers, Diana (1986) *Future Directions in Development Studies: The Case of Decentralization World Development,* Vol. 15, pp. 593-603

CPDO, (2009). "City Land Use Plan", City Planning and Development Office (CPDO). Tabaco City Government.

Ellis, F. (2000) *Rural Livelihoods and Diversity in Developing Countries.* Oxford: Oxford University Press.

Eric Schwartz, (2006). *A Needless Toll of Natural Disasters. Boston Globe,* March 23.

Goldsmith, M. (1993) :The Europeanisation of local government", *Urban Studies* 30, 4/5: 683-699.

Guzman, R. P. (1988) 'Decentralization as a Strategy for Redemocratization in the Philippine Political System' *Philippine Journal of Public Administration* Vol. XXXII, No. 3&4, pp. 217-225.

Hickey, S. and G. Mohan, eds. (2004) *Participation: From Tyranny to Transformation.* London: Zed Books.

Hoshino, C. (1994) *Land Development; Processes and Decentralization in Latin American Large Cities and Metropolitan Areas: Issue, Trends, and Prospects* Regional Development Dialogue, Vol. 15, No.2, pp. 29-60

Huizer, Gerrit: (October 1982). *Guiding Principles for People's Participation Projects: Design, Operation, Monitoring and On-going Evaluation,* FAO, Rome.

Hunger Project. (2000). *The African women food farmer initiative: Exclusion from development policy and programming equation,* New York.

Lightelm, A. A.& Wilsenach, A. (1993). "Development, poverty and the environment with particular reference to the Eastern Transvaal region". *Development Southern Africa,* 10 (1): 45-64.

Mckone, C.E.: (1989). *FAO People's Participation Programme: The First Ten Years - Lessons Learnt and Future Directions,* FAO, Rome.

Moseley, M. and Cherrett, T. (no date) *Involving People in Local Development,* (LEADER Dossiers series, Brussels: European Commission.

Mukherjee, A, (ed.). (2004). *Participatory Monitoring,* Delhi, Concept Publishing Company, 2004.

Mwamwenda, T. S. (1994). "Women and education in Africa". *South African Journal of Sociology,* 25(4): 143-147.

Narayan, D., Chambers, R., Shah, M. and Petesch, P. (2000). *Voices of the poor: crying out for change.* World Bank, Washington, D.C., USA.

Oakley, Peter and Dillon, B.: (April 1985). *Strengthening People's Participation in Rural Development*, University of Reading.

Reid, D. (1996) *Participation in Local Decision-Making; Examples of Local Action*. Scottish Natural Heritage.

Samuel, Paul: (1987). *Community Participation in Development Projects. The World Bank Experience*, World Bank Discussion Papers, The World Bank, Washington, D.C.

Senaratna, S. (2003). Community participation in research: Research undertaken in Sri Lanka 2002. Sustainable Coastal Livelihoods (SCL) Project Report, IMM Ltd, Exeter, UK.

Skutsch, M. (1990) Social forestry in integrated rural development planning, Sri Lanka. RWEDP, FAO, Bangkok, Thailand.

Tongzon, Jose L. (2005). "Trade Policy in the Philippines: Treading a cautious path". ASEAN Economic Bulletin, April 1.

UNDP (2004), *West Bengal Human Development Report*, Delhi, United Nations Development Programme.

United Nations Development Fund for Women (UNIFEM). (2000). *Women and economic empowerment*, New York.

Uphoff, N. Cohen, J.M. and Goldsmith, A.A.: (1987). *Feasibility and Application of Rural Development Participation*, A State-of-the-Art Paper, Cornell University, Rural Development Committee, Ithaca, New York.

Van Heck, Bernard: (1977). *The involvement of the Poor in Development through Rural Organizations, Framework for Research-cum-Action*, FAO. Rome.

White, S. and Pettit, J. (2004). Participatory approaches and the measurement of human well-being. WIDER Research Paper No. 2004/57

Index